REALITIES

realities

SIGNIFICANT WRITING FROM THE CATHOLIC PRESS

EDITED BY

DAN HERR *and* CLEM LANE

THE BRUCE PUBLISHING COMPANY
MILWAUKEE

NIHIL OBSTAT:

JOANNES A. SCHULIEN, S.T.D.
Censor librorum

IMPRIMATUR:

✠ ALBERTUS G. MEYER
Archiepiscopus Milwauchiensis

Die 3ᵃ Decembris, 1957

Library of Congress Catalog Card Number: 58–7669

ⓒ 1958 BY THE CATHOLIC PRESS ASSOCIATION
MADE IN THE UNITED STATES OF AMERICA

"WHAT is vital is to recover the moral and spiritual foundations on which the lives of both the individual and the culture depend; to bring home to the average man that religion is not a pious fiction which has nothing to do with the facts of life, but that it is concerned with realities, that it is in fact the pathway to reality and the law of life."

CHRISTOPHER DAWSON
(*The Commonweal*)

ACKNOWLEDGMENTS

GRATEFUL acknowledgment is made to the following publishers and authors for permission to reprint the articles in this volume:

America (329 West 108th St., New York 25, New York) and Gordon C. Zahn for "Catholic 'Separatism' and Anti-Catholic Tensions" (October 27, 1956).

The Apostolate (21 West Superior St., Chicago 10, Illinois) and Rt. Rev. Reynold Hillenbrand for "Five Point Social Program" (winter, 1955).

Ave Maria (Notre Dame, Indiana) and Most Rev. John King Mussio for "Politics, Corruption and You" (June 30, 1956).

Cadence (Loyola University, 820 North Michigan Ave., Chicago 11, Illinois) and Martin Gleason for "To All Its People" (spring, 1957).

The Catholic Courier-Journal (35 Scio St., Rochester 4, New York) and Most Rev. Vincent S. Waters for "How I Lost My Prejudice" (September 21, 1956).

The Catholic Messenger (407 Brady St., Davenport, Iowa) and Rev. E. M. Catich for "The Image of Christ In Art" (May 17, 1956).

The Catholic Messenger and Rev. Robert J. Welch for "Catholic Church and American Democracy" (January 12, 1956).

The Catholic University of America Bulletin (620 Michigan Ave., N.E., Washington 17, D. C.) and Thomas E. Murray for "Though The Heavens Fall" (July, 1954).

The Catholic World (411 West 59th St., New York 19, New York) and Sister Annette Walters, C.S.J., for "Catholics and Mental Health" (April, 1955).

The Catholic World and Rev. Francis P. Canavan, S.J., for "The Finality of Sex" (January, 1954).

The Commonweal (386 Fourth Ave., New York 16, New York) and Eugene J. McCarthy for "The Christian In Politics" (October 1, 1954).

The Commonweal and William Clancy for "The Area of Catholic Freedom" (November 5, 1954).

Community (4233 South Indiana Ave., Chicago 15, Illinois) and Helen Caldwell Riley for "If Your Son Should Ask" (April, 1956).

The Critic, formerly Books on Trial (210 W. Madison St., Chicago 6, Illinois) and Rev. John Courtney Murray, S.J., for "Literature and Censorship" (June–July, 1956).

The Homiletic and Pastoral Review (53 Park Pl., New York 7, New York) and Rev. John B. Sheerin, C.S.P., for "The Goal of Academic Freedom" (September, 1953).

Integrity (publication suspended) and Erik von Kuehnelt-Leddihn for "Pollyanna Catholicism" (July, 1954).

Jubilee (377 Fourth Ave., New York 16, New York) and Rev. John LaFarge, S.J., for "Christianity and the Negro" (September, 1955).

National Catholic Welfare Conference News Service (1312 Massachusetts Ave., N.W., Washington 5, D. C.) and Charles Lucey for "Hope For Tomorrow" (October 17, 1955).

The Review of Politics (University of Notre Dame, Notre Dame, Indiana) and Frank O'Malley for "The Culture of the Church" (April, 1954).

The Sign (Monastery Pl., Union City, New Jersey) and Most Rev. Karl J. Alter for "Industry Councils" (May, 1950).

The Sign and Rev. Ralph Gorman, C.P., for "One View of Four Viewpoints" (March, 1955; June, 1955; October, 1956; June, 1957).

Spirit (386 Fourth Ave., New York 16, New York) and Dr. George N. Shuster for "The Poet As Witness" (July, 1954).

Today (1700 West Jackson Blvd., Chicago 12, Illinois) and John Cogley for "Some Things Are Caesar's" (November, 1951).

Worship (Collegeville, Minnesota), The National Liturgical Conference (Proceedings of the 1955 Liturgical Week), and Most Rev. John J. Wright for "The Mass And The International Order" (February, 1956).

Worship and Willis D. Nutting for "Order and Apathy" (October, 1953).

INTRODUCTION

FOR as long as most of us can remember, abusing the Catholic press has been a popular sport among American Catholics. The Catholic press has been too radical, too conservative, too middle-of-the-road; it has been too nationalistic or too internationally minded; it has been too pro-labor or too pro-capital; it has printed too much news about bustling women's clubs or too little; it has been too high-brow or too low-brow; it has always been too something. In our opinion, it has been too little read by those who have been the most critical.

No one, least of all Catholic editors, will proclaim perfection for the Catholic press. Yet a more than casual reading should demonstrate that the modern Catholic press represents a solid achievement. Facing obstacles that the secular press has never known and, too often lacking the necessary encouragement and support from its readers, the Catholic press has steadily progressed. Today it is successfully striving for a more positive approach and a wider scope. It is far more critical of itself and of the activities of American Catholics than even the most optimistic prophet of the '40's would have thought possible. The head-in-the-sand days of ultrasensitivity are disappearing.

It might be well to remind our non-Catholic neighbors from time to time that this self-criticism should not be misconstrued. It does not mean that termites have been eating away at the Church in America, but rather that our healthy condition makes possible a long, searching look at our defects. At a time when we are decrying the lack of Catholic intellectual activity in America, for example, many

Catholics as well as non-Catholics might easily overlook what we have achieved in this area in a relatively short space of time. Our system of education, unparalleled in the Catholic world, is one example. An example, even more pertinent for us, is the Catholic press in all its variety.

For those of you who have not given the Catholic press the reading that we believe it deserves, we offer this collection of significant articles as a reasonable substitute. Our purpose, of course, is to entertain and inform, but we think that a new appreciation of the virtues of the Catholic press might well be a bonus for some of our readers.

When we were asked to edit this anthology, we were blessed with only the most general instructions: "to assemble from American Catholic publications nonfiction materials (appearing since 1950) worthy of inclusion in a permanent collection." The editors of the Catholic magazines and newspapers were asked to submit suitable material from their publications, a request which they acknowledged with a vengeance. As box after box tumbled into our offices, we became aware of the immensity of our job. Reading through this avalanche — a burdensome task which was compensated for by the increase of our knowledge of what's going on in the world — convinced us that our problem would be one of superabundance. As subsequent readings narrowed down the selections we found that the articles we judged best for the most part mirrored the awareness of Catholic editors of the problems facing American Catholics today. We do not insist the articles finally selected are necessarily the best published by the Catholic press — although we believe they are outstanding — or that they are truly representative.

Our chief regrets are that we could not include all the articles we admired and that this book reflects only to a limited extent the Catholic newspapers of America. This limitation should really surprise no one who will reflect for a moment on the purpose and function of a newspaper. Newspaper writers and editors are living very much in the present; they write and edit for the reader on the run, their work is to be read now and to be outdated by the next edition. Thus the aim of this collection — permanency — is for the most part irreconcilable with the function of a newspaper. Since one of the coeditors has been a newspaperman all his life, no one can accuse us of being prejudiced against newspapers, but we felt an explanation was necessary to avoid possible misunderstandings.

The articles themselves, we insist, can stand on their own and you will search in vain for words from us instructing the reader on their virtues. We hope that the quality of each article is such that the reasons for our selecting it are self-evident. You *will* find at the back of the book short biographical notes on the authors.

Advice and help have come from many people and we are grateful to them all. We are particularly grateful to William Holub — a man with broad shoulders who can and does bear mighty burdens with relative ease — Chairman of the Literary Awards Committee which initiated this project and selected us as editors, and to Monsignor John S. Randall, president of the Catholic Press Association, the Association Board of Directors, and the newspaper and magazine editors who sponsored this book and co-operated fully and generously with us.

THE EDITORS

CONTENTS

Contents   xvii

REALITIES

POLLYANNA CATHOLICISM

BY ERIK VON KUEHNELT-LEDDIHN

CORRUPTIO OPTIMI PESSIMA is an old Latin proverb implying that nothing is worse than the best things in their decadence, apostatizing from their essence and betraying their mission. A fallen angel like Lucifer, a treacherous apostle like Judas Iscariot, a rotten pope like John XXIII, a wicked king like Henry VIII — they all prove this saying without fail. Yet what is true of persons is also terribly true of nations — seemingly only very great nations can fall very low — and, in a way, can equally be applied to ideas, to verities, and even to divine institutions. In this case, of course, man himself is the corruptor. Small sects of little historic importance, one has to admit, have often achieved a remarkable degree of "limited perfection," but if we believe that the corruption of the best is the worst, then the Catholic faith and the Catholic Church must have produced the worst aberrations. This precisely is the case. The Plymouth Brethren never had in their ranks anyone like some of the late medieval popes, and the rectories of the United Southern Four Square Gospel Methodist Church hardly ever were such sinks of iniquities as some of our fifteenth-century convents. The very survival of our Church — as Boccaccio's Parisian Jew in his *Decamerone* knew only too well — is not the work of man, but of God. Without the divine promises and the fact that the Church is Christ's Mystical Body, we would have gone down the drain of history a long, long time ago.

1

Still, when we are talking about "Pollyanna Catholicism" we are not dealing with a grave and universal cancer on the body Catholic. This is a minor and localized disease which has the character of a wart rather than of a tumor. Yet a wart can have a disfiguring effect and on the tip of a fair maiden's nose it might prevent her enjoying the bliss of love or be an unsurmountable obstacle on her road to marriage. For this reason the beauty defects of our Church are no laughing matter and, in a way, have to be taken seriously. How many outside the fold caught glimpses of Catholic life which made them shudder and, sometimes, forever dissuaded them from taking another look at a closer range: the Presbyterian minister who once, out of a mixture of boredom and whimsical curiosity, opened a Catholic periodical which emanated an almost diabolic spirit of hatred, spite, and rancor; the sensitive Episcopalian lady who gasped with horror when she ventured into a Catholic church and there saw an orgy of all artistic monstrosities of the late nineteenth century; the inquisitive young Jew from the University of Chicago, fed a "Catholicism" consisting of oversimplifications, glib phrases, and other "short cuts" to truth everlasting.

All these men and women stumbled over a mere footnote of the Church. It certainly is their fault that they never arrived at the essence of truth on earth. It is their fault to have been thwarted by so little, theirs — *and ours*. Ours indeed, because *we* are responsible for the face and the expression of the Church. How can we go on expecting grace swiftly to surmount the needless psychological obstacles engendered by the frightful blemishes of a disfigured Mystical Body?

"Pollyanna Catholicism" exists only in English-speaking countries. In all our travels and trips we have not found it anywhere else. The term itself we have chosen because we are here face to face with a phenomenon which not only almost assumes the character of an "ism," but also because its essence is a naïve, childish — I would almost say girlish — gladness. Yet this "gladness" is not the deeper, inner gladness which is almost synonymous with joy, but rather the superficial happiness related to the "glad guy." The "message" of "Pollyanna Catholicism" is very simple: "Catholicism is fun." As a matter of fact it is a scream to be a Catholic; priests and nuns are the dearest, jolliest, sweetest, and killingest people under the sun; tragedy or sadness is only for the mentally deranged, for atheists and highbrow sourpusses. The truths, truisms, and common-places of our faith are so simple and so snappy that any child, movie actor, or music hall comedian could pick them up and digest them in a jiffy; to see insoluble problems in this world is sheer Jansenism. A cocktail of fragments haphazardly torn out of certain encyclicals plus a pêle-mêle of *Summa* citations served with a sauce of wisecracks copied from Chesterton solves *everything*.

To all this must be added the conviction that had we only the right cartoonists, nine more Jimmy Durantes, a hundred-thousand-bucks-a-year public relations man in Rome, Hollywood, Washington, and Radio City we might get, for our Church, Western civilization neatly delivered in a package. A better hold on television, an all-Catholic baseball team winning the World Series, and a copy of the *Cozy Catholic Convert's Catechism* in the night-table drawer of every hotel, alongside the Gideon Bible, would make the evils of the world disappear in no time.

These observations do not imply in the least that there is something basically wrong with America, Britain, Canada, and the other Dominions Beyond the Sea. Every nation has its virtues and shortcomings, its mediocrities and banalities. Humor *is* a wonderful thing and it is a concomitant of

Christianity because the disproportion between the sublime and the base, the perfect and the imperfect, the eternal and the temporal constantly will appeal to our sense of humor, an advantage the monistic-materialistic world certainly does not possess. The gospels, we must admit, never recorded that our Lord laughed or that He even smiled. These accounts *necessarily* are incomplete, yet if, indeed, Christ never gave external signs of having been amused, one might explain this from His divine nature because God sees everything at once in its "completeness" and (potential) fulfillment. The realization of the comic pertains to man's and, especially, to fallen man's psychological structure. St. Thomas was well aware of that and called lack of mirth positively sinful.

"Pollyanna Catholicism" is not genuinely humorous. It never evokes liberating laughters, because laughing expresses something extreme, and from extremes "Pollyanna Catholicism" naturally recoils. It stands for "small change." It is refined mediocrity. It is "Lilliput Catholicism" for religious pygmies. It is incompatible with sanctity because it is opposed to greatness. With all the joy the saints are carrying in themselves, they make us somewhat uncomfortable, or at least restless. "Pollyanna Catholicism" on the other hand puts us "at ease." It promises us a Mohammedan paradise (minus sex) on earth. It has no understanding whatsoever for the words of Léon Bloy: "Jesus, Thou prayest for those who crucify Thee, and Thou crucifiest those who love Thee."

Yet we are convinced that "Pollyanna Catholicism" has roots which are probably British rather than American, English rather than Irish, Welsh, or Scotch. It has been born in a spirit of analogy to a particular type of a (more or less) genteel Anglicanism aglow with an aura of all sorts of

niceties. This all-too-short allusion surely will be understood by all those familiar with a certain aspect of the
English scene dominated by a "dry humor" and a real horror
for all absolutes. Still, nursery-rhyme Anglicanism alone
does not explain the rise of "Pollyanna Catholicism." Equally
important is an old charge against our faith, to wit that
it is "medieval," mournful, reactionary, repressive, cruel,
morbid, and enslaving. And, indeed, in certain areas of the
Catholic world, medieval aspects of life and faith still
survive. The burial brotherhoods in some of the Mediter-
ranean cities, the Penitentes in the New World, the vaults
of the Capuchins in Rome where the skeletons of the
Princesses Barberini tastefully assembled as candelabras are
dangling from the ceiling, or the corridors of the Franciscan
Monastery in Palermo with the deceased brothers leaning
as mummies against the wall — all this is a little bit too
much for the nerves and dispositions of "enlightened" and
"progressive" British and American travelers — among
whom, oddly enough, we would have to include our "Pollyanna Catholics."

From Froude and Kingsley to Maria Monk and Coulton
there has always been a holy terror inspired by the Catholic
faith and Catholic forms as something magic, demonic,
and immoral. "Pollyanna Catholicism" came into existence
in order to deflate this very picture of an ancient, demon-
iacal, and sinister Catholicism and to represent it as something entirely harmless and tame. It rose from the pages
of Catholic humorists and apologists, from the drawing
boards of Catholic cartoonists and from the lips of Catholic
soapbox orators and after-dinner speakers. It was born
as a piece of clever defensive action, part mimicry, part
counterattack, and intoxicated primarily those busy in
manufacturing this brew. We have within our ranks real

addicts to "Pollyanna Catholicism," and there is a certain danger that it might become the *popular* form of the faith of a most important part of the Catholic orbit.

What then is the essence of "Pollyanna Catholicism"? First of all, it tells to the faithful and the infidels alike that the faith is by no means a "yoke" (the sweet yoke of Christ) but that to be a Catholic is great fun. It tells us that as soon as you become a Catholic almost every problem is solved, every intellectual question is answered, every dilemma disposed of. The cross which every Christian has to carry is naïvely forgotten. We are being told that there is nothing at all serious, tragic, profound, or esoteric about the Catholic Church and the Catholic faith, which are hilarious as a comic strip, easy to understand as an elementary reader, painless as a haircut, modern as a jet plane, chummy as an Elk convention, soothing as a cough syrup, smart and fashionable as a Dior dress, streamlined as a Studebaker and more advantageous for your mental health than five thousand dollars worth of brain surgery. There is nothing, so the argument goes, that we had not ages ago, that we have not the answer for. St. Augustine anticipated Charles Darwin; the mystics with their gift of ubiquity got better service than we from railroads or television; Chesterton, Belloc, St. Thomas, and Suárez had all the answers for all the questions. He who does not join the Catholic Church is a fool who misses the best things in life rather than — as in many cases — a tragic figure wrestling against terrible odds with the meaning of human existence. Hardly are we aware of the fact that some of those outside the Church have not seen anything but "Pollyanna Catholicism," this pseudo-Catholic clowning on a family circus level which has the tendency to branch out in all sorts of directions.

"Pollyanna Catholicism" rests on a profound error as to the true spirit of our faith. There is, as we have stated before, such a thing as Catholic humor and even, believe it or not, Catholic satire. But neither of these has anything to do with that cheap sweetness we get in the comic, darling little nuns with their pouting mouths like baby carps or the Father who looks like a clerical Dick Tracy, Jack Dempsey, and Bing Crosby rolled into one. Don't misunderstand me; a true Catholic is anything but a "clerical"; there are innumerable priests, friars, and nuns who are extremely comical and present excellent targets for humor and satire. There is nothing at all wrong in joking about the terrestrial aspects of the Catholic laity or the hierarchy. "Reverence" of that sort never characterized Catholic civilizations. Yet there is, I am afraid, nothing intrinsically amusing, funny, comical, or droll about *being* a priest or a nun. The decision for entering upon that state of life is deadly serious.

Every conscious imitation of Christ is deadly serious because the Savior's life on earth, thoroughly changing mankind's relation with God, was of unique importance — the whole life of Christ, starting with the dramatic circumstances of His Incarnation, birth, the flight to Egypt, and leading finally to the Garden of Gethsemani where the Son of Man was sweating blood, to betrayal, to the cruel death on the cross, the rising from the dead, Ascension, and martyrdom of almost all of His disciples. "Jesus will agonize until the end of the world; one ought not to sleep during this time." Naturally one can charge that Pascal, who wrote these words, was a Jansenist which, indeed, he was, but the fact remains that the agony in the Garden of Gethsemani, the darling little nuns and the two-fisted crooning priests from the Hollywood movies providing box office records, just do not mix. (Dom Camillo may be two-fisted, but we have seen him in terrible solitude, deserted, and with tears in his eyes. No pillar of "Pollyanna Catholicism" he!)

By concentrating on the frills of our faith, by remaining

deaf to the nostalgia of tortured souls and honestly inquiring
minds outside of our community, by cheapening down and
distorting the very character of the Gospels, by ignoring
the fact that God is still essentially to us a hidden God,
whom man frequently can only approach after terrible
struggles, ceaseless efforts, and desperate calls — we are doing
something truly negative. Of course, real despair for the
Christian is not legitimate, but the Christian certainly can
be *sad*. "Pollyanna Catholics" should take notice that this
earth is a "vale of tears," and that there is nothing Jansen-
istic or Manichaean about this passage in a great prayer.
A short moment of recollection reminding us of the diabolic
suffering of millions of fellow Christians east of the Iron
Curtain should predispose us to view the gay manifestations
of "Pollyanna Catholicism" at least with a slight air of
skepticism.

One repeatedly encounters a standard defense of this
"Catholicism in Six Easy Lessons." The average non-Catholic, so the argument runs, presented with this nifty and
charming picture of the faith and the Church, will drop all
his odious prejudices and immediately "fall" for the Mystical
Body. That this occasionally may be true, we will not deny.
Still, one has to doubt that by this sort of bait we will
attract the very best outside the Church, those who need
the truth and the light most. There is a definite danger
that this picture of the faith will primarily appeal to the
lightweights who, out of a certain emptiness and metaphysical boredom, are just "shopping around" and are happy
to find a "handy," arty, and charming religion which now,
losing its social handicaps, is getting a foothold in the
mink-coat set and also provides their flabby souls with a
snugly fitting corset. There is no escape from suffering, and
it is the cross which makes suffering *meaningful,* thus
eliminating despair which is the product of *senseless* suf-

fering. It was Strindberg who asked for the epitaph on his tombstone: *"Ave O Crux, Unica Spes."* From mere Fish-on-Friday people we, again, ought to become the depositaries of the cross.

No doubt the quest of the very best, of suffering souls and thirsting minds, will not effectively be met by the cheap images, the snap arguments, the sometimes arrogant salesmanship of "Pollyanna Catholicism" and "Catholic Smart Aleckism," the twin brother of the former. The latter reaches much further than Catholic cartoons, movies, wisecracks, *bon mots,* and rectory jokes. "Catholic Smart Aleckism" promises "all the answers to all the questions" and thus acts as the intellectual counterpart to the superficial sentimentalities of "Pollyanna Catholicism." "Problems? Only the others have 'em; we've solved them all," as a Catholic philosophy professor once declared to his students in class. "Catholic Smart Aleckism" implies that if only the papal encyclicals would be put into action, straight Thomism would be taught in Harvard and strict enough laws would be passed to prevent the sale of modern novels and the showing of films with D ratings, the Devil would be licked, the Kremlin would collapse, history would come to a standstill, and all moral, economic, psychological, and political problems eliminated.

It can be argued that this cocksure optimism has to be understood against the background of the ghastly failure of modern civilization, but modern man, however miserable and desperate, vaguely senses that our "Catholic Smart Alecks" overreach themselves. "The history of every human being is the history of a failure," is a sentence from Sartre, but in earthly relations it is quite correct. *We can hope for heaven, but not for paradise.* We cannot promise paradise because man's nature is a fallen nature, and because emphatically while having some answers, we do *not* have *all* the answers. *God alone has them.* To put ourselves in God's place is sheer blasphemy. For every answer we find (and we constantly find new, valid answers) there are ten or a hundred more new problems to be solved. To the uneducated or uninitiated in or outside the Church our knowledge looks like the huge, concrete surface of a giant airdrome, but once the plane is high up in the air the solid, immutable concrete mass appears hardly to be larger than a postage stamp.

Much of this particular evil, which repels rather than attracts the non-Catholic, is due to the training in Catholic colleges. Mr. (now Father) William B. Hill in a brilliant article published in *America* (March 13, 1943) acknowledged that "there is ample evidence that medieval philosophy and sixteenth century apologetics, as they are combined in our colleges, have been largely responsible for some of the imperfections of our graduates." No wonder that after leaving college the student's "tendency henceforward is to become an angry champion of faith and morals." He engenders "Smart Aleckism" on the highest level. Fully confident that he will crash the gates and shake the world by coldly building up mountainous arguments out of dry syllogisms he remains blissfully ignorant that "life lays a trap for logicians. The more logically sound they are, the less psychologically sound they may be."

Again and again we have witnessed discussions in which the Catholic participants have pulled out arguments with the ease and good-humored contempt of a magician pulling rabbits out of his top hat. Again and again we have heard concepts like the "Natural Law" glibly mentioned by these *terribles simplificateurs* as if its existence could be proved with a swift legerdemain. Boundless irritation on one side and the thinly veiled accusation of invincible ignorance suggested on the other, with the abyss wider than ever before, have been only too often the result of such "conversations" — conversations, not conversions. Yet invincible ignorance characterizes fallen man and we all are invincibly ignorant in *some* matters. No wonder therefore that this failing frequently appears where reason alone is bound to founder and ("incalculable") grace has to co-operate. Our faith cannot adequately be approached by an intellectual "Smart Aleckism" because its great mysteries will always escape the "deft handling" by "thinking machines," be they of a human order or a product of I.B.M. Of all this St. Thomas was acutely aware when years before his death he had laid down his pen.

And since we have alluded to the soap box before, let me remind you of a brilliant orator, the late Father Vincent McNabb, whose saintliness captivated and impressed all those who listened to him. Though certainly capable of "thinking on his feet" his honesty never permitted him to reply to hecklers and sincere inquirers with snap answers. Again and again he would humbly say, awkwardly smiling: "I just could not tell you," "I really don't know," "I would have to think that over." Yet curiously enough, each time he confessed his ignorance, he scored for the cause he defended.

"Pollyanna Catholicism" and "Catholic Smart Aleckism" with their racy clichés, their arrogance and oversimplifications have, to the "outsider," another meaning than to the addicts of these deviations within our ranks. These two phenomena help to convince the non-Catholics that the Church is something like a colossal industrial enterprise, a super Standard Oil with armies of devoted, slogan shouting, unthinking partisans on the march and a variety of circus performances as a "come on," running at the same time. Yet the Church is by no means a smoothly functioning mammoth institution of clowns and robots, directed by a general manager with twenty-four table phones and seventy secretaries. Neither is she an international chain of soul clinics and life guidance centers, nor is her theology a gigantic file of ten thousand little drawers with "all the answers" in form of a streamlined, divine "Information, Please!" Indeed it is good to be a Catholic, it is a noble thing and pleasing in the eyes of God to be a good Catholic, and God wants *everyone* to be a good Catholic. But it is by no means always "great fun" to be a Catholic. It may involve inhuman suffering — and not only from the hands of fanatic enemies of Christ and His Church. Worse than that: one may suffer not only with the Church, but also *within* the Church and *through* the Church.

This, our Church, is the Church Militant and this implies a real, *live* organism with all the human passions on the loose and which, therefore, can go through every imaginable crisis in which obedience is clashing with disobedience, loyalty with disloyalty, intelligence with stupidity, generosity with greed, sanctity with real evil, surrender to God's will with naked ambition. The two-thousand-year-old tradition, the rational character of our doctrines, infallibility on the highest plane — all this does not dispense the individual thinking, struggling Catholic from wrestling in a very personal way with each tenet, each new cognition, each problem in life. The tasks may be clear, but they have to be *mastered* nonetheless. The true Catholic is fully a human being, *homo sapiens, proles Dei,* dedicated to the quest of truth, "condemned to be free," exposed to all risks, called to create — and neither a clown, a parrot, or a robot.

HOW I LOST MY PREJUDICE

BY MOST REV. VINCENT S. WATERS

I AM a Southerner, I have been prejudiced. I had to get rid of my prejudice in order to get to be a little more Catholic. I shall tell you the story of how I lost my prejudice.

I remember the first time I boarded a streetcar in Baltimore, having come up from Virginia. A colored person sat beside me, I arose and got off the car. I had never had to solve that problem before and that was the way I solved it. At that time I was already thinking of studying for the priesthood.

I lost my prejudice not through any intellectual gymnastics or logic. Prejudice is not in the reason or the will, but is influenced by the emotions. Prejudice is where war and hatred are, where the devil works, in the emotions. The only way we will ever be able to lose prejudice is to allow the right emotions to influence our wills in the right way and to get rid of the wrong emotions. Our emotions should be subject to God and to reason, just as well as to our intellect.

I lost my prejudice by meeting a person, a colored person. He had come through Florida, up through North Carolina and Virginia, heading North for opportunity. He hoped to educate himself. He already had two years of high school. He was a Protestant. He had a good voice. He thought he

13

might get on the radio. He thought he might get a job at night and go to school during the day. He was outside Philadelphia looking around, as a colored boy would, at the public buildings. He saw a fine looking building, walked up and peeked in the door. Some very nice young lady said, "Won't you come in? This is a Catholic parochial high school. It has just been finished and we are having open house today." She showed him around and in a little while asked him if he would like to come to school there. He said, "Oh, could I come here? In Florida we don't have colored children with the white, and I am not a Catholic." To which there was the response: "Well, there will be some colored children here and we will even have some non-Catholics." "Oh, I would love going here," he answered. He got a job working at night, and went to day school. He was the only colored boy in his class. He was treated wonderfully well. He even became the president of the class. After a few months, he was so attracted to the Catholic faith that he asked the chaplain to take him under instruction. He became a Catholic and a good one.

At the end of his graduation year, in 1930, he told the priest: "Father, I will never be satisfied unless I have a chance to study for the priesthood." The priest said, "There are not many bishops in the country who will accept a colored student because they are unable to place them, but if you wish to study for our religious order we will be glad to send you to Rome."

He went back to Florida to tell his mother good-by. When she heard he was a Catholic, she wasn't too disturbed, but when she heard he was going to be a priest, she was almost willing to disown him. He gathered up his things to go back to Philadelphia and off to Rome. When he got back there he met with disappointment. His scholarship had been canceled. He did not have the money to go to Rome, but he knew he should go to Rome to be a priest. He went to all the Protestant churches and asked the ministers, "Permit me to sing for your congregation. I want to be a priest and I have to get enough money to buy my ticket to Rome." They gave him permission to sing and one said: "If this boy wants to be a priest, that's what we want him to be." They took up collections and by the end of the week he had enough money to get steerage passage.

He found himself on the ship a couple of decks below water, but when Sunday came he asked permission to go up and hear Mass. Mass was being offered in first class. One priest was serving another. He asked permission to serve in the place of one of the priests. At the end, the priest said: "Boy, where are you going?" "I am going to Rome to be a priest." A little inquiry showed that he didn't have enough money to get from Naples to Rome. Well, they gave him his transportation and enough money to be sure that he got to Rome.

When he finally reached Rome, he found the religious house, but when they finally got somebody down to the door who could speak English, they said: "Why did you come? We told you not to come. We canceled this year all American scholarships. We have no room. We can't even help you for tonight. We have people from all the other countries — they are even sleeping in the corridors." Someone said: "Well, there is another American community in Rome. They ought to be able to help him; send him there." There the priest was living in the sacristy and taking his meals at the nearby hotel. He couldn't help him but sent him to the North American College, because he was an American. Monsignor Burke, who was our rector at that time, was a wonderfully great man. He was big in stature and his heart was as big as his body. He said: "Sure boy, we will put you to work, and when you get enough

money we will send you back." He gave him a job in the
kitchen. I remember when he first came out to serve the
students with a white apron and a white cap, the whole
student body got up and gave him a cheer. They had not
seen a colored boy in four or five years.

Many of the Southern boys took a real interest in him
because they knew what difficulties he had overcome. He had
a very strict program for himself. He knew that he would
need the recommendation of the rector if he hoped to get
anywhere. It was very difficult for him to get any papers
from this country, even the baptismal certificate due to the
way he left the United States of America. After a few months
he became somewhat discouraged but he kept very close
to the college.

I think maybe this little incident had something to do with
the ultimate outcome. He borrowed books. He borrowed one
from me which interested him very much — it was *The Autobiography of the Little Flower*. I think that he got a notion
from that, because a couple of weeks later he came to the door
after night prayers, when we were not supposed to be talking.
He knocked, and I opened the door. He was trembling.
I said, "Come in, Charlie, sit down and tell me what's
wrong." He said: "I had to do it, I was getting nowhere."
I said: "What are you talking about?" "Well," he said,
"you know I couldn't even get my certificate or any recommendations, so I asked the Monsignor: "Monsignor, I must
have enough money to be sent home. I wonder if before
I go I could have an audience with our Holy Father."
"Sure, boy, put you on next week," Monsignor answered.

The next night he wrote a letter. He said: "Dear Holy
Father." And he told him his story. The next day, kneeling
in front of the Holy Father, he pulled out this letter and
gave it to His Holiness, Pope Pius XI, when he came to
kiss his ring. The Holy Father took it and gave it to an

attendant. A Cardinal was appointed to take care of the boy's case. The next day he was sent over to the Urban College and before the end of the week he was a seminarian.

That is a long answer, but you can see what that did to my Southern prejudice. That boy was more pious than I will ever be. And he certainly had more difficulties than I had to follow his vocation. So, I decided I had better help these poor Protestant colored boys coming through Richmond from the South, on their way to Philadelphia, where they might become Catholics and later seminarians, and priests.

The first thing I did when I was ordained was to volunteer for work among the colored people of the South.

THE CULTURE OF
THE CHURCH

BY FRANK O'MALLEY

AMONG the preparatory prayers of the Mass, there are these words from Psalm 42: "Judge me, O God, and distinguish my cause from the nation that is not holy." However inadequately accomplished, the purpose of this essay is to affirm and distinguish our cause as Catholic minds and human beings from the nation and from the world that are not holy — to affirm the strength and meaning of the world of the Church for our varied worlds of living and working. As Christopher Dawson points out in a remarkable essay, there is, even in the modern world, "a tradition of sacred culture which it has been the mission of the Church to nourish and preserve — and to nourish and preserve it even in the nation that is not holy. "However secularized our modern civilization may become," Dawson continues, "this sacred tradition [this sacred life] remains like a river in the desert, and a genuine religious education can still use it to irrigate the thirsty lands and to change the face of the world with the promise of a new life. The great obstacle is the failure of Christians themselves to understand the depth of that tradition and the inexhaustible possibilities of new life that it contains."

For many reasons it is regrettable that we have to be at all agitated about the problem of the Church and modern culture. Certainly, had the lives and works of modern men

18

been naturally and vitally integrated with the life of the Church, it would be quite unnecessary now to write or talk about the vitality of religion, of the world of worship, with respect to man's life and action in every field. It is most evident today that we are self-conscious about the truths and values we possess as Catholics. We do not take them naturally; we are not easy with them, since they are not, as they ought to be, the sustaining rhythm of our existence. Therefore, we feel the need of making them the objects of discussions, conferences, symposia, lectures and articles; and, as a result, what was and is natural and easy, in the rhythm of existence, may become artificial in effect, may sound complex and academical, large questions for forums and organizations and special movements created to consider them. The life of the Church, of course, is not to be dealt with or disposed of as a problem, a formula, or even as a philosophy, for the Church is a total existence, a living reality, a true "consciousness" that involves man and all mankind, one not to be reduced merely to the motions of dialectics or the abstractions of exposition. Yet our self-consciousness today is vastly more desirable than the state of death, the almost complete "unconsciousness" in which Catholics (and non-Catholics alike) have lived for too long, blind, somnolent, petrified, with only the rarest shattering of the composure of the liberal-bourgeois generations. And our very self-consciousness helps to make us aware and to convince us that the voice of the Word can still be heard among the men of our irreligious civilization, that the spirit of the Church is still strong at least in the spiritual underground of this embattled and explosive universe.

The Catholic intellect and art of the modern world have enjoyed a tremendous source of power in the liturgy, the cult of the Church. Many Catholics all over the world are experiencing the relation between the world of worship

(the cult) and the world of human experience (our civilization). And many important movements of Catholic life and
action in our own country regard the liturgy as their right
and necessary root or incentive and as the heart wherein
their various efforts will be refined and resolved (although
the liturgy is never to be thought of as a means simply to
practical solutions of individual or social difficulties or as an
instrument existing only to construct a brilliant aesthetical
or intellectual "culture"; nor is the life of the Church at any
time to be debased into a stamping ground for blundering
activists and reformists). Such efforts verify what has been
termed the resurgent wonder of the faith now at work, at
work clearly beneath the confusion and horror that blight
the surface of man's life in the twentieth century. There
were the first easy-flowing, peaceful ten years; and then came
the terror: World War I, followed by a lush and riotous
aftermath issuing into the economic depression of the
thirties, which closed in the disaster of World War II,
raging into the forties. Now well within the brink of the
fifties we look out, with a certain fear and anguish, upon
a more or less desolated civilization and brood about the
possibilities of universal catastrophe.

A great modern poet provides us with an appropriate
phrase and a figure by which to describe vividly our present
age and our present state of existence: "There are the noises.
But there is something here that is more terrible: the stillness. I believe that in great conflagrations there sometimes
occurs such a moment of extreme tension: the jets of water
fall back, the firemen no longer climb their ladders, no
one stirs. Noiselessly a black cornice thrusts itself forward
overhead, and a high wall, behind which the fire shoots up,
leans forward, noiselessly. All stand and wait, with shoulders
raised and faces puckered over the eyes, for the terrific

crash. The stillness here is like that." Nevertheless, in this
turbulent century of terrible noises and terrible stillnesses,
this century of extreme tensions, there has re-emerged — in
the depths indeed — a real and wonderful "consciousness"
as dynamic, diverse, and universal as the Church itself, a
life that has expressed itself in great achievements in art
and literature, in theology and philosophy, in sociology,
economics and politics, and in education — all of which, for
their authority and effectiveness, draw in some measure at
least upon the liturgy of the Church defined well as *the
public and corporate worship of God.*

When one considers the mangled and mangling "progress"
of the main events of modern history, this renascence and
capacity for renascence — everlasting in the Church — become all the more impressive and comprehensible. Indeed,
for many years, Dawson has been saying that the present,
overwhelming crises of Western civilization are due, precisely, to the disjoining of culture from its proper religious
motivation; and he has been insisting that the center of
culture is cult or worship. This insistence is one that Catholics especially should appreciate and grasp. For the Catholic,
above all, ought to realize that the meaning of the world
is to give God, in Gerard Manley Hopkins' language,
"praise, reverence, and service, to give Him glory," that
religious experience has, as Romano Guardini puts it, "a
unique relation to life . . . that it is itself life," and that
its effects must be the springing-up of all "vital forces and
manifestations." So requisite and so important is this acknowledgment of the heart of Christian culture as cult that
we are ready to accept the judgment that any Catholic
expression or effort, in the interest of the attainment of
Christian culture, lacking the sense of corporate worship
ignores reality and denies to itself "the special apprehension

of Catholicism proper to the twentieth century." As a consequence, it cannot sufficiently distinguish its cause or character from the nation that is not holy.

Thus we come to the central matter: what can or what must every Catholic today understand or derive, as he moves through time and civilization, from the liturgy, from the cult of the Church? Guardini, with exceptional brilliance, acuity and force, has provided us with the answer to this question. As he sees it, we are, whatever to the contrary we must witness, also the witnesses of an event of enormous significance: "That stupendous Fact that is the Church is once more becoming a living reality, and we understand that she truly is the One and the All. We dimly guess something of the passion with which great saints clung to her and fought for her. In the past their words may sometimes have sounded empty phrases. But now a light is breaking! The thinker, with rapture of spirit, will perceive in the church the ultimate and vast synthesis of all realities. The artist, with a force that moves his heart to the depths, will experience in the Church the overwhelming transformation, the exquisite refinement, and the sublime transfiguration of all reality by a sovereign radiance and beauty. The man of moral endeavor will see in her the fullness of living perfection, in which all man's capacities are awakened and sanctified in Christ; the power which contrasts uncompromisingly Yea and Nay, and demands decision between them; the determined fight of God's Kingdom against evil. To the politician . . . she is revealed as that supreme order in which every living thing finds its fulfillment and realizes the entire significance of its individual being. It achieves this in relation to beings and the whole, and precisely in virtue of its unique individual quality combines with its fellows to build up the great Civitas, in which every force and individual peculiarity are alive, but at the same time are disciplined by the vast cosmic order which comes from God, the Three in One. To the man of social temper she offers the experience of an unreserved sharing, in which all belongs to all, and all are one in God, so completely that it would be impossible to conceive a profounder unity."

It is in the wisdom of such utterance that we can comprehend the true strength and meaning of the cult of the Church. We know that for too long a period the idea of liturgy was reduced to signify the aesthetics of worship or the ceremonial rules, the externals. Today, however, we are able to know the liturgy in the fullness of the Pauline and Patristic meaning and with the complete value given it by the Church. The liturgy, holding all creation as signed by God's excellence and goodness, orders everything in existence — man, things, nature, civilization — to God, with grace and through prayer: "Creation as a whole embraced in the relation with God established by prayer; the fullness of nature, evoked and transfigured by the fullness of grace, organized by the organic law of the Triune God, and steadily growing according to a rhythm perfectly simple yet infinitely rich; the vessel and expression of the life of Christ and the Christian — this is the liturgy. The liturgy is creation, redeemed and at prayer, because it is the Church at prayer." The liturgy, expressing "a community of spirit and spiritual life," involves at once the Mystical Body, Christ and all Christians at prayer. It is the acceptance of this truth, with its wealth of personal and communal meanings, that today characterizes all those persons anxious to reveal and to live the profound and total life of the cult of the Church.

To those who do understand the grandeur and reality of the Church at prayer and who live in the greatness of the perspectives of corporate worship, no Christian will be seen, in reference to God or to the world, as a lonely and solitary creature. This was very clear to Cardinal Newman:

"Socrates wished to improve man, but he laid no stress on their acting in concert in order to secure that improvement . . ." Contrastingly, with the Incarnation, with Christ and the Christian order, there comes the reality of community, making the fellowship of Christians an unmistakable object and duty, and arising "out of the intimate relation between Him and His subjects, which, in bringing them all to Him as their common Father, necessarily brings them to each other." And Karl Adam has also stated what we mean, that with every Christian there is the complete Christ, the Head and fullness of His members composing one Body: "Consequently we do not face God in isolation and loneliness; we come before Him in Christ, united in a profound union with His only-begotten Son. Just as breathing and feeling and thinking are functions of our natural being, so living in Christ is a function of our Christian being. Christ is the new sphere in which our whole religious life is to be lived. . . . And even our natural activities, which must at bottom be controlled by religion, are exercised within this sphere: our daily work, our achievements, our struggles, our suffering and our dying. The Christian never toils and suffers and dies *alone,* that word is absent from his vocabulary. Christianity is a living and dying in full membership with Christ and His members." Hopkins, it may be added, has beautifully recreated this theme in the poetic experience of "The Blessed Virgin compared to the Air we Breathe":

> Men here may draw like breath
> More Christ and baffle death;
> Who, born so, comes to be
> New self and nobler me
> In each one and each one
> More makes, when all is done,
> Both God's and Mary's Son.

Claudel, likewise, writes of the community, accompanying a man as a Christian and in his Christian status, in the moving lines, from *The Tidings Brought to Mary,* spoken by Anne Vercors before he sets out on his pilgrimage to Jerusalem:

> I am not alone! A great multitude
> rejoice and depart with me! . . .
> And as it is true that the Christian is never alone,
> but is in communion with all his brothers,
> The whole kingdom is with me, invoking, and
> drawing near to the Seat of God, taking anew
> its course toward him,
> And I am its deputy and I carry it with me
> To lay it once again upon the eternal Pattern.

Catholic Christians, as worshipers then, cannot be isolated individualists. It is required of them to be persons, new selves and nobler men, in the community of persons. Appropriate to mention here is Jacques Maritain's now famous distinction between personality and individuality, made in a number of places in his work. In Maritain's viewing, a Christian is a person — and was a person in medieval culture, a culture organically informed by the Church. With the rise and advance of the modern world, the person became, it seems, strictly an individual. Yet the core of personality, Maritain declares, is the subsistence of spirit, of soul, whereas, for men as for all other things in nature, the core of individuality is to be found in matter: everything, whether mineral, vegetative, animal or human, is an individual of a species. Man alone has spirit, man alone dwells in the community of the spirit, is personal. So a Christian city, as Maritain defines it, remains as essentially and fundamentally anti-individualist as it is personal and communal. There can be no place for unbridled individualism in the Mystical Body — and when we have stripped our

civilization of unbridled individualism and all the selfish
brutality it suggests, when we are dominated by the communal idea, the deep consideration and reverence for our
fellow men, then we shall begin to live in the spirit of
community that receives its pattern from our community
of worship, our community of sacrifice, love, and order.
We are aware, however, in modern civilization of a strained
state in the relationship between the community and the
individual personality and even between the Church and
the individual personality — a ruinous condition contrary to
the nature of things. On this point, Guardini has spoken of
the special task of our time: "To see how the Church and
the individual personality are mutually bound together;
how they live the one by the other; and how in this
relationship we must see the justification of ecclesiastical
authority, and to make this insight once more an integral
part of our life and consciousness is the fundamental
achievement to which our age is called." To be successful
in such a task, we must reject the common and repressive
philosophies around us, like individualism on one side, and
communism or any form of totalitarianism on the other:
"Once more we must be wholeheartedly Catholic. Our
thought and feeling must be determined by the essential
nature of the Catholic position, must proceed from that
direct insight into the center of reality which is the privilege
of the genuine Catholic."

The privileges and truths of the Mystical Body are, of
course, best taken, best made into objective reality, by
genuine participation in corporate worship. It is said that
the law of prayer clarifies and instills the law of belief; and
we may append that it clarifies and instills as well the law
of action. So if the people who throng the churches in un-
countable numbers actually seized upon the truth that as
worshipers they enfold the entire Christian fellowship, that

they are living and moving (in the words from the Mass, itself a completely communal act) "through Him and in Him and with Him," as His Body and His members — they would of necessity distinguish their cause from the nation that is not holy, carrying over into the currents and cross-currents of their day laboring this wonderful consciousness of which they have repossessed themselves. In any event, the liturgical movement, the great protection of the culture of the Church, with all its social, political, intellectual, and creative manifestations, is a sure sign that the spiritual life and the community of the spirit are growing, even though they are not roaring, among the people. Despite all the weaknesses, waverings, and imperfections inseparable from human works, there is today, as Don Sturzo has discerned, "a reassertion of the character of Christianity as responding to all situations and all needs influencing by its teaching and its spirit every society, even those as refractory as ours of today. Nor should we pass over the great contribution made by the Church to the sciences, to letters and the arts, the modern growth of universities all over the world; the ever-expanding number of missions, the continuous increase of institutions, especially among women, for education, relief, charity, of which the most outstanding as examples of sacrifice are the leper settlements in Asia, Africa, and America." And Don Sturzo considers that, in the three great battles against the endemic naturalism of our time — the first against totalitarianism of whatever sort, the second against any economic system that preys upon the whole of society and the poor particularly, and the third for a universal construction of justice and peace making war impossible — it will be the spirit of love and of community that must provide the form for the action. This form is forever available to us in our corporate worship and instructs us as members of Christ's Church in our responsibility to be new witnesses to God, the persons who will "bear witness to Him among all peoples and in all ages to the end."

This then is the day for the new witnesses. But at this immense moment, when there comes distinctly before us our fresh and holy opportunity to bear witness in all the domains of living and learning, far too many of us falter and fail. It is sensible, therefore, to consider what elements or features or forces in our life diminish or destroy our effectiveness as witnesses, block up or dam the movement of "the river in the desert" which is the spirit of the Church in civilization, contribute to our failure to distinguish our cause in the nation or the world that is not holy. Our American civilization is undeniably one of the most potent of world civilizations. And it is a culture of freedom in which the life of the mind and the spirit should flourish. Yet some aspects of contemporary American civilization definitely interfere with and obstruct the life of the spirit. These same features surely taint the spirit of Catholics in this country and make them, in many important respects, indistinguishable from nonworshipers.

Sentimentalism: We can all become very tender about some poor child who must die before Christmas. But since our tenderness is not authentic goodness, a real principle of action and obligation in charity, a responsibility deriving from our need to recognize our right relations as individuals to the whole community, we are almost apathetic about the hunting and maiming of the Negro, the mark set upon the Jew, the poverty and disease that still afflict considerable numbers of our population. We like to have reality (the true nature and civilization of which the liturgy reveals to us) and the firm obligations of reality concealed from us. We prefer to feel good rather than to be good; we prefer to be deluded into static complacency by the soothing voices of orators, preachers, and publicists who assure us that we are beyond censure, beyond judgment. For the true form and strength of our magnificent act of worship we substitute the more pallid and more feeble formulas of minor pieties. In all this we retard the dynamics of the living Church. Today, against the formidable and perversely "religious" drive of Soviet metaphysical materialism and atheism conjoined with brutish physical power, we fortify ourselves, as John Courtney Murray has observed, with a practical materialism compounded with a sentimental moral idealism which equals for us the "American way of life." As Catholics we have in truth a firmer fortification — yet we do not seem to realize it. If we had a better sense of our life in the Church, we would have at this hour a better courage and a better power to confront the terrors of history and to resist the pressure of the age — upon leaving the consecrated precincts of the Church.

Commercialism: It is not necessary to cry this up, so obvious is it. Our lack of reverence for personality and communities of personalities is revealed in the instinct to exploit, often with high pressure methods, people or values or institutions for profit or fame or power or success of any kind — and what can be more horrible than the commercial exploitation of spiritual realities? Certain endeavors labeled Catholic seem to have dangers in this regard. They would force, through commercial techniques and means and even by commercial standards for achievement, the entrance of the Church — or the Church as their sponsors understand it — into society at large. But these movements merely force the note outrageously. For the Catholic Dale Carnegies are not likely, in the end anyway, to be distinguishable from their prototype, notorious for his commercial, exploitative approaches to human relationships. A Catholic Dale Carnegie-ism is not expected to be the salvation of the nation or the world. It is too much like, disconcertingly like, the world it imitates too much. It does not really distinguish its cause from the world that is not holy. When and if an organic Catholic or Christian culture develops in our country, it will not come from the rush and rampage of any ape-ing "how to win friends and influence people" evangel. Moreover, our resources as Catholics are infinitely greater — and decidedly more interesting and less tarnished — than those of the New York or Hollywood wits. With respect to any kind of commercial exploiter of the spirit, these words from Psalm 42 apply: "From the unjust and deceitful man, deliver me: for Thou art my God and my strength."

Sectarianism or Provincialism: Americans are often accused of not having enough appreciation of the ways and problems of other peoples and cultures, of lacking, on the spiritual and human level, universalization of point of view. There is considerable truth in this charge. And American Catholics share in this provincialism and display it in various disturbing ways. Consider, for instance, the current state of Catholic journalism, especially in the general run of Catholic newspapers. Nothing could possibly be more provincial or sectarian than the sadly unenlightening accounts of "Catholic" personages and "Catholic" doings, ironically summarized in the legendary but representative headline from a Catholic journal: "Catholic Plane Crashes on Catholic Meadow." Our newspapers by and large may be, in the narrowest possible sense, Catholic by denomination but they are hardly Catholic by inspiration or spirit.

Here, too, we may note the common attitude of Catholics toward a Catholic literature. They see it as something hopelessly sectarian, as the product of highly denominationalized mentalities and movements. But the truly great and serious Catholic poets and novelists of our civilization (Bloy, Bernanos, Mauriac, Undset, Claudel, Peguy, Hopkins, to mention only a few) show that a Catholic literature is in no way narrow or sectarian but rather fully and universally Christian (embracing "the whole world spiritually as a vast kingdom of realities"), that the significance of the Catholic writer is not to be found finally in his moralism or even in his aesthetic character or in his intellectual power. Instead it is to be seen that his way is essentially liturgical: his life and his meaning rest at the heart of the world of the Church, the world of worship; his own world of intellect and art moves vitally within this world of worship. As Guardini writes, "A religious process of incalculable importance has begun." In this process a powerful Catholic literature has been created. And Catholics should understand this process more fully and vitally themselves. Then they may arrive at and acquire a genuinely Catholic world view. Without it they shall be — and ought to feel — segregated, sullen, and arbitrary.

Catholics everywhere, speaking in the main, have too determined a tendency to restrict the limits of their activity or influence in constructively spiritual and intellectual directions. Of course, in this country, some Catholic persons and organizations, uninhibited as well as of exceedingly limited outlook (that of a primitivism combining sometimes a pseudo-Americanism with a pseudo-Catholicism) have never hesitated to rush onto the streets, practically with club and gun, to uphold, in ways unspiritual and rude and dubiously Catholic, the name and dignity of the Church. The profound point is: we say, as Conrad Bonacina declares, that Catholic Christianity is the universal religion of humanity. But then the question comes: what good is our saying it, "if we show by the whole tenor of our apologetic that we really believe no such thing, that when it comes to the point we are not equal to the logic of such a tremendous conception?" Actually, if we as Catholics in America do believe in Catholicism as the universal Kingdom, as the Church of all mankind, a requirement of faith, "then it behooves us to think out the implications and see to it that our *Weltanschauung* as Catholics accords with them." Our Church has an historical mission which it must gravely regard and we must ourselves gravely regard its demands upon us. Jean Danielou now acquaints us with our true vocation: since Christianity must become incarnate among and transfigure different civilizations and cultures, it unavoidably becomes our vocation to circulate or disseminate through the alien world and never to seclude or enclave ourselves. Going out among others, "we must become one of them, but we must without question avoid being contaminated by our contact with them. All is lost if, when we go out among them, we become like them, instead of their becoming like us." In such an event, we have failed utterly to distinguish our cause from the nation that is not holy.

Externalization: In our civilization, too much stress is laid upon external and artificial devices, upon techniques, practices, processes, analyses, and activities. We do not realize sufficiently the importance of development, of growth, of synthesis, of creation. We are great believers in efficiency, in the mechanical and industrial manipulation of all our resources. And in a culture which understands machines and formulas rather than spiritual form, there cannot be too much chance for religion and spiritual regeneration, for those creators of culture who see existence under the aspect of eternity, eternal form.

Nowhere does the barbarism of externalization more unpleasantly show itself than in our universities and colleges. What is the formula by which we conduct our schools? It seems to be: bureaucratic organization and oppressiveness plus busyness plus competitiveness sometimes amounting to murderous connivance. Contrarily, what should the form

for the Christian school be? This: respect, reverence for
the personalities of both teachers and students plus development (for "what ultimately matters is not activity, but
development," a sentence which should be the sign manual
for Christian education) plus a real sense of community. The
grievous question is: in how many of our schools does this
form shine? Or, in how many Catholic schools and colleges
is any serious effort made to achieve a Christian community
and a Christian culture? There are, naturally, here and there
the valiant efforts and programs of those who struggle away
to reveal the relationship between religion and culture and
to establish the synthesis to which the decent mind aspires.
But on the whole there are only opportunities for parochial
pieties on one side and the academy on the other — and
nothing or no one to join the two. We have, in too many
of our colleges, either religion without culture or culture
without religion and, broadly reflecting, our intellectual
works are indistinguishable from those accomplished in the
schools normally stigmatized as secular or "unholy." Routine
is preferred to revelation. That sense of *mystery* which characterized early Christian education is lost or ignored. Our
effort now is chiefly distinguished by our almost passionate
desire for the tangible and an extravagant confidence in
machinery as if it were itself an absolute, a confidence which
Matthew Arnold long ago called the besetting danger of our
civilization. And having removed practically all traces of our
real form, our real aim and meaning, we have, in the mood
of fanaticism and even frenzy, accelerated our operations.

We should, however, come back to our Christian senses,
and to a new realization of that impetus which would
release us from the traps of routine. Christian education, as
Dawson envisages it, was once "a process of catharsis, an
illumination which centered in the sacred mysteries, and
which was embodied in a cycle of symbolism and liturgical

action." In such a process, "Christian education was not only an initiation into a Christian community, it was also an initiation into another world: the unveiling of spiritual realities of which the natural man was unaware and which changed the meaning of existence." We shall have to agree with Dawson when he specifies that modern education has failed to provide this extraordinary kind of initiation. We shall have to agree, further, when he affirms that in our modern education there is "no sense of revelation." Modern education, in the Catholic colleges no less than in the others, "is accepted as instruction — sometimes as useful knowledge, often as tiresome task work in preparation for some examination, but nowhere do we find that joyful sense of the discovery of a new and wonderful reality that inspired true Christian culture." With Dawson's stimulation, we shall have to remind ourselves that "all true religious education leads up to the contemplation of Divine Mysteries, and where this is lacking the whole culture becomes weakened and divided." Dawson realizes that some may protest that there is here involved the world of worship rather than the world of education. But he points out firmly that "it is impossible to separate the two, since it was largely in the sphere of worship that the Christian tradition of education and culture arose and developed. The first Christian education was the initiation into the Divine Mysteries in the liturgical sense, and it brought with it a development of religious poetry and music and art which were the first fruits of Christian culture."

Now those of us who are Catholic teachers or scholars or students today are faced with the grave problem of how, in our various realms of science and art, to discover and display that "wonderful reality" informing Christian culture, of how to provide at least the minimum means for education toward Christian culture, of how to draw the works of the mind within the world of worship. Etienne Gilson is right when he insists that piety — or religion — does not dispense with technique. But it may be added that technique does not dispense with transfiguration. And Gilson poses the problem for all of us: "To serve God by science and art, it is necessary to begin by practicing them *as if* these disciplines were in themselves their own ends; and it is difficult to make such an effort without being taken in. So much the more difficult is it when we are surrounded by savants and artists who treat them effectively as ends. Their attitude is a spontaneous expression of naturalism, or to give it its old name, which is the name for all time, of paganism, into which society ceaselessly tends to fall back because it has never completely left it. It is important, however, to free ourselves from it. It is impossible to place the intelligence at the service of God without respecting integrally the rights of the intelligence; otherwise it would not be the intelligence that is put at His service; but still more is it impossible to do so without respecting the rights of God: otherwise it is no longer at His service that the intelligence is placed. What has to be done in order to observe this second condition?" This is indeed the question — *what has to be done in order to observe this second condition?* — on which all of us, in any way responsible for the education of Christians, must constantly meditate. Otherwise we do not justify our reason for existence or justify the existence of our schools.

Surely one of the terrible obstacles to the work of synthesis so absolutely necessary is the sense of inferiority with respect to, the lack of pride in their faith, which has led Catholics, as Newman once chided, to surrender their sacred life and tradition so as to get on better with the world: "In proportion as you put off the yoke of Christ, so does the world by a sort of instinct recognise you, and think well of you accordingly. Its highest compliment is to tell you that you disbelieve." Gilson has made a precisely similar observation: "What is the greatest praise that many among us may hope for? The greatest the world can give them: he is a Catholic, but he is really very nice; you would never think that he was one." But this sense of inferiority is also, oddly, accompanied by a partisan optimism and complacency about Catholic affairs. What Gilson regrets and what we all must regret — is "that instead of confessing in all simplicity what we owe to our Church and to our faith, instead of showing what they bring to us and what we would not have without them, we believe it good politics or good tactics, in the interests of the Church itself, to act as if, after all, we distinguish ourselves in no way from others."

Perhaps all the weaknesses of modern culture, ours and those of other countries, can be caught up into the one great vice of spiritual mediocrity, described by Georges Bernanos as "a colorless and odorless gas; allow it to accumulate undisturbed and suddenly it explodes with a force beyond all belief. . . . The dire omen for all of us . . . is not that Christians should be less numerous but that the number of mediocre Christians should increase. Smile, if you like, at mediocre Christians, the power they still can wield is vast." This is the strange power of those who are spiritually powerless. They are the ones who fear truth and reality and the voices of truth and reality in any field of action. Their dead or dying hands seize and do not release until crushed the life of the soul, of the mind, of culture.

There is the danger that, in the sight of all this spiritual mediocrity, of the frailties of Catholics themselves, some of us — who know better — might become perfectionists, inclined, without warrant, to withdraw from or reject the world. Since we do not find it as we want it, we shall have none of it. The perfectionist, in Waldemar Gurian's evaluation, "professes to be exclusively interested in the absolute good, and therefore, he regards everything that is not perfect as bad . . . [he] observes that the ideal is not realized in his environment; therefore, he emphasizes the weaknesses of his surroundings and is a defeatist by his very readiness to admire and understand far-distant worlds" and no other than utopian worlds. But his abandonment of the world to the devil is not perfection — just perfectionism. To be exact, there is in the Church a legitimate perfectionist way of life, the higher life of the pure contemplative. Yet the great men and women drawn, with justification, to this life have not disesteemed the importance — and perplexity — of worldly existence; nor have they felt that it was somehow unnatural and out-of-joint with true Christian living. They have realized, in the perspective of the Incarnation-Redemption, that it is necessary for men to move through and with matter to the fulfillment of the spirit. Most of us cannot and will not be anchorites. We shall have to live as Christians in civilization; and in this solution civilization will be accepted in all its density and regarded as capable of Christian transfiguration. Actually, all the claims of our secular state-in-life, of our *natural* life, are in themselves good, can be the basis of spiritual development and can serve to bring us toward the highest perfection of supernatural life.

The Christian man knows that his achievement of intellectual and moral virtue ought not to set him at severe odds with the society in which he finds himself. It is not a question of his compromising with the too frequently false standards of modern civilization or of submitting all the high and treasured quality of his meaning as a man and as a mind to what may seem to him the lower character of workaday existence. The necessity for the Christian man, exercised in the Christian understanding of life and of the movements of history and contemporary events, is to comprehend the

world in all its weaknesses and terrors no less than in its
glories and wonders. With his Christian understanding of
and sympathy for the plight of people in a difficult and
dangerous civilization, the Christian man must try to illuminate, for himself and for others, the difficulty and the
danger. Because of the human deficiencies inevitable in the
Church itself on earth, the deficiencies which are Christ's
very cross, he knows that he cannot expect perfection from
ordinary humanity, that he cannot isolate himself from men
and the real world, that he must live in the face of all sorts
of exigencies and evils and strive to alleviate them. The
Christian knows that he must live as a Christian in the
more or less un-Christian world. Having this knowledge
he will show himself courageous and hopeful in the darkest
moments; and his Christian courage and Christian hope
will help him to make sense today.

The Christian man, as the Christian in civilization and
making sense of the senseless world, realizes that the greatest
source of his own power and strength in life is his membership in the Church. It is in the Church that he finds forever
renewed his faith and hope and charity; it is in the Church
that he is enabled to approximate the Christian idea of
man, in the dignity and beauty of his prudence, fortitude,
justice, and moderation. Having experienced the vitality of
the sacraments, of prayer and worship, the real freedom
given by conformity to the moral law, the relevance of
belief for every realm of human action, the Christian man
cannot forsake the religious rhythm of his life. The action
of the Christian in the Church must be something more
than the negative, verbal fealty displayed (notably at times
when the Church is attacked) by those nicely pinioned as
marginal or fringe Catholics, half-lost men clinging to the
Church by their fingernails. The action of the Christian
must be a constant, living, positive action sustained by

prayer; indeed the action of the Christian must grow out of prayer. The Christian man knows that this positive and living action is best taken in reference to the parish to which he belongs. The Christian in the Church knows that he can find his opportunity, not merely in massive organizations and meetings and in well-publicized crusades but in the comparative quietude and unpublicized integrity of his works with and for the people who are joined with him as worshipers in the closeness and unity of the parish.

Fortified by the communal reality of his life in the Church, the contemporary Christian will carry over, into his daily works, the virtues of his living. The Christian man knows that — whatever his vocation, his function in the world (in the secular priesthood and religious orders, in teaching and scholarship, in the creative arts, in journalism and public communications, in law, government and politics, in medicine, in science and engineering, in business and industry, in the military) or whatever his status (as employer or employee, as director or directed) — he must animate his function and his works with the Christian spirit. This is not easy. But this he must do, if he is to change the world; otherwise the world will change him, spoiling him and even destroying him. Toward the people who work with him or for him in any job or profession even as toward his own family, the Christian shows respect, indeed reverence. He does not exploit them or *use* them to his own savage advantage. In a real fraternity of labor, he stands ready to sacrifice the momentary gain or profit, ready to sacrifice himself. He knows his obligation to be joined with his fellow workers in the true community of self-giving, in the true community of a friendship that the followers of Dale Carnegie can never understand. The Christian in civilization may not, by the notions of conventional publicity, become a neon-lighted name. But in his own humble universe of the parish of which he is a faithful, prayerful, and active member, of the family to which he is deeply devoted, and of the job or vocation or profession in which he unselfishly exercises his special talents or skills, he can let the light of genuine Christian personality, "God's Kingdom in the soul," shine. It is this light that will brighten and help to save the dark world.

Catholics then, almost without exception, men of "the people" and men of "culture" (and the Church, in the interest of wholeness, would not separate them: "There is no place for a Church of aesthetes, an artificial construction of philosophers, or congregation of the millennium. The Church man needs is a church of human beings; divine, certainly, but including everything that goes to make up humanity, spirit and flesh, indeed earth.") will have to live, not as fugitives oscillating between materialism and asceticism, but as Christians in civilization. As such, we will have to manifest, as Nicholas Berdyaev reflects at the close of his autobiography, "more than a mere rejection of or adaptation to 'communism,' the grapes of which are so sour to [us: we] will have to show a power to move men *in extremis,* without looking to the right or left, coupled with a genuine sensitiveness to the issues of our time." And we are quite cognizant as Christians that there will be seen "no solution of the betrayal of the world by Christians or the betrayal of Christianity by the world until history is ended. Only beyond history is there victory for the spirit of God and man." But we are sure, in the wisdom of Divine Providence, that for all its fierce plunging, history advances toward this apocalyptic victory. We know that we must remain, that we must work and strive in the best ways open to us, live with bright and ungrudging readiness in the midst of our present, painful history, in the history that is, as the liturgy makes clear to us, a mysterious jumble, an imperfect and entangled thing that will not be rectified, with the good wheat separated from the disturbing chaff, until the world is done. So, no matter what confusions, frustrations, and persecutions befall us, we must have the endurance of Christians, the marvelous endurance told by Christ in the twenty-first Chapter of the Gospel of St. Luke: "There were some who spoke to him of the temple, of the noble masonry and the offerings which adorned it: to these he said, The days will come when, of all this fabric you contemplate, not one stone will be left on another; it will all be thrown down. And they asked him, Master, when will this be? What sign will be given, when it is soon to be accomplished? Take care, he said, that you do not allow anyone to deceive you. Many will come making use of my name; they will say, Here I am, the time is close at hand; do not turn aside after them. And when you hear of wars and revolts, do not be alarmed by it; such things must happen first, but the end will not come all at once. Then he told them, Nation will rise in arms against nation, and kingdom against kingdom; there will be great earthquakes in this region or that, and plagues and famines; and sights of terror and great portents from heaven. Before all this, men will be laying hands on you and persecuting you; they will give you up to the synagogues, and to prison, and drag you into the presence of kings and governors on my account; that will be your opportunity for making the truth known. Resolve, then, not to prepare your manner of answering beforehand; I will give you such eloquence and such wisdom as all your adversaries shall not be able to withstand, or to confute. You will be given up by parents and brethren and kinsmen and friends, and some of you will be put to death; all the world will be hating you because you bear my name; and yet no hair of your head shall perish. It is by endurance that you will secure possession of your souls."

This is the endurance — an endurance of honor — of Christians in civilization. In the exercise of this endurance, we have the benefit and the creative freedom of the new life of the Church, which is striking in our age, despite our age's spiritually deteriorative features. Inspirited by, made strong within the culture of the Church, we shall be relieved of the burdens of sentimentalism, commercialism, sectarianism, externalism, activism, and perfectionism; and we shall worship, live, think, and work — even suffer — so as to distinguish our cause from the nation that is not holy. For it is a certainty that if we fail to distinguish our cause, God will judge us and judge us severely. But if we do distinguish our cause, send forth into civilization, His transfigurative light and truth, then His light and His truth will ultimately conduct us to His holy hill and into His tabernacles.

ONE VIEW OF FOUR VIEWPOINTS

BY RALPH GORMAN, C.P.

The Ultraconservative Catholic

THERE'S been a lot of talk about liberal Catholics. We haven't heard much about ultraconservative Catholics, although we think they are more numerous. We haven't sufficient space to describe the species but here are a few general characteristics.

The ultraconservative Catholic has great difficulty accepting labor unions. He may not deny explicit Church doctrine that workingmen have a natural right to organize. His attitude is: "Unions are all right, but . . ." It's the "but" that matters. He never finds a union without defects, so he never finds one that is acceptable. To him all unions are Red or pink or leftist or corrupt or gangster-ridden or predatory. If he applied the same rigid norms to other groups, he would have to reject every organization functioning in this poor world of ours.

The ultraconservative Catholic also has an allergy to anything that smacks of international co-operation. In fact, the word international is in itself derogatory. He can understand charity between individuals, but not between nations. He is often generous in aiding the weak, the needy, the orphan, the homeless. But let Uncle Sam do the same thing on an international scale and he immediately cries out in alarm. He is suspicious of all moves to lessen restrictions on

43

immigration so that some of Europe's pitiful escapees, refugees, and expellees can be admitted to this country. Without
realizing it, his attitude is expressed in the cynical question
of the first fratricide: "Am I my brother's keeper?"

The ultraconservative Catholic belongs to an international
organization in the religious sphere, but he just can't accept
an international organization in the secular sphere. Few
would be so silly as to deny the defects and weaknesses of
the U.N. as it is now organized and functions. But that it
should be disbanded and its buildings closed is quite another
thing. At least the U.N. is a step in the right direction. It is
accepted as such by the Holy Father, to whom our ultraconservative friends could listen to their great advantage.

The organization within the U.N. that almost gives the
ultraconservative a stroke is Unesco. Like its parent organization, Unesco has defects, but it's good enough to secure
the co-operation of the Holy Father. The Pope has shown
his good will by sending a permanent observer to Unesco.

The ultraconservative Catholic has something in common
with Hitler, Mussolini, and Peron. In this, he is usually the
wealthy, employer type. He thinks ecclesiastics should be
confined to the sacristy and to mouthing general religious
principles without applying them to the hard realities of
daily economic life. To this type, Westbrook Pegler is a
minor deity, although his knowledge of Catholic social
teaching just about equals a Hottentot's. In a recent effusion,
Pegler declared with ultrapontifical certainty: "The right-
to-work or open-shop issue is a political problem within
the authority of the States. Any religious counsel, whether
of the Vatican or any council of ministers or rabbis is
only advisory."

There are a lot of ultraconservative Catholics who agree
with Pegler in spite of the forceful denunciations of these
laws by some of our bishops. Such laws involve a moral

issue, a question of justice. They are in a sphere in which the Church has a right to teach. Pope Pius XI made this principle clear in his Encyclical *Quadragesimo Anno:* "The deposit of truth that God committed to us and the grave duty of disseminating and interpreting the whole moral law, and of urging it in season and out of season, bring under and subject to our supreme jurisdiction not only the social order but economic activities themselves."

The explanation of the ultraconservative Catholic lies in his ignorance. He is unacquainted with Catholic social teaching. He has no knowledge of the great documents in which recent popes have given us their divinely authorized guidance to help us solve the problems that we face today.

As a beginning we would like to prescribe for the ultraconservative Catholic a daily reading of papal declarations in place of his favorite right-wing columnist.

The Ultraliberals

Some time ago we dissected the ultraconservative on this page. Our little homily on the subject kicked up a minor storm. Now that the dust has settled, we'd like to take on his opposite number, the ultraliberal.

The ultraconservative and the ultraliberal are quite different and yet they have much in common. Both have adopted labels that don't belong to them. The ultraconservative is not a conservative nor is the ultraliberal a liberal. Both are hidebound in their addiction to slogans and a party line. Label a viewpoint conservative and the ultraconservative is for it even though it's reactionary; label it liberal and the ultraliberal is for it although it's leftist or even pinko. Both are very dogmatic in their views. In this, the ultraconservative is the more logical since the ultraliberal is so utterly dogmatic in denouncing dogma.

In many respects the ultraconservatives and the ultraliberals are at opposite extremes. For instance, the ultraconservative overrates the danger of Communism in American
life, while the ultraliberal underrates it; the former is prone
to equate accusation of Communism with guilt, while the
latter finds it difficult to accept any evidence of guilt; the
one overemphasizes the importance of Congressional investigations while the other opposes them on principle; the one
is lenient toward Fascism, the other toward Communism;
the one is a flagwaving superpatriot, the other looks down
his nose at patriotism as a sort of primitive impulse.

The ultraconservative is so shortsighted that he seems
unable to see beyond the borders of the U.S.A., the ultraliberal so farsighted that one wonders at times whether his
heart belongs to Uncle Sam or to some visionary world
government of the future; the former despises the U.N.
and all its works, the latter exalts it above all its merits;
the one tends to be pro-management, right or wrong, the
other equally pro-labor; the one favors a *laissez-faire* economy, the other hankers for the welfare state; in doubtful
cases the ultraconservative always advocates censorship and
the restriction of civil rights, the ultraliberal exaggerates
liberty to a point where it becomes license.

The ultraliberal has certain distinctive marks of his own.
He considers it "liberal" to be pro-Israel and anti-Arab. He
has an antipathy for nationalism and racialism and adopts
a rather supercilious air toward religion. Yet he plumps all
out for a state founded on race and religion. He is extremely
sensitive to the sufferings the Jews have endured — and in
this we praise him — but he is as cold as a clam toward the
plight of nearly a million Arab refugees. He would rather
be accused of robbery or adultery than of anti-Semitism
and yet he allows himself a sneaky indulgence in anti-
Catholicism — the anti-Semitism of the pseudoliberal.

This sort of fellow can be more than annoying. He can be dangerous. During World War II, he sold the American public on good old Uncle Joe Stalin and Soviet "democracy." He and his fellows damned as Fascists any writers who dared tell the truth about Soviet Russia and international Communism. He helped to engineer the greatest fiasco in American diplomatic history when he convinced the Administration that it was useless to waste money on "corrupt" and "Fascist" Chiang Kai-shek and that, anyway, his enemies were not Communists but agrarian reformers. Right now he'd like to keep Spain out of Nato because Franco accepted help from Hitler and Mussolini in the Spanish civil war. He conveniently forgets that throughout World War II we were allied to cutthroat Stalin who was as bad as Hitler and worse than Mussolini.

When Catholics move into the ultra field, they become ultraconservatives rather than ultraliberals. We don't have a ready explanation for this but we think the facts bear us out. We must confess that we don't know any Catholics or Catholic publications that would fit our description of the ultraliberal. Perhaps there are some. We have a suspicion, however, that they are the product of the perfervid imagination of the ultraconservatives to whom anybody to the left of George III in social outlook or political views is a dangerous radical.

The Progressive Conservative

Since we're against the ultraliberals and ultraconservatives, some of our readers would like to know just what we stand for. For want of a better term, let's say we're progressive conservative — conservative in keeping what's good, progressive in reaching out for better.

It would take a small library to treat the subject adequately. On a single page we can give only a brief sketch of the progressive conservative as we picture him and then only in a limited field.

The type we are describing is Catholic, so he realizes that the Church teaches in the realm of morals as well as of faith. He knows that the social teachings of the papal encyclicals are binding in conscience on the faithful and may not be dismissed as mere unauthoritative counsel. He doesn't look to the Church for a solution of the technical problems of modern industry, but he does look to it for guidance in the solution of its moral problems.

The progressive conservative doesn't look on the state as an enemy, nor does he regard it as an evil. He doesn't think that the sole function of the state is to act as a policeman. He recognizes that the state has a right and duty to aid him in his search for security, a reasonable prosperity, and the better things of life. He knows what socialism is and why it has been condemned by the Church, so he doesn't use this term to smear all legislation to aid the poor, the unemployed, the sick, and the aged.

On the other hand, he doesn't look on the state as a sugar daddy, responsible for all his needs from the cradle to the grave. He has a healthy fear of big government as a threat to individual liberty and he refuses to turn over to the state anything that can be accomplished by smaller and lower groups.

The progressive conservative recognizes the right of private property, but he holds that this right is not absolute but implies social obligations. He knows that there is such a thing as precedence of rights. He accepts the statement of the "Bishops Program of Social Reconstruction" that: "The laborer's right to a decent livelihood is the first charge upon industry. The employer has a right to get a reasonable living out of his business, but he has no right to interest on his investment until his employees have obtained at least living wages."

The progressive conservative doesn't think that capitalism has been canonized by the Catholic Church. He knows that some of its evils have been excoriated by recent popes in no uncertain terms. He doesn't think that free enterprise is free from the moral law and the just regulation of the state. He condemns the laissez-faire capitalism of the rugged individualist as strongly as the collectivism of the leftists.

The progressive conservative recognizes the workingman's natural right to form unions. He acknowledges and opposes abuses and corruption in labor unions but respects the principle the Prohibitionists forgot in 1919, that abuse doesn't take away the use. He recognizes the danger of big labor just as he does that of big business and big government, but he knows that only big labor can deal with big business on an equal footing. He is aware, therefore, that it is a union-busting maneuver to attempt to restrict unions by state lines in dealing with huge, nationwide capitalism. While he realizes that higher wages often mean higher prices, he knows too that higher profits have exactly the same effect, so he doesn't ask labor to desist from seeking wage increases without asking capital to limit profits.

In concluding his splendid work, *Catholic Social Principles,* Father John F. Cronin, S.S., writes eloquently of the task of Catholics in working for a sound reorganization of society:

"Time and again, the present Holy Father has called for courage and resolution in the face of the present crisis. He considers those who isolate themselves from the fray or who minimize the social duties of Christians as virtual traitors in the face of the enemy. He calls us to a crusade more urgent and vital than those of old."

We would say that one of the marks of the progressive

conservative is that he doesn't lend a deaf ear to that
urgent appeal.

The Thinking Catholic

You can't tell a Catholic from his neighbor by the style
of his hat or the cut of his coat or the baseball team he
roots for. But you should be able to distinguish him by the
principles he holds and by his outlook on the world.

The Catholic has the Sacred Scriptures and the teachings
of the Church to provide principles of action. He has the
declarations of the popes, especially the encyclicals, as well
as the whole body of Catholic social principles expounded
by specialists, to help him apply these teachings to his daily
life.

Since the Catholic recalls the parable of the Good Samaritan and understands the doctrine of the Mystical Body of
Christ, he is inclined toward an international outlook. He
knows that Christian charity isn't limited by national boundaries, nor can it exclude Jew or Gentile, Russian or American, black or white. He is naturally inclined to favor
organized efforts for international co-operation. While loving
and serving his own country, he dislikes chauvinism and is
nauseated by the raucous boasts and constant flag waving
of the extreme nationalists.

Such a person advocates generosity to less favored nations
— even if it means fewer good roads and Cadillacs for
himself. He believes we should welcome refugees, whatever
their national origin or the color of their skin. He condemns
efforts to segregate the Negro as an implicit denial of the
Faith and an affront to the Son of God who shed His blood
for all of us without distinction.

The kind of Catholic we're writing about has distinct
ideas on the sacred character of the individual and on

the rights and duties of the state. He is a middle-of-the-roader, avoiding the extremes of socialism and excessive individualism.

He believes in the right of workers to organize in unions. Since recent popes have spoken clearly and definitely on the subject in teaching the universal Church, he may not believe otherwise.

The Catholic has very strict standards, however, for union officials, since they are so largely responsible for the material well-being of workingmen. In fact, he looks on them as men performing an almost sacred function and he demands of them higher standards of morality than those of the ordinary citizen.

The true Catholic doesn't vote for a candidate simply because he is a Catholic. In fact, he is stricter on him than on the non-Catholic, because the Catholic should follow a rigid code of morality and gives scandal when he doesn't. He is ashamed of those politicians, ward heelers, party leaders, and machine bosses who have grown rich at the public expense while posing as Catholics to attract the "Catholic vote."

The Catholic believes that the heat of a political campaign is no excuse for lying, that graft is sinful, and doubly sinful in a Catholic because of scandal, that a man who accepts an unnecessary job as a political reward is stealing in taking his salary, that a public official sins by accepting a bribe to do his duty or not to do it, that a man in public office has no right to take advantage of official information to enrich himself, that he sins against the virtue of religion when he breaks his oath of office, that he has an obligation in conscience to select the best candidate for an appointive office.

The thoughtful Catholic is in some respects an individualist. Having definite principles to guide him, he doesn't need to follow blindly a commentator, columnist, politician, or demagogue. In cases of doubt he leans toward the side of liberty and civil rights. He doesn't believe in illegal short cuts or in doubtfully constitutional methods of action even in times of danger. He believes that Communists are enemies conspiring to overthrow the Government, but in dealing with the Communist threat he holds that accusation is not proof, that a man is innocent until proved guilty, and that it is gravely sinful to call a man a Communist or pro-Communist if it is untrue or even doubtful.

We know there's a lot more than all this in being a Catholic, but at least these are a few distinguishing marks of a Catholic, especially of a thinking Catholic.

CATHOLICS AND MENTAL HEALTH

BY SISTER ANNETTE WALTERS, C.S.J.

BOTH physical and mental suffering are hard to accept, but it is easier for most people to understand that physical suffering can, with the help of God's grace, be made a means of participating in the passion of Christ. It is not so easy to see that the mentally ill person, while not suffering physically, may be sharing in the agony of Christ in the garden of Gethsemani.

When it is a question of mental illness, particularly of the milder but still very annoying varieties, we tend to take the position of Job's comforters and assume that the person suffering from such an abnormality must have something the matter with him that separates him from God. Often the person who desperately needs professional treatment is told that if he will only go to confession everything will be all right. Advice of this kind not only does not help, but may actually do much harm. It betrays a profound ignorance of the basic psychological principles underlying mental health and mental illness. And since this lack of understanding is so common, it might be well to examine some of the misconceptions common among Catholics concerning the relationship of mental health to religion.

Perhaps the commonest misconception is this: if you are straight with God you will be mentally healthy. This view is usually held by the extreme extrovert who lives on the

surface of life and who has never had to grapple interiorly
with excruciating personal conflicts. Typically, he is the big
muscle man who seeks relief from his worries in physical
activity — shoveling snow, boxing, or playing basketball. Or
(if it is a woman), relief is sought in taking down the curtains, waxing the floors, or cleaning out the attic.

This point of view reflects confusion concerning the
relationship of the natural to the supernatural. It assumes
that mental illness is a moral disorder and that it has its
roots in the supernatural rather than in the natural life of
man. It assumes, moreover, that a cure can be effected by
supernatural grace alone without the natural helps of
psychotherapy, environmental therapy, or any of the other
therapies used in the treatment of emotional disturbances
and mental illnesses. Both of these assumptions are false.
It is no more true to say that you can cure a mental or
emotional illness by supernatural means alone (barring, of
course, a miracle) than it is true that you can cure a physical
illness by supernatural means alone. Only the so-called
"Christian Scientist" would expect to cure a cancer or
pneumonia by prayer and meditation alone.

In considering mental health it is important to remember
that supernatural grace does not supplant or take the place
of nature, but that it builds on and perfects nature. If
this were not so, rectors of seminaries and religious superiors
would not be so concerned as they are about examining the
natural dispositions and emotional stability of their candidates before admitting them to the seminary or novitiate.
Although it is certainly true that people can use both
physical and mental illnesses as means to acquiring sanctity,
it is significant that in many of the collects of the Mass
the Church bids us pray for "health of mind and body"
in order that we may serve God more faithfully. We are
explicitly encouraged to regard health of mind and body

as natural helps to reaching our supernatural goal of union with God.

The clinical psychologist is professionally concerned with the natural factors that influence mental health and the growth of a healthy personality. This is true whether he is a Christian or not. But the Christian psychologist in so far as he is zealous for spreading the kingdom of God, has an additional motive that inspires his work. He wants to help people attain to that state of natural perfection in which the supernatural life can flourish. He wants to help people to control their unruly impulses, to develop good habits and, in general, to develop the natural dispositions and virtues which will facilitate the growth of grace in their souls.

Closely related to the above misconception, namely, that if you are in the state of grace you will necessarily be mentally healthy, is the equally erroneous notion that psychological treatment or psychotherapy is not necessary for emotionally or mentally disturbed persons if they will only use the confessional correctly. Unfortunately, these disturbed people often cannot use the confessional correctly until they have received help with their emotional problems. It is true, of course, that a normal person (and, at times, an abnormal person) may be greatly helped and even restored to mental equilibrium by the guidance and encouragement that he receives in the confessional. But for the person whose mental health is threatened or already destroyed, something else is needed. A mentally sick person may receive advice and help over and over again in the confessional but his sick mind may prevent his profiting by it in any way.

The psychotherapeutic treatment of the majority of mildly maladjusted or neurotic persons has little in common, except accidentally, with what goes on in the confessional. The role of the priest in the confessional is almost diametrically opposed to the role played by the psychotherapist in a psychological clinic. The psychotherapist usually should not and does not assume a role of moral authority in dealing with his patient. The priest, as judge, must and does adopt a role of authority in the confessional. True, it is not his personal authority but the authority of God that he is exercising. And it is for this reason that his exercise of authority does not increase the tendencies of a neurotic person toward an unwholesome dependency but rather provides him with an opportunity to practice the virtue of obedience to God's representative.

The skillful psychotherapist does not assume such a role of authority in his relations with his patient. Above all, he does not take upon himself the responsibility for making decisions that should be made by the patient if he is to be cured. He seeks rather to create a situation in which the patient's anxieties are so alleviated that he is not afraid or unable to take the responsibility for making his own decisions and for accepting the consequences of his decisions should they have unpleasant results.

Basic to a therapeutic situation is the interpersonal relation existing between the psychotherapist and his patient. Maladjusted people characteristically have unwholesome relations with other people. They can be restored to health only by a satisfying and constructive relationship with another person. Before any kind of help can be given to the patient, the relationship between the psychotherapist and the patient must be defined. Creating the appropriate personal relationship and sustaining it is an essential feature of the psychotherapeutic process.

In the confessional, on the other hand, the personal relationship existing between the confessor and the penitent is unimportant. There are, it is true, some confessors who are more understanding than others. But such understanding is relatively independent of the personal relationship that exists between the priest and the penitent. Then, too, it appears that the best use is made of the confessional when the penitent ignores the person of the priest and sees only Christ in him. The sacramental grace of the confessional does not depend upon the personality of the priest nor upon the amount of warmth that he can radiate to the penitent nor upon the penitent's emotional identification with the confessor. Yet all of these considerations do have an important bearing upon the success or failure of psychotherapy.

Another common misconception is one that has been built up by some of the molders of Catholic opinion who write for Catholic newspapers, and who approach this subject with more heat than light. This is the view that psychologists and psychiatrists are immoral materialists who are likely to lead you into sin if you go to them for help. Psychologists will supposedly insist that you get rid of your repressions and, consequently (so the uninformed layman reasons), you will necessarily be put into an occasion of sin or even forced to commit a sin if you seek professional treatment for your emotional maladjustments.

Usually this notion is attributed to Sigmund Freud who, according to the journalists referred to above, taught that people can be mentally healthy only by giving full and uninhibited expression to their sexual urges. Now actually Freud's theory is not nearly so alarming as the journalists would have us believe. Freud did, it is true, hold some strange and unacceptable views concerning religion and human relations, views which a Catholic cannot accept. But, at the same time, Freud was too keen an observer of human life ever to suggest that a man could be perfectly happy and healthy by giving free reign to all of his unruly impulses. Freud pointed out that repression leads to symptoms of mental abnormality. But repression is a technical psychological term that is easily misunderstood. Repression is not the same thing as self-control. You may, for instance, be fully aware of your impulse to kick someone. Must you kick him if you want to be mentally healthy? Not at all! Even Freud would not ask you to do that. What any good psychologist would insist upon, however, is that you recognize the fact that you have had this desire and that you are the kind of person who has such evil impulses.

In other words, to be mentally healthy, you must not repress the knowledge you have of your own limitations. You must not run away from the painful occasions that give you an opportunity to know yourself and your human weaknesses. You must not only open your mind to the fact that you are the kind of person who can think such mean things but you must somehow learn to accept emotionally the fact that you are this kind of person and to live happily with yourself in spite of this fact. Such self-knowledge and self-control are not at all the same thing as repression; they are, in fact, incompatible with repression. It must have been this attitude that led St. Philip Neri, in watching condemned criminals being led to the gallows, to beat his breast and exclaim, "There, but for the grace of God, goes Philip!"

Let us try now to answer a question frequently raised, "Should there be an official Catholic point of view on mental health?" To this the answer is "No!" But if the question is re-phrased to read "Should Catholic psychologists have a Catholic point of view?" the answer is an emphatic "Yes!" People frequently ask Catholic psychologists such questions as, "What is the Church's stand on psychoanalysis?" "Does the Church approve of the use of hypnosis?" and the like. Often they are astonished when they are told that the Church has taken no official stand on these specific questions. The inquiry then follows: "Why hasn't she? Shouldn't the Church give us some directives in these matters?"

It is well to remind people who raise such questions that the Church does not legislate in matters of science but only in those of faith and morals. It is only when science encroaches on the sacred preserves of faith and morals, and thus goes beyond its own legitimate sphere of inquiry, that the Church raises her voice in protest. Thus, the Church has never pronounced for or against any specific system of psychology, although individual Catholics have been loud in their praise or denunciation of various of these systems.

Pope Pius XII, in his address on April 13, 1953, to the International Congress on Psychotherapy and Clinical Psychology, after commenting on some of the recent developments concerning the psychological structure and function of man, pointed out that "these questions, which lend themselves to the examination of scientific psychology, belong to your [that is, the psychotherapist's] competence. The same may be said for the use of new psychic methods. But theoretical and pratical psychology, the one as much as the other, should bear in mind that they cannot lose sight of the truths established by reason and by faith, nor of the obligatory precepts of ethics." The Holy Father in this address clearly stated that the scientific study of man and the choice of methods to be used in studying him were the responsibility of the psychological scientist and practitioner. But he also explained at length "the fundamental attitude which is imposed upon the Christian psychologist and psychotherapist."

Thus it seems clear that, although there is not a specifically Catholic point of view on the subject of mental health, yet any view adopted by a Catholic psychologist must be consistent with the Christian view of the nature, origin, and destiny of men.

With the exception of the splendid and original work of Dom Thomas Verner Moore (now a Carthusian — Rev.

Pablo Maria), American Catholic contributions to the psychological study of mental health were, until a few years ago, virtually nonexistent. Not only lay people but even Catholic scholars were blind to the tremendous possibilities of this new science for improving the mental health and balance of the modern man, who must live in a disintegrating world of values and who often lacks the natural stability upon which grace can build. The Catholic scholar who works in this field has the enormous task of separating the wheat from the chaff in psychological theory and practice. But the scholar, if he is truly Catholic, must not stop there. He must go on to the next stop — that of gathering the wheat into the barns instead of scattering it with the chaff to the four winds!

Catholic molders of public opinion have been prolific in their negative criticisms of contemporary clinical psychology and have created a climate of opinion in which the study of modern psychology has been avoided as though it had been invented by Satan himself. Yet the importance of this profession in modern life cannot be overestimated. Let us hope that our Catholic colleges will teach their students to respect truth wherever it is found and will thus enable them to rise above the narrow, parochial, and in the last analysis, un-Catholic prejudices that prevent them from learning what is true and valuable in modern psychology. Only if this is done can we expect to produce first-rate clinical psychologists and psychiatrists who are capable of viewing their professional specialties in the clear light of their Christian faith.

THE GOAL OF ACADEMIC FREEDOM

BY JOHN B. SHEERIN, C.S.P.

ACADEMIC freedom has been a fiercely controverted topic for the past year. In the face of threatening Congressional investigations, educators have demanded the privilege of exemption from scrutiny. It is a privilege which, they claim, has its origin in the very nature of the teaching process. A teacher can do his best work only if he operates in an atmosphere of free inquiry and unrestricted discussion. Once a teacher becomes aware that he may have to answer, outside the classroom, for opinions expressed in class, his intellectual curiosity will be repressed and his teaching initiatives inhibited. So goes the argument of certain educators, and they view Congressional committees investigating subversives on the campus as a revival of the Inquisition and a menace to academic freedom.

The American Association of University Professors, for instance, has stated its policy in these words:

> There is, then, nothing in the nature of the teaching profession which requires the automatic exclusion of Communists, and the attempt to exclude them would threaten our educational system with real dangers. Discrimination against Communists would readily lead to discrimination against teachers with other unorthodox political views, and the exclusion of such teachers would mean the exclusion of some of the liveliest intellects and most stimulating personalities on our campuses.

Academic freedom means the right of a competent professor to teach his class without any control except that of his own conscience. This is a definition which, I feel confident, would find favor with any member of the teaching profession. What does it mean? First, it does not mean the right of a teacher to instruct as he pleases. Freedom implies not only that we are free from coercion or pressure, but also that we are free for something.

John Foster Dulles, in an address to the General Assembly of the National Council of Churches, recently pointed up this lesson of freedom as a positive thing. He said that freedom is a naked concept (freedom from something), but that it must be clothed in a high moral purpose; else it is formless. Our Founding Fathers did not shake off their chains and then ramble around in irresponsible liberty. Such would have been mere license. But they did create a democratic charter that expressed the positive goals toward which America would direct its energies.

So, too, academic freedom cannot be an irresponsible freedom. It cannot be mere freedom from restraint and dictation. It must be the freedom of men using the intellect for the purpose for which God made it, the acquisition of truth. The scholar should be a dedicated man, a man consecrated to the task of pushing back the curtains of ignorance by discovering the truth.

Today we hear much of the rights of academic freedom, but little of the moral responsibility of the scholar. As Dr. Grayson Kirk, president of Columbia University, said at Commencement on June 2, 1953:

> It is more pleasant, always, to talk of freedom and rights than of duties and obligations. Unhappily some of our academic brethren who are the first to man the ramparts in defense of freedom, seem less eager to talk of those responsibilities which are the pre-condition for the freedom which they defend.

We can sympathize with the universities when they are besieged by alumni, or wealthy benefactors, or by politicians who attempt to direct the policies and the teaching programs of the faculty. Academic freedom certainly means that a university should be free of such pressures. Constant interference from outsiders would deflect the university from its true function. It is not an agency for the propagation of private theories or even an arm of the government for the dissemination of propaganda. It is a place where competent professors should be free to teach and study the truth.

Academic freedom implies, therefore, the moral responsibility to teach the truth, the whole truth, and nothing but the truth. We Catholics find it quite incomprehensible, however, when advocates of academic freedom claim a professor should be free to teach what the rest of the faculty regards as error. Sidney Hook, professor of philosophy at New York University, maintains that a university should harbor any and every "heresy" as long as the professor is technically competent in his field and is honest in presenting his evidence. Hook would not expel a professor for teaching even the most hare-brained and ridiculous notions.

> If he has pitted his own independent judgment against the weight of scientific evidence, then, even if he is a thousand times wrong, he must be protected against dismissal.

This reveals a fundamental fault in American education today. A teacher must not be dismissed "even if he is a thousand times wrong." Why? The basic reason must be this, that the university authorities are not sure of any truth. They do not believe that absolute truth exists. To them, all truth is relative, and, therefore, their assent to any proposition is necessarily hesitating and provisional. They fear to condemn an obvious error for fear it may become true tomorrow. This is the attitude of numerous policy-making educators.

This position is not only absurd: it is a tragic abdication of the university's responsibility to its young students. The university dedicated to truth must be the unremitting enemy of error. Indeed every professor should be possessed of a fierce and pitiless hatred of error. It is commendable for the university to create an atmosphere of free inquiry and bold experiment, but, after all, these are only means to an end and the end is the attainment of truth. A university more interested in free discussion than in truth is like a quarterback who is more interested in talking over plays than in making touchdowns. If the authorities of a university tolerate unquestionably erroneous teaching, they are subverting the very purpose for which the university exists: the communication of truth.

Yet, as I have already said, they allow error to go unchallenged because they do not believe in absolute truth. Indeed you will find that many of the professors look with disdain upon men who believe in absolute, unchanging truths and who possess firm convictions about these truths. Catholics, in their opinion, have closed minds and are drugged by supernatural dogmas into a state of mental assent which prevents intellectual growth. Not only Catholics, but any "absolutists" are to be reprobated. John Strachey, writing for the *Nation* (October 4, 1952) in an article called "The Absolutists," reproaches the anti-Communists for their fixed convictions. He says they are just as deplorable as the Communists with their addiction to dogmas and definite ideas. Contrary to Whittaker Chambers, who divided mankind into two classes, the religious and the antireligious, Strachey asserts there is still a third and happier breed of men, the experimentalists.

> It must be far harder to define this second world outlook, for its very essence will lie in a certain relativism, in a cooler temper and a lower claim.

There you have the mind of many educators, the experimental mind which is never quite sure but that tomorrow's experiment may not upset all of today's knowledge. For that reason they refuse to give unconditional assent to any proposition, nor will they condemn any notion no matter how silly it seems. Sidney Hook quotes Justice Holmes to the effect that it is the mark of the civilized mind to have questioned one's own first principles. The experimentalists in the classroom are forever questioning all their first principles, arriving at no conclusions and leading their students up dead-end streets.

Justice Holmes at least had a makeshift criterion of truth.

> . . . the best test of truth is the power of thought to get itself accepted in the competition of the market.

If a notion is generally accepted, then, according to Holmes, it is true. How an external circumstance such as popularity can make an idea true is beyond me. The experimentalists, however, do not have even this criterion of truth.

Fortunately, some educators refuse to go the full way: they place some restrictions on so-called academic freedom. They will not tolerate the teaching of an ideology that constitutes a serious and imminent threat to the safety of the State. In other words, they are much more certain of an idea's consequence than of its truth. (Or is it, perhaps, their common sense which is asserting itself?) At any rate, they say that if the expression of an idea constitutes a clear and present danger to the welfare of the State, it should be proscribed. Justice Holmes stated:

> I think that we should be eternally vigilant against attempts to check the expressions that we loathe and believe to be fraught with death, *unless* they so imminently threaten immediate interference with the lawful and pressing purposes of the law that an immediate check is required to save the country (quoted by Howard M. Jones in *Atlantic Monthly*, June, 1953, p. 40).

In other words, a professor may with impunity utter the wildest and most revolutionary challenges to his class. He will not be disturbed unless "an immediate check is required to save the country."

Sidney Hook, however, in his *Heresy, Yes — Conspiracy, No* (John Day: 1953), objects to any restriction whatsoever. As long as a professor is not affiliated with some authoritarian organization that would dictate his thinking, Hook would not expel him no matter how dangerous his ideas. If he were a member of the Communist Party and, therefore, a partner to the Communist conspiracy against the Government, he would dismiss him, but he would not dismiss him for his advocacy of Communism in the classroom. The title of his book gives the clue: as a heretic in the classroom, the Communist should be safe; as a conspirator, if he is a conspirator, he should be punished.

A large number of university professors, on being questioned by the Congressional Committee, refused to answer or took refuge in the Fifth Amendment. They insisted that the Committee was interfering with academic freedom. Dr. Einstein recently made a statement in which he called upon all intellectuals to protect the cultural welfare of the country by refusing to testify.

> The reactionary politicians have managed to instill suspicion of all intellectual efforts into the public by dangling before their eyes a danger from without. Having succeeded so far they are now proceeding to suppress the freedom of teaching and to deprive of their position all those who do not prove submissive. What ought the minority of intellectuals to do against this evil? . . . Every intellectual who is called before one of the Committees ought to refuse to testify, i.e., he must be prepared for jail and for economic ruin, in short, for the sacrifice of his personal welfare in the interest of the cultural welfare of his country.

I believe it was Father Gannon who was asked about one of Einstein's regrettable utterances on the nature of God, and he answered: "This shows you what happens when a good first baseman goes out on a golf course." But Einstein's latest indiscretion points out a phenomenon that is very curious. Einstein was hard on the Nazis, but he is soft on the Communists. This vein of softness seems to run through the academic world. Sidney Hook has pointed to the contrast between the anti-Nazi "ferment and stir on American campuses from 1933 to 1939" and the lack of moral indignation on the campus today. Mass demonstrations and picketings were a regular daily occurrence when the students and professors were excited about Nazism and Fascism. But in 1948, when Hook tried to organize a protest against the cold-blooded execution of Czech students by the Communists, he could get only a corporal's guard. Hitler's crimes could not measure up to the Kremlin's in savagery and magnitude, and yet men, like Einstein, are not worried about Communism. Bertrand Russell in 1940 wrote that any propaganda likely to promote subversion should be prohibited: today he is stern in his condemnation of any effort to prohibit subversive propaganda.

In the matter of testifying before Congressional Committees however, Einstein has received only a trickle of support from a few educational confreres. The general academic reaction is that professors should testify. The Association of American Universities recently issued a statement in which they said:

> If he (the Professor) is called upon to answer for his convictions it is his duty as a citizen to speak out. It is even more definitely his duty as a professor. Refusal to do so, on whatever legal grounds, cannot fail to reflect upon a profession that claims for itself the fullest freedom to speak and the maximum protection of that freedom available in our society.

What should be the thoughts of a Catholic on this question of academic freedom? (I express only my personal opinion of what a Catholic should think: there is no official Catholic attitude.) We define academic freedom, not merely as freedom from coercion (such as governmental coercion under the Soviet regime), but also as freedom for the acquisition and teaching of the truth. A scholar is a man dedicated to the truth, and, if he is in a position of influence in a university, he should not tolerate the teaching of any doctrine that is obviously false. Second, the professor does not live in an ivory tower, but his teaching is of great potential benefit or injury to society. Therefore, Congressional Committees have a right to question him to discover if he is teaching Communism. If he is found guilty, he should be dismissed by the university even if he is not a member of the Communist Party or a participant in any crime. Joseph Alsop, in an article in the *Atlantic Monthly* in June, called upon his Alma Mater, Harvard, to lend no aid to Congressional Committees. He claimed that no university can do its job unless its members feel free to think new thoughts and say new things. Any Catholic, and indeed any man of good sense, must respond: we can well afford to do without original thinkers who are laying down the patterns for destruction of the American way of life. Academic freedom does not imply the right to overthrow the institutions that protect and guarantee all our fundamental freedoms.

THE IMAGE OF CHRIST IN ART

BY E. M. CATICH

THE function of religious art in all ages is to help people in their devotional needs; to help them approach more easily and understand more clearly divine truths; and ultimately to move them, by the aid of grace, to closer union with God. To the extent that religious art does not do this it is not good religious art, whatever other merits it may possess in the areas of technique and aesthetic delight.

I have a threefold purpose in this article:

1. To show how Christ has been historically pictured.

2. To explain the presence of much vulgarity that passes for "Christian art" today.

3. To suggest some positive artistic and theological principles by which we may produce a Christian art (particularly images of Christ) which will avoid vulgarity and fulfill the function of religious art as defined above.

This is, of course, a complex subject which cannot be adequately treated within the compass of one article. The most I can do is to indicate some of the main features of the matter and their relationship.

The first thing we notice about our subject — the image of Christ in art — is that we have no pictured information to tell us what Jesus looked like — we have no art images

made of Him while He was on earth. While this may seem
to complicate the work of Christian artists, introduce in-
superable difficulties, actually it affords us a clue as to how
the artists must approach their work and it exerts a liberating influence on the artists who produce that work, the
image of Christ.

We are told that the reason why we have no images of
Jesus contemporary with His life on earth is because the
first Christian converts, chiefly Jews, had an ingrained fear
of idolatry, they had not completely escaped the influence of
the Jewish law which prohibited the making of images of
living individuals. Some respected biblical authorities even
suggest that had Jesus lived elsewhere than in Palestine
we would have had graphic and plastic likenesses of Him.
After all, so the theory goes, we know what Caesar Augustus
looked like from the many proved historical monuments.
We even know what Alexander the Great, Philip of
Macedon, and others (who antedated Jesus by centuries)
looked like from the evidence of their coinage, seals, and
other representations. Had Jesus lived in a Greek or Roman
culture, would we not also have had images of Him?

Under normal conditions, a portrait of a great man would
be among the very first mementos of him. In the age of
Caesar Augustus, portrait painting reached its highest point
in Roman art, yet we have no such portrait-memento of
Jesus, nor does history record even the rumor of the existence
of one.

True, we do have literary, Messianic idealizations in the
Old Testament, one showing the Messias as "The Man of
Sorrows" (Isa. 53:2), the other, a symbolic epithalamium
(Ps. 44) but these prophetic references can hardly be used
as supports for the human visualization of Jesus.

I think the absence of artistic images of Christ in His
time has another explanation which is more plausible and,

if correct, has an important bearing on the work of producing visual pictures of Christ.

The Jewish stricture against images was not as rigorously enforced or exclusive as we might think. The First Commandment injunction is aimed principally at the first and last clauses — "no strange gods" and "thou shalt not adore them." Many interpret that as an absolute prohibition of all images. Yet how can we reconcile that interpretation with the lawful use of bulls and lions supporting the temple basins, carved garlands of plant life, the images of the lions and bulls on the king's throne, the cherubim of the covenant and the brazen serpent (prefiguring Christ) which Moses caused to be elevated in the desert encampment? All through the Old Testament there is a sanctioned use of delineations of living things. We know, too, that Jews practicing their Jewish religion in Rome during the first century painted pictures in the Jewish cemetery of Vigna Randinini.

Nor did the first Christians fear idolatry. There are numerous catacomb pictures dating back to Apostolic times (second half of the first century). These artists — mostly Jewish converts — decorated the catacombs not only with human and animal types but they even appropriated suitable pagan symbols to serve Christian religious art and the devotional needs of their Christian community.

I cannot, however, bring myself to believe that the absence of portraits of our Lord is accidental. It may well have been part of God's plan that we were to have no pictorial statement of the Christ. This theory is reinforced when we recall that we do not have even a factual, verbal description of what Jesus looked like. The silence of the Apostles and disciples on this point is resonant. This unanimous silence is almost as if inspired by the Holy Ghost. It may well be that God withheld from us virtually all knowledge of Christ's hidden, personal life because such knowledge was not deemed essential for our salvation. Consequently, I suggest that personal portraits of Christ were denied us so that each age and people could assimilate Christ as their ideal.

The art in the catacombs is instructive here. The representations of the Apostles Peter and Paul, for example, are unvarying and were undoubtedly based on some strong oral, written, or pictured tradition. St. Peter is consistently pictured with white hair and a short, cropped beard; St. Paul with bald head and a brown, pointed beard. This continuity over the centuries suggests a kinship with the original appearance of both Apostles, or studied attempts to record that appearance.

On the other hand, Christ is always pictured as an ideal type, one which varies with each age and culture. Sometimes He is depicted after the fashion of the classical Roman. At other times, He is patterned after the Greek philosopher type. For the first three centuries, Jesus is usually pictured as a beardless adolescent with one exception — a fresco painted about the year 300.

The earliest studies of Jesus in the Catacomb of Pretestatus, painted sometime during the first half of the second century, show Christ being crowned with thorns, healing a woman afflicted with the issue of blood, and conversing with the Samaritan woman at the well of Jacob. In these Roman catacomb scenes, the beardless young Jesus is garbed in the clothing common to Greek philosophers.

After the first centuries, there is no consistency in the portrayals of Christ. In the catacomb frescoes, Jesus is sometimes painted as a mature man, sometimes as an adolescent about 15 years of age. And in several of the baptism scenes He is shown either as a very small boy or a midget, about half as tall as St. John the baptizer. A fresco in the Catacomb of Domitilla of the second half of the second century shows

Christ seated among sheep, playing a lyre, in the guise of Orpheus, the mythological Greek hero.

The point is that the ideal and not a portrait-likeness of Christ was sought by Christian artists.

St. Clement of Alexandria, writing in the "Pedagogue" in the year 190, says that the full beard agrees with the Christian character. Yet, during these same centuries, Christ, the Christian's ideal, is beardless. This is a curious contrariety made even more curious when we recall that in the early fourth century Constantine introduced the custom of shaving the beard — yet, a short while later, Jesus is mostly shown bearded. My explanation is that in both these ages of early Christianity theologians and artists were attempting to emphasize the divinity of Christ. They rightly feared that likening Him to the ordinary man of those ages might give the distinctly erroneous impression that He was only man.

The modern notion of Christ with beard and long hair reaching to shoulders appeared for the first time at the end of the fourth century. From the fifth century through Romanesque times, Christ is pictured both bearded and beardless, with the beardless face more frequent.

Medieval and Renaissance likenesses of Jesus were influenced in good part by the ideal essayed in the apocryphal "Golden Legend" of the Dominican, Jacques de Voragine, who probably was inspired in his description of Jesus by the Davidic epithalamium. The "Shroud of Turin," which it is claimed gives us a true image of the dead Christ as He lay in the tomb from Good Friday until Easter, may also have been inspired by de Voragine's legend. I dismiss the "Shroud" as a fourteenth-century fabrication.

Until recent centuries, then, the history of Christ's image demonstrates that Christian artists were not preoccupied with making particularized portraits of Jesus. Most artists did not attempt "authentic" likenesses of the Saviour.

Rather, the artists and their theologian-directors and clients used the ideal man of their culture as a point of departure for representations of the Saviour type.

Examples multiply indefinitely on how various ages used their ideal as the formal exemplar for their Christ-image. Usually the pattern is based on their notion of the highest type of man — most often the emperor, philosopher leader, apollo, warrior, or king.

In Byzantine art, we have the all-powerful Pantocrator molded on the emperor prototype. During the ages of the barbarian migrations the ideal stems from the leader-warrior — for example, in a Ravennate mosaic, Christ is smooth-shaven and garbed in the costume of military leader. In Caroline art, the classical Roman emperor re-echoes in figures of Christ. In Romanesque, Ottonian, Visigothic, early Gothic, and Insular cultures, Christ is fashioned after the model of the crowned king, usually seated on a throne.

This is not to say that there have been no literary and pictorial attempts to establish the "authentic" portrait of Christ. In Constantine's time, after the horror of the crucifixion had diminished following its extirpation as a criminal penalty, new interest in the person and relics of Jesus arose. For a short while after the relic of the True Cross was found we have the mature, bearded Christ. The artistic practice after the fourth century veers again to the picturing of the ideal. In general, this idealizing process continues into the Renaissance where it is re-molded in terms of Greek and Latin statuary. But here in the Renaissance a sly over-emphasis occurs, hardly noticeable on the surface but nevertheless harmful to the whole symbolic process and consequently damaging to religion.

Before examining in detail this critical error in much Renaissance art, I must clarify the mechanics of symbolism,

for symbolism is at the very core of religious art, indeed
of religion itself.

St. Thomas states as a principle of theology that symbolism is used in arriving at our knowledge of God. He
says: "We cannot speak of God except metaphorically" (C.
G. Lib. 1 cap. XXX). Practically all our notions of supernatural realities we get from symbolic comparisons of things
in the natural order — except, of course, in the case of those
favored souls far advanced in the "unitive way" who are
directly illumined by God concerning divine truths.

In the broad sense, a symbol is the expression of an idea
in a material. In the restrictive sense, a symbol is that which
stands for or suggests something; which calls to mind something (usually abstract or unpicturable) by association, relationship, or convention, but not by intentional resemblance;
it is a visible sign of the invisible; it is an act, gesture, or
thing which, by analogy, directs our attention to some
spiritual concept.

To illustrate: the ship's anchor in the storm-tossed sea
is the sailor's assurance of safety. It is his hope, his security,
for without the anchor the ship and its sailors are helpless
and hopeless. Accordingly, St. Paul, writing to the Hebrews,
says: "This hope (Christ) we have as a sure and firm anchor
of the soul. . . ." The anchor, therefore, from the earliest
times, was a symbol of the Christian's hope in salvation
through Christ's promise. It reminded the Christian of old
that no matter how storm-tossed he might be in the angry
sea of life he had a secure anchor, Christ crucified, who
guaranteed him safety in eternity provided he remained
steadfast to Truth.

Now in symbolic usage the anchor is but a means, not
the end; hence it must always be subordinate to the end. In
religious art, any symbolic anchor which is too particular-

ized, complicated or "realistic" loses its symbolic quality. It calls attention to itself as a mariner's tool; it distracts the symbol-user who has difficulty seeing the anchor as a symbol of Christian hope and sees instead merely an illustration of a ship's tool.

When the symbol reference (analogic predication) is lost or removed we have a superstition (from the Latin *superstat*) that "stands over" an empty shell (symbol-thing) with little or no vital, inner life (idea) to which it should point. Superstition and idolatry are not restricted to the worshiping of statues and the burning of incense to idols. In fact, the broad definition of idolatry and superstition is defective symbolism. We must clearly understand that a symbol "stands for" something while a superstition "stands over" that thing.

This, then, the derangement of final cause, the wavering between illustration and symbol, is at the bottom of all disorder in idolatrous, vicious, bad and tepid religious art. When the details in a religious painting become too detailed, when they are loved for themselves, when they illustrate mores or are merely documents of archaeological research, such a painting loses its symbolic nature and much of its religious usefulness since, at best, it only meagerly helps people to satisfy their devotional needs. Instead of being a steppingstone to more effective devotion, such art becomes a stumbling block.

The history of religious art and symbol making is filled with examples of the pendulum's swing between the symbol-thing and the idea to which the symbol refers and for which it stands. In periods of pioneering and experimentation, when new cultures are emerging, generally the idea is predominant and the visible expression of that idea in symbols is inferior so far as technique is concerned. In other periods, marked by growing traditions, craft accretions, iconographical expansion, hieratic discipline, familiarity with fixed religious types and needs, the emphasis in symbol making frequently (and sadly) veers to the technique itself and to the material expression of the idea.

Obviously the greater damage in religious art occurs when the shift is away from the idea toward the thing being made, since the idea is the final cause and if that is frustrated by preoccupation with technique, overt personalisms, and digressions, the harm is most serious. The ages in which there is a delicate balance, a poise between idea and thing, are few.

Up to the Renaissance, events in the Old and New Testament were conceived as happening in the artist's own environment — his land, climate, clothing, buildings, flora, fauna, gesture, age, and people. Flemish artists, for example, used the Flemish landscape as the background for scenes of the Passion and Crucifixion, even though they well knew from the Crusades and travelers that such backgrounds bore no resemblance to the physical Holy Land. The pre-Renaissance artists in Italy (the Sienese and Umbrians) for other examples, similarly painted sacred subjects in terms familiar to Italian eyes.

I shall return to this point later, showing the validity of portraying sacred ideas and scenes in contemporary terms. I mention it here as one of the impressive pre-Renaissance developments in the history of sacred art.

True humanists prior to the sixteenth century, as much as any other group of artists before or since, achieved a superb balance in their sacred art between the natural and the supernatural, the visible and the invisible, the symbol-thing and its reference value, the idea. Such artists include: St. Francis, Dante, Giotto, Duccio, St. Thomas, Matteo di Giovanni, the Lorenzetti, Martini, Memlinc, Vivarini, to mention a few. Their art, whether considered under the aspect of symbol-thing or expressed idea, was truly lofty. Their art production was a meeting place for natural, human, aesthetic qualities and didactic, persuasive, religious values.

The Renaissance, however, ushered in a new era in which man, not God, was to become the center of interest and attention. This egocentrism both nourishes and is nourished by a rediscovery of classical culture and an intense desire to recreate classical motifs, classical themes and ideas. This intoxication with the power and splendor of natural man, this naturalistic humanism, though it resulted in some magnificent artistic productions, rendered to religion a service which was not always wholly desirable.

The Renaissance shift toward classicism was not a sudden occurrence. It began, as a good usage, during the Middle Ages and blossomed in the later age. Actually, Christianized classical allusions were present in Christian art almost from the beginning.

But the uncritical canonizing of classical things in the Renaissance introduces to the history of religious art paintings and sculpture with little or no religious symbol value, art which points to itself and to man rather than to religious ideas and God. So we see Nativities located in classical ruins; figures in the classical contrapposto and solidity of Greek statues; detailed excursions into the land of anatomy, chiaroscuro, perspective, landscape, architecture, flora-fauna, rocks and rills, mythology, drapery, texture, and light problems.

In such an age, it is not difficult to understand why artists produced so many pictures of St. Sebastian — it gave them an opportunity for exploiting and demonstrating their newly acquired anatomical information. Or why so many portraits of seminude women could be given the facile title, "St. Mary Magdalene." Or why the star of the desert-saints, Jerome and Anthony, was in ascendancy — the artists had a splendid opportunity to exhibit their technique in painting rocks, lizards, lions, monsters, and imaginative desert landscapes.

It is undeniable that artistic genius, in itself, reached its highest peak in the Renaissance. What is significant, however, is that when this artistic genius turned to religious work, too often man and not God's realm was the center of attention. This is a very difficult problem not made any easier by the astonishing magnificence of artistic production. Perhaps someday we may have more exacting norms for evaluating the properties fundamental to true religious art such as we have, for example, in liturgical music.

Coming closer to our own times, we find that the rise of the Academies, along with the neoclassical school of painting in the eighteenth and nineteenth centuries (officially sanctioned by the French court) pushed art even deeper into false realism. Pictures were judged according to their historical-archaeological accuracy. Art had taken on the aspect of antiquarian science; painters like Greuze and David offered the public a view of authentic antiquity down to minute details of swords, armor, and shoelaces. It was the age of the artist-commentators, the documentary "you-are-there" program, much like what Metro-Goldwyn-Mayer is now doing in illusionistic, three-D, colored "biblical" movies.

The Nazarenes and pre-Raphaelites of the nineteenth century, sensing confusedly the error of Renaissance, Baroque, and neoclassical religious, artistic ideals, especially classical antiquarianism, tried to remedy the error by making one of their own: they would return, as far as they were able, to "realistic" biblical antiquarianism, to the actual conditions in Christ's time. Thus, the pre-Raphaelite, William Holman Hunt, could make a trip to Bethlehem in his search for traditional carpenter's tools used there 1900 years ago; he could talk at length with native carpenters, use native models for the picture of Christ in the carpenter's shop and, in his finished picture, show Christ with upraised arms casting a shadow of the cross on the wall of the shop.

The interacting influences of the pre-Raphaelites, Nazarenes, neo-Classicists, and Romanticists combined in good part to produce the neo-Christian art at the end of the nineteenth century and the banal repository-Barclay-street art which still plagues the Church today.

I have already indicated the danger of making religious symbols excessively realistic, of making them call attention to themselves rather than suggest and point to religious ideas and concepts.

Two further examples of defective images must be mentioned before we go on to an investigation of some positive norms and principles for effective religious art.

The first is an accenting of the body at the expense of spirit. A too-human Christ invites a de-emphasis of His divinity. We are then dangerously close to the heretical position of viewing Christ as Christ-Man, the great teacher, psychologist, social worker, healer, rather than the true recognition of Him as Christ-God-Man.

The second type of defective image is the effeminate portrait of Christ. We are all familiar with this type, we see it everywhere: the upgazing eyes; soft, downy beard; long, slender, ladylike hands and fingers. Our age is burdened with millions of reproductions of this hermaphroditic portrait-type that suggests not the Incarnate Word of better ages but a bearded lady fit only for exposition in the world of the circus and carnival side show.

There are beard and beards. A fresco made in the second half of the thirteenth century on the walls of the Cyriacus-kirche in Niedermendig shows St. Christopher bearing the infant Christ on his shoulders. The infant has a beard, something which may amuse twentieth-century Christians who may think the artist was naïve, that he was ignorant of infant anatomy. The point that this artist well knew was that it was his duty to paint a childlike not a childish Christ-child, not what we would recognize today as a "North-Star"-blanket illustration of a cuddly baby. The thirteenth-century artist wanted to make absolutely certain that no one would err in reading his picture; he wanted all to see that the infant on St. Christopher's shoulders was not an ordinary child but a special, unique Child endowed with Divine Wisdom. He, therefore, added what undoubtedly was the accepted attribute in his age and clime of manhood and wisdom, a beard.

I must also mention a third kind of abuse in religious imagery which has entered as a kind of reaction to the abuses described above — I mean the exaggerated abstract symbolism, the abstractive, contemporary art in which the human configurations and features of Christ, for example, are eliminated or distorted unduly in an attempt to communicate pure spiritual ideas or "religious" emotions. The dangers of such art are obvious. Pure abstraction implies a denial or at least a serious dilution of the fact that the Word was indeed made Flesh and dwelt among us. Abstraction also invites the viewer to read into such art what he wishes to read, encouraging "personal" religion and devotional relativity. The Catholic religion, on the contrary, is specific and concrete; it has definite norms and beliefs which cannot be placed at the mercy or disposal of arbitrary personal interpretations.

What, then, is the right approach to religious art today? What is a fitting "image of Christ" for our time?

We may state as a fundamental principle that religious art must, above all, be theologically correct. This correctness excludes not only direct statement of theological error but, in so far as it is humanly possible, all statements which may unwittingly lead viewers into theological error.

The Church is the final arbiter on the theological qualities of any work of religious art. Her concern is theology. She uses art to help communicate theological truths. The artist composing a religious hymn or carving a crucifix is teaching theology; he is communicating religious ideas to those who hear and see his work. The Church, because of her sacred mission, is abidingly concerned with the kind of religious ideas these artists propagate, since religious art is, as it were, a minor branch of theology. The religious "statement" in a work of art is always the final cause, the determining cause; the art itself is the material cause and, therefore, subordinate.

I have already pointed out some of the most gross errors in religious art, both past and present: excessively human portraits of Christ which minimize His divinity; excessively abstract symbols of Christ which deny His humanity; effeminate portraits of Christ which belie His virility and manhood; excessive realism and particularization of details which destroy, or at least attenuate, the symbolic function of sacred art and distract the viewer from the greater truths the symbols are meant to convey; preoccupation with historical-archaeological problems and personal artistic excursions which are not central to religious truth.

In order, then, to arrive at sound norms and principles which will guide his work, the artist must know as much what errors to avoid as what habits to perfect. He must know, for example, why a painting of a Crucifixion or Resurrection scene which is scrupulously exact concerning the historical accidentals of first-century dress and clime is, theologically, less desirable than the same scene represented in contemporary terms, in terms, that is, of our own age and culture.

Christ's life, death, and resurrection are, indeed, historical facts. Yet these facts are not ordinary history; they have an immediacy and relevancy for all souls in all ages. A religious picture which, by inordinate attention to the historical accidentals surrounding these facts, would relegate Christ and His Redemption to a certain period of history, runs the serious risk of leading present-day Christians into the belief that they are but detached and passive spectators of these truths. It is a dogma, for example, that our sins, in 1956, help crucify Christ. But it is difficult, indeed, to feel the force of this truth when we view Crucifixion scenes which, by freezing the meaning of the Crucifixion as a first-century event, encourage us to believe that the guilt belongs exclusively to the Jews and the Roman rulers and soldiers.

I suggest, therefore, that a basic principle of religious art is that we must express religious truths in contemporary terms; we must use the things proper to our own age. God chose to call us into existence in this age rather than another. For all of us now living, this is the very best age.

We cannot go back to any other age for a contemporary expression of Christ in art, not even to those earlier inspirations (Umbrian, Sienese, Medieval, and early-Christian) which were authentic, which were truly peaks in the history of religious art. We may learn much from the *manner of operation* of those authentic artists; we may not imitate the *external expression* of those artists who were producing religious art well ordered to their time.

Nor ought we, as I have frequently indicated, clothe Christ in the garb of biblical Palestine. Religion is not a masquerade nor a costume party. The Gospel tells us nothing of clothing styles. We translate the Bible into the language of those who are to use it — verbal language as well as visual-artistic language. Should we all learn Hebrew and Greek because those were the original languages of the

Bible? In order to understand Christ's teachings, must we all learn Aramaic because He used that language?

I sometimes wonder whether the preference of some for Christ pictured as a merely historic figure, a stranger from faraway places living in a remote age may not reflect a type of spiritual escapism. Such a representation of Christ in art does not disturb us unduly; it provokes no embarrassing questions about our part in His Crucifixion. If, on the contrary, Christ is portrayed as a member of our household, and our city, a person of our land and language, we are thrust uncomfortably close to truths we perhaps would rather not examine for fear of their personal implications in our lives.

The function, then, of the religious artist of every age is to state the eternal truths of Christianity in new, fresh, acceptable terms accommodated to the true devotional needs of his particular audience.

The prudent artist must guard against allowing his visual language to become stale and trite from overuse. But he must also guard against seeking novelty for the sake of novelty in his art.

Above all, the good religious artist not only avoids but actively fights against all forms of sentimentality in art since sentimentality bypasses reason and substitutes emotionalism for Faith's intellectual assent to religious truths.

Earlier, I said that each age makes pictorial statements of Christ in terms of the ideal of its time. What is the ideal of our time? I cannot answer that question with any finality, at least not for some time. One reason is that we no longer have kings, epic heroes, emperors, and other serviceable prototypes for the ideal.

Meanwhile, until we do have an ideal to serve as our artistic prototype, there is nothing to prevent religious artists from parting company with the sentimental abominations now prevalent in religious art. Images of the effeminate Christ, referred to earlier, confront us everywhere: in homes, schools, seminaries, hospitals, convents, and churches. This is a serious problem demanding full and immediate attention. One of the first duties of Catholic artists is to restore to Christ His Manhood which has been stripped from Him in recent centuries.

In ages of sentimentality, it is a most serious obligation of the artist, I am convinced, to register his distaste for such sentimentality by producing works of art which will correct the error. In the case of the effeminate Christ inflicted upon the faithful, it is necessary to go for a time to a clearly masculine ideal until that wretched error is buried. In our time, one sign of manhood is trousers which, as garb for Christ, are a useful artistic device in the needful masculine-restoration process now demanded. Conversely, slacks for the Blessed Virgin would be inappropriate because repugnant to the idea of her sacred maternity. In the task of showing divine qualities in the image of Christ, the artist is, of course, confronted by formidable artistic difficulties. It is impossible to discuss this delicate problem in great detail here. We may note, however, some elementary premises. The artist must use those forms, lines, shapes, and colors which, by unprejudiced artistic consent, symbolically suggest higher values. To suggest power, for example, the artist would not use weak, effeminate, soft, overly rounded lines or shapes, but rather more straight lines, verticals, horizontals, strong curves, and starker contrasts suggesting solidity and strength. To indicate eternal beatitude, as another example, the artist would not use violent lines, shapes, or colors — which may well be apt for picturing chaos — nor would he employ delicate posturings suggestive of daintiness which is incompatible with what we know about Christ.

In expressing Christ in contemporary visual language, I do not mean to imply that in the matter of clothes, for instance, we should strive for the latest "fashion." To put Christ in a Brooks Brothers suit, or to make Him a candidate for one of the Ten Best Dressed Men of the year would be to return to that error of overemphasis on the details of the clothes at the expense of the sacred Person. The clothes given to Christ should be neither too old nor too new. They should be a general type, acceptable to our time, to indicate that its Wearer is living among us, that He is a partner to our secrets, sorrows, and joys; that He is one to whom we can go with full confidence in the knowledge that He is sharing our lot.

There is no universal "Catholic style" in art. That is to say, there is no one permanent artistic expression of Christ, frozen for all time. Each piece of good Catholic art is a unique expression uttered by the Mystical Body, an expression most fitting for the time and place where it occurs.

If God did, in fact, withhold all graphic and literary records of Christ's physical features, there must have been a reason. The reason cannot be, as some might infer, that we are meant to have no pictures at all of Christ. We need religious images. It is true that some select souls, far advanced in virtue, and some philosophers can dispense with the usual symbols and pictorial images in arriving at divine truths. The great majority of people, however, must have pictures. As St. Thomas says: ". . . it is fitting that divine truths be expressed under the figure of less noble than nobler bodies; . . . especially in the case of those who can think of nothing nobler than bodies" (S.T. I, 1, 9, ad 3).

I have suggested, earlier, a possible reason why we have had no literal picturization of Christ: so that "each age and people could assimilate Christ as their ideal."

A more detailed examination of this possibility will conclude this discussion.

Could it be that God, in His infinite wisdom, withheld the pictorial, literal image of Christ from us in order to discourage that type of idolatry which suggests that some special national or racial group was favored and superior to all others? True, the Jews were once the chosen people. God rescinded that choice and invited non-Jews to His table. All who are Catholics are now the "chosen people," chosen, however, by Grace not by race.

By taking from us the temptation to particularize on the features of the Redeemer, the Church is able to preach more effectively the truth of Jesus who is "all things to all men." To limit the image of Christ to a particular ethnic or racial strain is to impede the unreserved acceptance of Christ by the great variety of ethnic and cultural groups in the world. Insisting that Christ's image be Latin because the Church is Roman is as much a blunder as demanding that the image be Jewish because He was born of a Jewish maiden into a Jewish people.

The Catholic Church is indeed catholic. She does not, and cannot, identify herself with any particular culture. While she molds cultures, she is above them. She cuts across centuries and remains true to her divine direction to commend herself to all cultures in all times.

This is crucial in these days of a shrinking world. The doctrines of white supremacy, Nordic ascendancy and superiority, and kindred evils are diabolisms of the worst kind. Certainly, religious artists of all people should be on guard against unwittingly giving credence to these malicious myths. To project one kind of image patterned after a special, physical, and racial type as the "true Christ," is bigotry (either conscious or unconscious), injurious to the Faith and

a contradiction of St. Paul who, inspired by the Holy
Ghost, wrote:

> With the Jews I lived like a Jew, to win the Jews; with
> those who keep the law, as one who keeps the law (though
> the law had no claim on me), to win those who kept the law;
> with those who are free of the law, like one free of the law . . .
> to win those who were free from the law. With the scrupulous,
> I behaved myself like one who is scrupulous. I have been all
> things to all men to bring salvation to all (1 Cor. 9:20–22).

May we any longer say that a Mongolian Madonna with
slanted eyes is wrong? May we object to Arctic natives making an Eskimo of St. Joseph? What is the legitimate visual
ideal of Christ for a normal, black native in Africa?

These are not academic questions. They are terribly important theologically, artistically, and, as we are beginning
to see in our own country and throughout the world,
culturally and socially. Their implications are enormously
wide and deep.

THE CHRISTIAN IN POLITICS

BY EUGENE J. MC CARTHY

Is THERE a Christian politics? Christian political thinkers and leaders have defined and described what they consider the ideal Christian State. Some have seen this ideal State in the medieval synthesis of State and Church and looked to the restoration of a similar order today. For others, the ideal Christian State is conceived as a monarchy, with the Christian monarch defending both faith and country. Others envision the Christian State as a democracy founded upon the natural law or the papal encyclicals.

If the concept of Christian politics is to be justified, or if any historical State is to merit the label "Christian," it must be of such kind that, as Franz Joseph Schoningh, editor of *Hochland,* pointed out in the April, 1949, issue of that magazine, "fundamentally, through its Christian character alone, it differs from every other."

Neither history nor political theory establish any basis for the application of the label "Christian" in any absolute sense to politics. Recognition of Christianity by the State does not make the State itself "Christian," nor does official approval of certain Christian forms and practices. Neither does the fact that all citizens of a State are Christians make that State a Christian State. A government might be distinguished as more or less Christian to the degree that it has either succeeded or failed in establishing a greater measure of justice; or, a form of government called Christian to the extent that it depends upon the inspiration of the Gospels for its fulfillment, as does democracy. Such qualified application sets the limits on the use of the word "Christian."

Although the existence of a purely Christian politics cannot be established, there remains an obvious need for Christians in politics, that is, for Christian politicians. Every human society is political and every adult member of such a society must of necessity assume political obligations. A Christian must assume these obligations as a citizen, and more particularly as a Christian citizen. He must, as Pope Pius XII pointed out in his message correcting the misinterpretations of the directive "Return to the Spiritual," be actively present in political life — "wherever vital interests are at stake; where laws concerning the worship of God, marriage, the family, the schools, the social order, are being deliberated; wherever through education the spirit of a nation is being forged. . . ."

The calling of a Christian is not to judge the world, but rather to save it. In the conflict between good and evil, in which great advantage is given to evil by neglect, the Christian cannot be indifferent to so important an area of conflict as that of politics.

Not everyone has an obligation to run for public office, or even to become active in party organization. The measure of participation required of an individual depends on many conditions of personality and circumstances. There is no excuse, however, for complete neutralism and detachment. It is not even possible, under all circumstances, to justify the position of the "independent voter," or of the nonpartisan citizen. These forms of political activity can be enjoyed only because others are actively engaged in party politics. It is important to keep in mind the testimony of history to the need for party politics in domestic government. In the United States party factions preceded the adoption of the Constitution itself, and government, since that time, has depended upon political party activities. Good government depends on good political parties.

In approaching politics, the Christian must be realistic — politics is a part of the real world. In politics the simple choice between black and white is seldom given. The ideal is seldom realized, and often cannot be advocated. For example, a Christian politician in a society in which many marriages are broken, may have to advocate and support divorce laws for the sake of public order. Trade, diplomatic relations and co-operation with nations whose conduct he condemns may be made necessary by circumstances. Political leaders may, in what Maritain describes as "regressive or barbarous" societies, have their freedom of choice reduced to the point where they must take a position which is questionable, rather than the alternative which is simply and completely bad. Prudence may require the toleration of evil in order to prevent something worse, and may dictate a decision to let the cockle grow with the wheat for a time. In making decisions of this kind, the Christian in politics, whether he is the official who makes the decision, or the citizen who supports the official and his decision, runs the risk of being called un-Christian or anti-Christian. This is a risk which he must be willing to take.

Despite these difficulties and complications it should nonetheless be possible to distinguish the Christian in politics. If such distinction could not be made there would be no point in urging the participation of Christians in political life.

What are the marks of a Christian politician? He is not necessarily the one who is seen most often participating in public religious activities, or conferring with religious leaders. He is not necessarily the one who first and most vociferously proclaims that his position is the Christian one and who attempts to cover himself and his cause with whatever part of the divided garment that is within his reach. He is not necessarily the one who makes of every cause a "crusade" presenting himself as Carlyle described the crusader as "the minister of God's justice, doing God's judgment of the enemies of God."

The Christian in politics should be judged by the standard of whether through his decisions and actions he has advanced the cause of justice, and helped, at least, to achieve the highest degree of perfection possible in the temporal order. He has available to him a great body of teachings on secular matters. He should know and understand those teachings and should seek to apply them.

When a political problem can be reduced to a simple question of feeding the hungry or of not feeding them; of ransoming the captive or of refusing to ransom him; of harboring the harborless, or of leaving him homeless — there should be no uncertainty as to the Christian position. Problems of overpopulation, of displaced and expelled peoples, of political refugees, and the like are in reality not always reducible to simple choices. As a general rule the inclination of the Christian should be to liberality. His mistakes and failures on problems of this kind should be as a consequence of leniency rather than of a fearful self-interest; of excess of trust, rather than of excess of doubt and anxiety.

The Christian politician must, of course, hold fast to the moral law remembering that the precepts of morality do not themselves change, even though the way in which they are applied to concrete acts may be modified as society regresses or is perverted.

On the basis of moral principles, he must strive to separate good from bad even though the line may be blurred or shifting. He must remember and honor in action the rule that the end does not justify the means. He should carefully avoid confusion such as that which is manifest in Cromwell's reply to Wharton's protest of Pride's purge and the execution of the King. "It is easy to object to the glorious actings of God, if we look too much upon the instruments. Be not offended at the manner. Perhaps there was no other way left."

The Christian in politics should be distinguished by his alertness to protect and defend the rights of individuals, or religious institutions and other institutions from violation by the State or by other institutions, or by persons. He should be the first to detect and oppose a truly totalitarian threat or movement and the last to label every proposal for social reform "socialistic."

He should protect the name of Christ from abuse and profanation, and should himself avoid unwarranted appeals to religion. He has a very special obligation to keep the things of God separate from those of Caesar.

The Christian in politics should shun the devices of the demagogue at all times, but especially in a time when anxiety is great, when tension is high, when uncertainty prevails, and emotion tends to be in the ascendancy.

The Christian in politics should speak the truth. He should make his case in all honesty — aware that any other action is as C. S. Lewis states, to offer to the Author of all truth the unclean sacrifice of a lie. He should not return calumny and slander in the same token, but combat them with truth and honesty, risking defeat for the sake of truth. He should not resort to the common practice of labeling, which by its falseness violates justice, and by its indignity offends charity. Powerful personalities may be able to stand against these forces. The weak are likely to be destroyed. It is these who must be the concern of Christians.

In addition to distinction on the basis of actions the Christian in politics should be distinguished by his manner of approach. He should normally be optimistic rather than pessimistic. The optimism would not be blind or foolish, without awareness or recognition of reality, but rather manifesting hopeful confidence, despite the difficulties of a situation and the potentiality of men and human society for failure.

The Christian should show respect for the opinion, judgment, and motives of others. This he can do without any abject denial of the certainty of his own position and without agreeing to disagree, or conceding that those who disagree with him may be right.

The Christian should be humble, reflecting in his actions, his awareness of the great mystery of redemption, and the shared mystery and dignity of all men.

Altogether these seem to be difficult standards and demands. Their fulfillment requires sanctity. There is, however, no other measure which is valid for Christians in politics or in any other way of life. As the great politician and saint, Thomas More, observed, "It is not possible for all things to be well, unless all men are good — which I think will not be this good many years."

THE FINALITY OF SEX

BY FRANCIS P. CANAVAN, S.J.

KINGSLEY DAVIS, of Columbia University, some time ago wrote an article on "The American Family: What It Is — and Isn't" (*New York Times Magazine,* September 30, 1951). As he sees it, the American family is "marriage-centered," that is, its primary purpose is conceived to be the happiness of the two parties contracting marriage. This explains our insistence on complete freedom from parental interference in choosing a mate, our strong interest in the trials and tribulations of courtship, and the young age at which we marry. In saying this, Mr. Davis disclaims any judgment of value. "I am," he says, "simply describing some salient features of our family system." The significant point is this:

"One should realize that the salient features are all connected. The preoccupation with courtship and the cult of marital happiness not only reflect the degree to which our family is 'marriage-centered,' but they are also integrally related to other features which some groups at least find objectionable, such as our low birth rate, our young age at marriage, and our high divorce rate."

The root therefore of the modern notion of what marriage should be is the orientation of the institution to the happiness of the two individuals who marry. There is no idea of a subordination of the individuals concerned to a higher purpose, a purpose which imposes obligations on

them, and in the fulfillment of which they fulfill themselves. The supreme good of marriage is the happiness of
the individuals concerned, as they themselves see it, and
whatever standards govern marriage derive from this goal.
Here we have the pivot on which contemporary thought
about marriage is swinging from a Christian idea to a
distinctively modern one.

It is well known that the Catholic Church is at odds
with the rest of the world on divorce and birth control.
What is not so generally known is that this disagreement
arises from a far more fundamental disagreement over the
basic purpose of marriage. Mr. Davis indicates the true
source of the opposition when he says: "If marriage exists
for the purpose of individual happiness, if it is entered into
and maintained because of personal attraction, the decision
to have or not to have children will be made by the couple
themselves in terms of their own wishes. They may be so
happy that children would seem an interference." The same
line of reasoning explains why "marriage is not nearly so
irrevocable as it once was. If the initial venture turns out
to be irksome, divorce is easy to obtain."

What has happened is that the finality, or purpose, of
marriage and of sex itself has been changed. What was once
an institution primarily for the procreation and rearing of
children is now primarily a means of achieving individual
happiness. Marriage was once the seedbed of the family;
now the family is an adjunct to marriage. Once the social
function of sex was held paramount; now it may legitimately
be subordinated or even denied.

This suggests that the sexual drive has been liberated
from the restraints of traditional morality and made free to
determine and strive for its own goals. The sexual drive,
as the term is used here, does not connote merely the craving
for the animal satisfactions of sex, but rather the whole

complex of physical and psychic urges which impel people to a more or less permanent sexual union. What is important is that "sex," in however wide a sense the term is taken, is now an end in itself.

Therein lies the difference between modern and Christian sexual morality. Contrary to what can be read in many books written by those who ought to know better, Christian morality does not consider sexual satisfaction an evil to be tolerated if one must, and abolished if one can. The question to which Christian writers on sexual morality address themselves is: what is the right use of sex? — a question which obviously supposes that there is a right use. The answer they give depends, as any answer to the question must, on their conception of the purposes of sex: here is the truly crucial point.

I say purposes, because the moralists have traditionally recognized a plurality of ends which the sexual function of its nature is intended to achieve. Human nature being an animal nature, there must be a legitimate satisfaction of animal desire. On a higher level, there is the expression of mutual love. Finally, there is the procreation of children, which in its full meaning includes their full education to maturity. This last Christian morality has always recognized as the primary end or purpose of marriage and of the act of sex which marriage, as it were, enshrines.

It is undeniably antipathetic to modern ways of thinking to assert that sex is primarily for the sake of procreation, so antipathetic that I am sure that many who consider themselves devout Christians will strongly resent the assertion. So conditioned are we by the romantic notion of love that we almost instinctively think of sex as finding its ultimate justification in love. We have therefore found it easy to accept the corollaries of birth control and divorce. It is to be feared, however, that if we persist in our individualistic view of marriage, we shall find ourselves accepting still other corollaries which will make it unmistakably clear just how far we have departed from marriage as Christian civilization has always understood it.

For the modern position certainly implies at least this: procreation is not the primary natural purpose of sex, nor therefore of marriage. This is the reason why the practice of contraception is considered morally permissible. But it also follows from the same premise that procreation is not even a necessary purpose of sex. The acceptance of contraception as legitimate, for whatever reason, is a denial that there is a necessary relationship of purpose between the sexual act and procreation; in other words, it is an affirmation that sexual activity is morally autonomous and free of any subordination to procreation as its goal.

It is no answer to say that most people who practice contraception do so only to limit the number of children they will have, and not in order to have none at all. The argument is from the nature or essential structure of the sexual act. If it is morally right to perform it with a contraceptive in any instance, it follows that there cannot be an intrinsic and necessary connection between the act and procreation as its purpose. It is with the consequences of this position that we are here concerned.

Two consequences have already been stated. The first is that marriage is not the seedbed of the family, except as a matter of free choice on the part of the individuals concerned. As Mr. Davis says, a couple "may be so happy together that children would seem an interference." The second consequence is that the continuance or termination of a marriage ought also to depend, primarily if not exclusively, on the free choice of the parties to the marriage.

Aldous Huxley said some years ago: "There are already

certain American cities in which the number of divorces is equal to the number of marriages. In a few years, no doubt, marriage licenses will be sold like dog licenses, good for a period of twelve months, with no law against changing dogs or keeping more than one animal at a time" (*Brave New World*).

It may seem that Mr. Huxley is merely being clever in a coarse way. Yet what he says is in the logic of the modern position on sex and marriage. If sexual activity is not of its nature purposeful and subordinated to procreation, there is no intrinsic reason why it must be kept within the bounds of marriage at all.

What has caused adultery and fornication to be regarded as morally wrong is, ultimately, that they produce a situation in which it is a wise child that knows his own father and so they are an attack upon the very purpose of the family. But now that modern science can guarantee that there will be no child to ask embarrassing questions, modern morality may well wonder why self-sterilized sex activity has to be confined to the marital union.

The only answers that can be given are, first, that as far as individuals are concerned, romantic love demands fidelity, and second, as far as society is concerned, social welfare demands stable marital unions. Neither argument, however, affords any solid ground on which to build an enduring monogamy. Romantic love furnishes no reason for prohibiting a wide range of premarital experimentation, and can at most demand that polygamy be successive (as in Hollywood) rather than simultaneous (as in Arabia).

Nor can a concept of social welfare, which accepts contraception and divorce to begin with, frown on pre- and extramarital sexual activity, provided it be sterile. If marriage has no necessary relation to the family, and if, moreover, society is willing to take over most of the functions of the family, why should society concern itself to confine sexual activity to marriage?

Or, for that matter, why should society concern itself to confine sexual activity to persons of opposite sex? An English woman psychiatrist, Laura Hutton, has suggested homosexual love affairs as a substitute for marriage for women who, perforce, can get nothing more satisfactory (*The Single Woman and Her Emotional Problems*). The suggestion will be shocking to many, as Dr. Hutton herself recognizes, yet it is in the logic of contraception.

Simone de Beauvoir, in her recent book, *The Second Sex,* asserts that modern woman is gaining equality and freedom as a result of her "sharing in productive labor and being freed from the slavery of reproduction." Mme. de Beauvoir also writes approvingly of premarital sex experimentation, adultery, lesbianism, free love, and abortion. These are merely the conclusions that flow naturally from freedom from the slavery of reproduction. For if sex may morally be made sterile and deprived of any necessary relation to procreation, then there is no compelling reason why it must realize its desires through complementary organs of generation.

Or, to put it another way, if the organs of sex are not morally as well as physically organs of generation, then it is a matter of subjective preference whether one uses them with a person of one's own or the opposite sex — or whether one brings another person into the action at all. Most people, of course, will retain a preference for normal sex relations, but it is difficult to see why normality should be made equivalent to moral obligation. *Chacun à son goût* — and let joy be unconfined.

At least, it is difficult to see why there is any obligation to act normally in sexual matters on the basis of the modern assumptions about the nature and purpose of sex. The entire case for contraception, for instance, rests on the proposition that sexual passion, as between man and wife, cannot or ought not be controlled. Let us leave aside the question whether this is true. Even if it is true, this proposition has no claim to being considered a rational approach to the question of sexual morality. Rather it is an abandonment of rationality and an assertion of the primacy of passion.

But if passion has the primacy in marriage, it must also have it outside of marriage. That being so, on what grounds can one argue against sexually abnormal conduct? Not on the grounds of the natural purpose of sex, for that has already been denied. Not on the grounds of rational self-control, for that has been asserted to be ultimately impossible. Not on the grounds of love or even of pleasure, for those are matters of which the individual must judge for himself. *Once the intelligible natural purpose of sex has been denied, reason has been deprived of the only standard by which it can distinguish between right and wrong in sexual conduct.* Then everything is right which society does not choose to forbid.

All this seems farfetched, no doubt. So too does Aldous Huxley's novel, *Brave New World*. Huxley therein depicts a society in which sex has been so completely divorced from procreation that all children are generated in bottles, and motherhood has become a dirty word. At the same time, and as a direct consequence, marriage has been abolished and everyone has been conditioned to accept a carefree promiscuity as normal and right. This is, if you will, farfetched. But the point remains the same: it is in the logic of modern ideas about sex and marriage.

I certainly do not expect Mr. Huxley's brave new world ever to eventuate in reality, and I doubt that Mr. Huxley does either, though in the preface to the latest edition of his novel he professes a growing pessimism. But the only reason why the brave new world will not eventuate is that human nature will revolt against the inhuman when it becomes sufficiently obvious.

The consequences of the concepts of sex and marriage on which modern man is now acting are, in strict logic, the inhuman consequences described above. Man will, let us devoutly hope, stop short of the full consequences, but he will do so only by abandoning the false philosophy that leads to them.

The abandonment of the false philosophy and the elaboration of a rational philosophy of sex will demand a return to traditional theism, at least to the extent of recognizing God as the intelligent creator of a rational universe. This will involve the recognition of human nature as a product of the Divine Reason. (Here is reintroduced, quite frankly, that climate of opinion in which Carl Becker's modern mind could only gasp for breath. But if the modern mind wants rationality in its morals, it has to gasp for breath.)

Human nature, in this view, has an intelligible structure and is endowed with a hierarchy of natural purposes. That is to say, the various powers and organs of a human being have by nature their proper functions and purposes. The eye is not merely an organ by which we see, it is an organ *for* seeing. So too the digestive system has as its natural purpose the nourishment of the body.

As applied to sex, this principle means that the organs of sex are organs of reproduction, not merely in physical fact, but also in the intention of nature. A man and woman may join themselves in the act of sex out of passion or love. But in so doing, they are performing an act that of its nature aims at and intends procreation. That mutual love should desire to express itself physically is understandable, for the body is as natural to man as the soul. But that love should have a natural inclination to express itself in precisely *this* act is unintelligible unless we look beyond love to an intention of nature. On analysis of the structure and operation of sex, it is evident that this intention can only be the reproduction of the species.

But since human nature is the work of God, the "intentions of nature" are intentions of God, who made human nature and determined its purposes. And if the intentions of nature are God's intentions, it follows that they must be respected. All things that fall under human power, including man's own body, were given to man by God, and given that they might be used. But man may not do whatever he wills with them. He may use them or abstain from using them: it is legitimate to close one's eyes, and one need not always be eating. But man may not abuse the gift of God by using it in such a way as to frustrate its divinely intended purpose. There is no obligation for a married couple to use their reproductive powers to the utmost, but if they do use them, they may not in the same act render them sterile. Nature is man's servant, not his slave.

This is the keystone of the whole Christian position: that the natural structure and purposes of sex and marriage are determined, not by man, but by God. A man is free to marry or not to marry, and to marry this person or that. But if he marries, he must marry a woman and enter with her into a union designed by nature for the reproduction of the species in an adequate way. Since the species in question is the human species, the only adequate union for reproducing it is a permanent and exclusive union founded on mutual esteem and love. No merely temporary union based on passion or emotion will do. Human nature demands nothing less than truly human marriage. That is to say that God demands nothing less.

Against all this the argument can be advanced (it is really

the only argument that ever is advanced), that it involves at times a restraint of passion which most men and women would find intolerable. Sexual passion today is forming in the minds of men a concept of marriage which is no marriage, but a sterile and unstable partnership in a selfish quest for happiness. Against this adversary one strives in vain with reason alone: only the grace of God will suffice. But there may be some value in defining the point at issue. The point at issue here is whether sex and marriage are to be regarded as instruments of human desires or as rational expressions of the will of God.

THE POET AS WITNESS

BY GEORGE N. SHUSTER

WE HAVE recently heard a junior voice in the councils of elders of the nation urge the police to keep a close watch on professors. Why not on poets, too? Or rather, why not on poets first of all? For these are not merely some unforgettable ones, crowned with laurel or trailing clouds of glory, who give to the spiritual quest by which their time lives, its permanent name and image. The poet is also one of the many folk on whose spirits some human experience, dear or savage, has been etched so clearly, troublingly, beautifully, that it cries out for its saying in transitory words. He enters the lists where that which is more enduring than bronze is fought for, however uneven the handicaps may be. And in a higher sense poets are like the obedient angels who, St. Thomas surmised, are assigned to govern the rolling in space of the stars, being charged with keeping night-watches on the meaning of created things. They live by the axiom, for them at least an axiom, that a fleck of dust in the sunlight is no less mysterious than is the whole of cosmic space. Any contour, familiar but breathtaking, may be a symbol of the fruition of beauty which for some inscrutable reason God has desired to reveal to His people. Inscrutable? Yes. For this people is the crowd of the perennially dirty, the unaccountably dissolute, every one of whom has nevertheless been ushered into this world with "Destination Immortality" branded over his heart. We must try to

believe Him when He says of them all, even the illiterate
and cruel who have latterly overrun a beleaguered outpost
in South East Asia, that they were born to experience His
affection, not as roses and rabbits do, blindly, but as angels
immured in the flesh might if they only knew.

Good it is therefore that never were so many poets
amongst us as there are now. They drape sonnets over the
lampposts of every village and city. They sit in farmhouses
writing of love and death. They praise the stability of
earthly existence in the midst of traffic. They lament the
passing of time, perched on the imperturbable stone fences
of New England. They echo Dante in night clubs. It is the
habit of some of them to be simple and straightforward,
while others are as cryptic as runes. Of not a few it must
be said that they are sillier than any prose writer could be;
and of others the critic will report that they are glutted with
the canned meat of learning. Only here and there amongst
them rise the voices of prophets, speaking a few lines that
only after a century men will be able to comprehend.
Heaven seems, then, to be scattering the poets with a
prodigal springtime hand, little caring that for ancestral
reasons only a few rise tall in the sun.

I surmise that this is as it is because the soil has been
stripped so bare — because there has been a kind of dust
storm in the spiritual realm of creation, wiping the granite
ledges clean. Civilization has become a kind of huge pump
over an enormous well, hauling to the surface immeasur-
able, ungovernable things. Of knowledge and of power.
But also of brutishness and evil, such as have not been seen
since the dawn of time. Science can now put to death, with
a flick of what is in a capsule, gruesome fiends within the
body who in former days mowed down millions. But it can
also, with another twist of the wrist, wipe out us all. In like
manner the idols which the age adores are not grim and

discernible creations, like Jupiter or Baal, but appalling
mysteries of iniquity which move behind locust-like swarms
of planes and tanks. They spread about them plagues of
hatred and idea, striving to compress what remains of time
into a wineglass of assumed eternity. Meanwhile the little
man is ground into something eerier than bone meal in the
machines of slavery. There seems to come from this ghastly
product an odor which induces madness.

Therefore let the poets say and let us repeat with them
— "Glory be to God for all dappled things" — for the
crazy quilt of what is little and individual and warmly,
deliciously human, for laughter and love, for what is half-
witted and full-bodied, above all for the bravery which
reminds us of Don Quixote on his ridiculous horse. For
here is the true meaning of our culture and our faith.
That the little thing (or poem) is sacred because no other
thing can reflect as it does the Divinity which has made
it — this is true by reason of the same fiat which measured
out to each of the planets its radiance. In the days of yore the
saints were wont to criticize humankind because there was
always too much zest in every human creature. He sang his
wassail songs too lustily, and drank overmuch of ale as he
did so. In order that he might endure the season of Lent,
he made a fool of himself during Mardi Gras. But few of
the blessed could foresee an hour during which millions of
little men, women, and children would be only numbers in
a chain gang, only bloodless symbols of a collectivity. And
so while we are yet free let the poets speak with frenzy of
freedom. Let them praise with rapture their sapphire flowers,
their true loves and their bold prayers, so that there may be
a mighty torrent of stanzas, each one of which will not be
a drop in the stream merely but truly itself, with the sunlight in it and something like wine as well.

We have these days read of a soldier in the great tradition — far-off with hordes assailing him and with little chance of succor. Is this not again he "whose loss is laughter when he counts the wager worth"? We shall assuredly have to behold many who are like him before the battle is done. For this is the only way in which man can effectively symbolize the adventure of immortality. Alas, there must be on the other hand the dire anguish that follows battle — the loss of what is dear because it is different, of each separate martyr in the arena of the world. Glory and sorrow must appear in divers forms if liberty is to abide.

Sometimes, of course, I am tempted to think — as no doubt have you — that the poets are too eager for recognition. They publish magazines for the purpose, and not infrequently pay the printer for their books. And yet having thought the matter over carefully, I am prepared to praise them mightily for this. They are giving testimony. It is the yearning to stand before men and to be counted by them which mirrors the ultimate fact that in the end each must kneel alone before God. We do not believe in anonymity and collectivity because these are the supreme illusions. I remember a French soldier whom I saw mortally wounded in the wartime of my youth. Before he died he passed his hand carefully over the ribbon which symbolized his Cross of the Legion of Honor, so that he might be sure that it was clean. I have not forgotten him because by this gesture he proved that he was a Christian and of the West. And so I hope that our poets will likewise keep on pressing their verses to their hearts.

THE AREA OF CATHOLIC FREEDOM

BY WILLIAM CLANCY

A CATHOLIC, by the profession of his faith, has the advantage of possessing a large area of certain knowledge — the area of those first truths on which the Church has spoken with authority. Here the Catholic is relieved of questions; he has only answers: *Roma locuta est; causa finita est.*

Rome does not speak often, but she speaks clearly and magisterially at those times in history when great issues are in doubt, when the human spirit is assaulted, when she herself must choose between divergent paths. At such a time the Church looks to herself, to her own nature and destiny, and gives final answers. Much of the nineteenth century was such a time. During the pontificate of Pius IX the spirit born of the Enlightenment and Revolution reached its full strength and, under the name of Progress, threatened the very existence of the Church. Pius IX responded by condemning wholesale those principles and slogans most valued by the Enlightenment and Revolution. He denied that the Church could or should reconcile herself with such liberalism or progress as they represented.

There were Catholics who had hoped for a different resolution of the conflict between the Church and modern civilization. Newman and Acton in England, Lacordaire and Dupanloup in France — the great liberal Catholics of the nineteenth century — had sought to avert so decisive a break

between the City of God and the City of Man. They had
worked for a greater restraint on the part of men in both
camps. But this was not a time of restraint, and the moder-
ates lost. The rupture between the Church and the world
seemed complete.

But was it complete? Ninety years after Pio Nono's famous
Syllabus it seems less so. What perhaps could not be recognized in the hot atmosphere of 1864 seems true now: the
work of Pius IX in the area of the Church's relation to
modern culture was essentially negative. This is not to
deny its necessity or its value. It had to be done. With
Italian armies beating against the gates of Rome the Pope
could not linger over nice distinctions between what was
totally unacceptable and what was redeemable in the spirit
of the Risorgimento. What Pius IX named was a spirit the
Church could *not* reconcile with her own spirit. He did not
attempt to explore — nor, probably, to understand — what
the Church could accept in the modern world.

Those Catholics who did attempt this during Pio Nono's
reign were destined to frustration and defeat. They lived
too soon. But the questions they raised have still to be
answered. Lord Acton's writings are relevant today. The
basic facts of the Church's unalterable opposition to materialism and relativism were settled in the nineteenth century; the more complex issues of the practical relationship
between Catholicism and modern culture are still unresolved.
Paradoxically, their resolution should be more possible because of the reigns of Pius IX and St. Pius X. The dangers
of theological Liberalism and Modernism have been made
clear. The limits of orthodoxy have been drawn. No informed Catholic should fall into errors against which he
has been so forcefully warned. We should therefore be able
to consider things more calmly and more safely than was
possible before the Syllabus and the Encyclical *Pascendi.*

What are the things we have to consider? What are the unresolved issues which hang over from the great conflicts of the nineteenth century? They seem to me to fall roughly into the general questions of the areas of freedom possible within the Church, the relation of Catholics to the political life of their time, and the attitude to be taken by Catholics toward modern culture. In each of these questions we know what is *not* possible. We are plagued however, by ambiguous attitudes toward what *is* possible. Here we must still explore and discover, for the sake of both the Church and the world.

And here we can expect no syllabus to show us the way. These are areas primarily of attitude rather than of definition — areas in which no easy guideposts are possible. There are Catholics who think that the important questions have all been solved, that we need only consult the manuals to discover the answers. They would bind us in a nineteenth-century strait jacket as we attempt to grapple with twentieth-century complexities.

Such an attitude is as impossible as it is imprudent. Contingent problems cannot be solved in advance of their appearance. Each generation must face the problems of its own age. It should be guided, of course, by the experience of previous generations, but should not be deceived into thinking that the two experiences are the same. Many of the problems a Catholic must face in 1954 are radically different from the ones Pius IX answered in 1864. We have, as Catholics throughout history have had, a unique present with which to deal.

The situation, for example, which faces Catholics in the United States cannot be met by an appeal to the Syllabus. This country has known none of the fierce antireligious, anticlerical tradition of European democracy. Our institutions were developed in a spirit of respect for religious

values. Liberalism and Progress never meant in America
what they meant to Pius IX when he condemned them. In
all this the United States and the Church have been especially favored. What was impossible in nineteenth-century
Europe because of the antireligious bias of the age might
therefore be possible here.

There is another reason why the United States offers an
especially opportune climate for the working out of tensions
between the Catholic spirit and modern culture. The Church
itself is, in this country, vigorous and united. In Europe
during the nineteenth century whole classes were lost to
Catholicism and the fight today is to recover them. France,
and in some ways Italy, have become mission countries in
which the Church must fight a day-to-day struggle against
organized forces encroaching upon those rights she still
retains. Spain, still Catholic, is an island apart from the
modern world, a country divorced by force from the main
currents of the time, and thus has little to offer toward
the solution of the time's problems. In this country, however, the best in the modern liberal faith and the strongest
in the ancient religious faith find themselves together and
in this fact there is reason for hope.

But serious problems also exist and it seems foolish to
ignore them. In spite of — perhaps because of — its favorable situation, the Church in the United States is distinguishable by its conservatism in certain key areas of
politics and culture. The churches are full; the people are
faithful. Why, it seems, should we unsettle this happy state
of affairs by brooding on our imperfections? Why should
we risk dividing the unity of Catholic opinion in this country by a public display of differences within the Church?
Why indeed, except that complacency in the long run can
be deadly and the absence of self-criticism may place us in a
permanent state of arrested development.

In the meantime American culture grows increasingly secularized and Catholics do little or nothing to halt this because they are, on the whole, cut off from the major cultural developments of their times. It is easy to denounce modern culture for its subjectivism, its materialism, its relativism; it is easy to use the words "liberal" and "progressive" as epithets to hurl at our contemporaries. It is much more difficult, however, to distinguish what is valuable from what is perverse in modern culture, to take hold of it and turn it, wherever possible, from its suicidal ends toward ends compatible with man's nature and destiny. This demands a positive engagement rather then a negative withdrawal. The great challenge facing Catholics today is the challenge of maturity; of facing rather than evading the problems of their age; of saving rather than condemning the world. If this challenge is to be accepted we will have to face the broad questions of Catholic freedom, politics, and culture much more positively than we have in the past.

What is the legitimate area of freedom within the Church? Obviously, it does not extend to dogma, discipline, or the received traditions of Catholic teaching. It does not include what is commonly understood as the Magisterium of the Church. Pope Pius XII has warned against the dangers of "lay theology," that is, against a theology developed independently of the Church's tradition and authority. Whatever falls within the area of that authority, he reminds us, is not the laity's to tamper with.

But the Holy Father has warned not only against "lay theology." He has warned also against a too rigid, and hence unhealthy, unanimity of opinion among Catholics on matters which do not fall within the scope of the Church's teaching office and which, of their nature, admit and demand diversity of views even within the Church. It seems that most questions Catholics are practically concerned with in the United States today — questions of the attitude to be taken toward particular political and cultural issues of our time — are included within this area of freedom. And so it would seem that here a healthy pluralism of opinion should be encouraged within the Catholic community, as well as a mutual respect among Catholics who disagree.

But this situation does not always prevail and to the extent that it does not we have failed the Church by setting her up as that monolith which her enemies consider her to be. To make the Church appear partisan and parochial is to betray the Church's spirit, which is catholic. To fear that Catholic unity cannot admit open discussion and disagreement among Catholics in areas outside the Church's teaching authority is to sell short the vigor of the Church.

In reality, what scandalizes the world and causes fear of the Church is the sight, not of Catholics' disagreeing, but of Catholics in unanimous agreement on everything under the sun. And quite rightly, for such an image is a monstrosity; it should frighten Catholics too. We all know the ancient formula: in essentials unity; in doubtful matters liberty; in all things charity. We have tended, in the face of assault from a hostile world, to emphasize the first clause. Perhaps we should now begin to lay greater stress on the second and third.

Should a layman, for example, be burdened with the charge of "anticlericalism" if he takes public issue with a cleric in some question of temporal affairs, over some political or cultural problem, some legislation, politician, or play? It does not seem that he should, but he frequently is so burdened today if he exercises what at an earlier time in the Church, or in different countries today, would be considered his legitimate freedom of speech within the Church. Again, what causes real scandal in these matters, uniformity or diversity?

No Catholic can be anticlerical, obviously. But there is a sense in which every Catholic should be anti-"clerical." The distinction of the two is a constant necessity for the health of the Church. The one is life, the other death for the Church's welfare. To charge a fellow Catholic with anti-clericalism because of His disagreement with a nonessential position held by his fellow Catholics — whether in politics or in the arts — is in itself a perversion of clericalism properly understood; it is a manifestation of "clericalism" at its worst.

A first and necessary step toward a Catholicism more able to enter into and influence the age seems to be, therefore, the cultivation and encouragement within the Catholic community itself of a livelier pluralism, a more vigorous diversity, in all matters nonessential to the faith. And presiding over this freedom, tempering and directing it, there must be a spirit of charity, a reluctance to advance one's own position as *the* Catholic position at the expense of the orthodoxy of one's opponent.

This spirit is not something that can be accomplished by decree or easily defined. It is an attitude that must be built slowly along the way, and it is possible for a Catholic only if it is firmly based on dogma and kept open to the Church's teaching authority. But we must realize that in the Church on earth, as in the Church in heaven, there are many mansions, and that the freedom of the sons of God is something wider than those outside the Church can sometimes see or understand.

The temptation which betrays many Catholics into diminishing the area of freedom possible within the Church is the same one that leads them into an excessive rigidity in political and cultural affairs. It might be called the "principled" temptation, and it is based on an error we might characterize as the "essentialist" error.

We are proud of our richness of principle and quick to deplore a lack of principle in our opponents; we are quick to seize on essences — to get to "the nature of things" — and ever ready to denounce the superficiality of those whose view of reality stops at mere externals. But this attitude has its own pitfalls. We frequently tend to pronounce upon complex realities as if they were merely principles, merely essences stripped of their particular existences. It is thus easy, too easy, for us to categorize reality, to distinguish our "friends" from our "foes," at one quick glance, and to demand of others conformity to our own judgment if they are to pass as "right-thinking" citizens. This is the ancient folly of the *bien pensants*.

Jacques Maritain has written of "the terrible general tendency of the conservative world to link the defense of its material interests with the defense of religion." This tendency is surely the danger in a purely "principled" approach to the temporal order — whether in the area of politics or the arts. We establish something as being, in principle, friendly to religion and, without further ado, identify the cause of religion with the cause of this thing. Therefore, if a political party professes a "militant" anti-Communism it deserves our support; if a novel takes an optimistic view of all things Catholic it is good. And the reverse holds too. If a political party or a novel does not do these things we denounce them. In all this we are betrayed into slogans and into a distortion of reality itself which, being complex, demands a complex judgment.

The great betrayal is to identify the cause of the Church with what are essentially temporal causes, to bind the Church to contingent things, to multiply "Catholic" positions without necessity. And, in this country at least, such a multiplication comes more frequently from quarters which pride themselves on strict orthodoxy than from those Catholics loosely known as "liberal." We are thus frequently presented with a "Catholic" position on every particular problem that arises to vex us — on every politician, every novel, every play. The admission of Red China to the UN? No Catholic can consider its possibility. Faulkner's novels? We should ban them. The Hollywood Production Code? We must fight any effort to change it.

Doubtless, such rigidity is a caricature of the Catholic position. Unfortunately, this caricature is all that many non-Catholics see as they observe some of the more articulate manifestations of Catholicism in America today. This is the problem we must recognize and, to the extent that it exists, change if we are to contribute significantly, as Catholics, toward resolving the larger political and cultural problems of our milieu. We must work toward a Catholic climate that is more open to the problems of the world, and that approaches them in a spirit of humility rather than with an attitude of despair.

Too much of our thinking seems a hangover from the Church-State conflicts of the nineteenth century, a purely negative rejection of our age. Indeed, many of us seem determined to add to the Syllabus of Pius IX, to build up our own private appendix to that famous condemnation. It would be better to leave such tasks to the Holy See, which will warn us quickly enough when warnings are needed. In the meantime our work should be the more positive one of building whatever bridges are possible between the Church and the world. And this we can accomplish only through an expansion of freedom, charity, and tolerance for those both within and outside of the Church.

IF YOUR SON
SHOULD ASK...

BY HELEN CALDWELL RILEY

COMMUNITY asked me to write an article about being a Negro parent in the South, and I have been putting it off for two months because I can't think of the words that can describe what this means. I asked my husband Jesse to help me, and he gave me a few ideas.

What stumped us both was how to tell the truth and remain charitable at the same time. So here I go now, doubtlessly rushing in where angels fear to tread because I don't know how to walk softly as I ought.

My husband has the same problems doubled since fatherhood is so new to him (he is my son's stepfather) and we both are feeling our way prayerfully. We both know what we want for Butch and for all the children we may have.

First, we want him to love God, and out of this love, love the Church, her liturgy and sacraments, and love the multitudes who make up the members of the Mystical Body. We want him to have respect and reverence for the priests who administer these sacraments and for the sisters who teach him in school.

Next, we want him to love his country, to respect its laws and Constitution. We want him to be a credit to his community and to feel personal responsibility for the achievement of co-operative good within it. We want him to be humble without being fearful or subservient. And because we believe these things to be impossible otherwise, we want Butch to be a whole person — intelligent, obedient, courageous, and charitable.

I guess all parents want these things for their children plus the right and opportunity to form them in the framework of a good society. And every parent, I guess, finds in society problems which make these things difficult to accomplish.

But what other problems, if any, does the Negro parent in the South find? I think he finds a great many more, a multitude of things on every level which make it harder to raise his child.

Butch learns at school about the Mystical Body, and to call God his Father and all men his brothers. But outside the classroom he finds two churches — one for him, and one for his white brothers.

He may live very near the "white one" and very far from the "colored one." Although he is colored, he may sometimes go to the white one, but he does not "belong."

Again and again even in the friendliest white parish church (not to mention the more common indifferent or downright unfriendly white churches) things are done and said to remind him that he does not and cannot belong.

To be honest, this has been the exception in the case of our own son, but then we live near a white church which I know to be an exception. At this church very little is done or said, and then only inadvertently, to indicate we do not belong.

Even in the house of God, color determines whether or not one belongs. It is a terrible thing for a child not to belong.

Butch sees that only colored children go to his school. In the Catholic school he passes there are only white children. He plays in a park with colored children only, and rides in the section of the bus reserved for colored people. He knows that this is not his own choice nor ours, but the way things must be.

He sees that the finest movies, the biggest parks, the newest, most modern schools (at least until recently, when we see things changing here in this big city of Memphis but not in the country towns around us yet) all are for white only.

When he passes a work gang he sees a white man giving orders while Negroes do the manual work, the dirty, hard, thankless work. If he goes to town he sees that all the sales clerks, the office workers, the bus drivers have white faces.

No matter what we tell him, Butch can see for himself, and think for himself, and he wonders. We don't want him to feel inferior, but what does this combination of things beyond our control contribute if not a feeling and sense of inferiority?

"Why am I different? Why can't I do the things that other children do? Why must I always take the back seat on the bus? Or the last place in line while others who come later get served first?

"Why is a special place reserved for me alone? That Chinese boy, his father owns the grocery down the street, he goes to places I can't go to. Why, when he isn't white either?

"Some of the Spanish girls at the white school are darker than some of my classmates, but they are white and my classmates are colored. . . .

"Mother, what does 'colored' mean?"

In a child's way of expressing himself, I think, from what I have seen and what Butch has asked, that these are the things that run in his mind. I know these are things I wondered about as a child.

And what answer can I give? I don't want him to feel inferior, yet I don't want him to hate and resent people either. He is too young to understand abstractions and the complex philosophy which might charitably explain these things without justifying them.

Children are extremists, and see only blacks and whites, not the fine shadings of gray that adults learn to utilize.

For them things are good or bad, true or false, that is all. People are friends or foes. The friends are people who do nice things for me. The foes are people who hurt me.

We tell Butch that he is as good as anybody. That it is not the color of his skin that is important, but what he is inside.

When he then asks, "Then why do people make a difference?" we answer "Because they don't love God enough." But then he wants to know about the priests, why they don't tell people better, and he wants to know if they don't know either.

Perhaps it is only an evasion which can't last long, but I say, "It's because most of the people aren't Catholics and wouldn't believe the priest if he told them."

So far Butch accepts that. When he does not, by then perhaps I'll have a better answer for him.

In our own home we welcome both white and colored friends. He sees here an equality of friendship between the races which silently supports the things we have said to him.

We also visit the home of white friends occasionally, and the parents talk while the children play, all on a friendly, equal basis, just as if we were all white or all colored. We hope this will offset the harm of enforced segregation which he meets everywhere else and consequent feelings of inferiority.

In his presence we try to avoid uncharitable generalities about white people though every now and then, when something terrible happens between the races, we forget. Then we are ashamed.

But we know from this weakness in ourselves how easy it is to speak harshly of others because of color, and identify people as good or bad on that basis. We hope we can overcome this soon, for it is, I believe, a fault equally ugly whether in the Negro or in the white person.

We buy Butch books and tell him stories which show the Negro as an ordinary, or heroic, or good person, as well as books which tell of blond fairy princesses and fairies with skins like milk. We want him unconsciously to absorb a feeling of security and equality as naturally as other circumstances in his environment tend to make him absorb feelings of inferiority and insecurity.

As far as possible we try to discourage well-meaning relatives and friends who go to either of two extremes in talking to Butch or before him. One extreme would make him ashamed of his color and race, which he can't change. The other would make him hateful and resentful of all white people, waiting for a chance at revenge. Conversations like these present a problem, especially with older relatives, and I haven't figured out a real solution yet.

I've told the things we want and the things we believe, and it is for these things we work. As a Catholic parent I know that I must teach my child and be a good example to him as he grows up in an environment where there are unfriendly feelings between people of different races.

As a very young parent I don't claim to have a blueprint of the way this can or ought to be done. Rather I confess to a great ignorance and admit that in raising our child, we hope in darkness lightened only in faith. We hope in the ultimate providence of God which will result in good for those who trust Him and work as well as they know.

And all the time we pray. We pray that through it all we may yet love God and each other and other people and so become like Him.

POLITICS, CORRUPTION, AND YOU

BY MOST REV. JOHN KING MUSSIO

IT's A dirty business! How often have you heard this said of politics? The implication is that politics and rackets are synonymous. Out of this mismating is born the idea that the politician is a free-wheeling grafter who slaps backs, kisses babies, and squeezes the last dime out of the taxpayers' pockets. Wherever the political scene is marred by the big-time illegal operations of organized vice and controlled by bosses who are nothing but higher-bracketed thieves, you can be certain the responsible citizens have forgotten the meaning of their citizenship.

Sometimes the good people of the community are more concerned with their selfish little interests than they are with the essentials of good living. They are stirred from their lethargy only when higher taxes try to shrink their pocketbooks. Let them go undisturbed and they will not ruffle the water of community officialdom no matter how putrid it becomes. These good people do not hesitate to seek special privileges such as having a parking ticket torn up, traffic violations "fixed," certain ordinances twisted, at times, to fit their own convenience. They are really nothing more than little chiselers aping the grafters they tolerate in office. By feeding the selfishness of these good citizens in the hale and hearty manner of good comradeship, the gang in power tightens its stranglehold on community control.

When politics resembles a pork barrel and the politician a leech on the community's back, it is because the good people have been more concerned with their own selfish interests than with the essentials of good government. And this doesn't make them exactly the good people they think they are.

Apathy in a citizen toward his civic duties breeds corruption. A politician wants to be elected to office and he wants to stay in office. To do this he must place both his platform and his qualifications for office before the electorate. He needs money for his campaign. This he must either borrow or receive as a political contribution. If he is going to receive contributions, they should come from those who, as right-minded citizens, are interested in good government. If such citizens are unconcerned, the contributions come from the special interests — always with an angle. Provision should be made by the community for the proper presentation of issues and personalities before the electorate without the necessity of recourse to private backers.

What happens in many instances is that a candidate or the political party, in order to function as a party and to elect its slate of candidates, is sorely tempted to receive money from gamblers and other illegal racketeers. When such money is accepted, there is always the payoff — and it is the citizen who pays and pays and pays. Once these racketeers get control, the gates are thrown wide open to the camp followers of organized vice: prostitution, numbers, dope, unlicensed joints, and the shakedown technique masquerading under a thousand different extortionistic forms. Soon the office holders as well as the party chiefs find themselves caught in a vicelike grip. The racketeers have the "goods" on the boys and hold them in line by threat of exposure. The final picture is of a citizenry that shied away from paying higher taxes for better government finding itself now paying the tremendous cost of a breakdown in law enforcement. Vandalism, petty and grand larceny, extortion, gang wars and increased uncontrol of juveniles demand a tribute in money that is astronomical. This is just a dollar and cents appraisal of the situation. The moral implications are terrifying.

Perhaps the most terrifying aspect of this moral stagnation is the broken spirit of the community. People caught in the snare of corrupt government despair of better administration. They think themselves powerless to destroy the monster they nourished by their own apathy. Vice is looked upon as a necessary evil that one must learn to tolerate in community life. It isn't that these citizens do not want better government; they do not think they can have it. This is the disease of mind that invigorates civic corruption. As a result, men of quality, ability, and honor will not offer their services to the community. They fear the below-the-belt tactics of the machine. They know that neither their home, reputation, nor personal integrity will be spared an attack that knows no bars. Politics has become a dirty word and the politician an equally dirty person.

This is the attitude the racketeers want. Their best protection is in keeping "beaten" men in office, men they control through the force of fear and greed. They know that once a man of high principle has the backing of the electorate their own reign of graft and self-interest is over. And so they keep a blind electorate happy with little services that are paid for a thousand times by the very people who think they are getting something for nothing. It is time for us all to realize that it isn't politics that is corrupt nor the politician as such that is an enemy to public service. What is corrupt is the man who uses the office and the service for his own selfish ends and also the electorate that is not concerned with the ends of good government.

What do we mean by politics? Since it is concerned with

government, then it has to do with authority. If it has to
do with authority, then it has to do with God. For all
authority is from God. Politics has been defined as the
administration of public affairs in the interest of peace,
prosperity, and the safety of the State.

Even better than that, it has been called the special
application of the principles of morality and religion to
the service of the State. In this function, politics participates
in the great apostolate of Christ. For God's Word is order.
It must, then, permeate everything we think and plan and
do if we are to realize our final perfection. Since by nature
we are social beings, since we must live together, and work
together, and help one another in order to live normal,
full lives that lead to God, it naturally follows that this
social structure must be ordered and directed by the rules
which God has established for our salvation. Living without
good order is disastrous. Politics, by applying to the services
of the State those rules and regulations which God has laid
down for social living and administration, finds the purpose
of its existence and the dignity of its profession. Politics
brings the Word of Christ down into the warp and woof of
the fabric of government. It is that administration of government which results in man being directed rightly to
his ultimate perfection. If you are in the habit of counting
your blessings, count politics in.

The politician, then, is a dedicated man with a high
mission and a stewardship entrusted to him by God. He
confers a real boon upon his fellow men by a service that
is indispensable in our modern society. And, inasmuch as
politics carries out, in its sphere, the purposes of God in
regard to man, the politician is likewise, in an official way,
a servant of God. This is a dedication that puts the politician
in very high company.

It is imperative, then, that exemplary Catholic young

men of exceptional intellectual and spiritual qualities aspire to the work of the politician. Their training in Christian morality, in the Catholic philosophy of government equips them, in a very special manner, to fulfill the duties of political office. Service to people is fulfilled in a right sense only by those who have a deep sense of their responsibility to the common good. This demands very great qualities of spirit as well as a discipline of character which can result only from high moral principles derived from religion, pure and undefiled. When a capable, dedicated young man desirous of a political career declines to serve because of the battle ahead then he has already eliminated himself from the list of desirables. Fearlessness is a quality of moral integrity . . . they are inseparable in the true politician.

We have suffered enough from these Catholics in name who have exploited the field of political service for their own profit and advantage. It is time to show the real power of our faith for dedicated public service in the contributions of our young, intelligent, representative Catholic men to the cause of good government and conscientious service. Such men must not wait until the omens are propitious. Rather they must enter the lists and wrest the victory from men who are unworthy to carry its high responsibilities.

Corruption, with its system of bribery, vote fraud, propaganda of lies and tactic of division can be wiped out. But this will never come about by the "hands-off" policy of worthy men. The aspirant for political power must be motivated by the highest ideals of public service. He must want to serve God in this service to his fellow men. He must be convinced that there is no service except a good service — and by good I mean that which is based upon sound morality.

He must know that above fame and fortune in this world there is the approbation of a good conscience and the preservation of God's grace in the soul of man. He must interpret love of fellow men in terms of a service to that common good from which every man receives what is best for him. He must hate corruption because it is sin; he must want orderly and good government because this is virtuous and virtue is the badge of his service. Considering the tremendous sop to a man's greed, to his vanity and to his pride of life that corrupt politics offers to a community and to its public servants, it is quite evident that only a man who is bigger than his own ambitions and personal interests can fight and defeat entrenched selfishness in our civil government.

There is another side to this political picture. The voters have an obligation to vote into office right-intentioned, capable men, and more than that, to keep them in office as long as they fulfill conscientiously the duties of their office. In our American way of doing things, government is basically in the hands of the people. A community is nothing more than the reflection of its people. In fact, the community is its people. Corruption in community management reveals corruption somewhere in the thinking or in the attitude of that people toward their duty as citizens. It is thoroughly dispiriting to hear people deploring bad government, rotten politics, despoilers in office when they themselves neglect to vote. The vote of the citizen decides the kind of government he gets. Good men will give a good service to the community when we are ready to support good order even at the cost, when necessary, of our own private interests and personal projects. The real freedom of man to serve his God according to his conscience will be protected and served by government only when votes are cast from the sense of a religious as well as of a civic duty, in fact, they are truly one and the same obligation.

Every citizen has a duty to vote. This is a moral obligation, an obligation of legal justice. Young men coming of age are not to look upon the voting privilege as a sign of manhood but as the responsibility of manhood and the obligation of their citizenship. It is the greatness of our American way of life that the citizen and his vote are important to its very existence. Under our republican form of government, good order comes from the proper exercise of our duties as citizens. Our obligation to uphold good order is likewise the obligation we have to vote. We violate the common good when we neglect what is most important to its preservation. And by that violation we offend God Himself, the very source of order, the foundation of all right authority.

In the American concept of government, we, the people, are the government. We govern through the vote, through those chosen to wield the authority that molds our civic life as God would have it be. A man who does not vote renounces, in a vital way, the responsibility of his citizenship. By his failure to vote, this civic slacker opens the way for grave abuse in public service. This neglect to vote is a form of crime. For the failure to vote is in raw fact a vote cast for a rule by graft and greed.

But it is not enough just to vote. A citizen must vote intelligently. He must know the aim of good government; he must be convinced that it takes more than a good man to hold office but a good *capable* man. The citizen will vote for those dedicated to good government only when he himself is dedicated to good government and to its preservation. Any deliberate action through the vote which makes possible the rule of graft, favoritism, personal profit, trafficking in immoralities is a grave sin. A man who deliberately damns the good government of his community likewise damns his own soul. It is that simple and that serious.

A citizen must vote without rancor. He must in no way

penalize a candidate because of religion, race, or color. The candidate must have the capability of performing the duties of the office to which he aspires. His character must be such as will command respect and honor in the fulfillment of duty. His integrity of life must be without question. The voter must not be blinded by the "windbags" who promise everything for nothing. Nor must he seek revenge through the vote on someone who might have slighted him or, through line of duty, justly decided against him. It is that same common good which must be served both by voter and by official alike. Ofttimes the official who goes against our own selfish aims is complimenting us by living up to the high purposes for which we put him into office in the first place. Be fair.

Voting should not be subject to whims. To vote is a duty the citizen must himself perform with fidelity and great care. He must not be turned aside from this duty by bad weather, by worldly occupations such as a cake in the oven or fish in some pleasant stream asking to be hooked. Nor must he let laziness blind him to his obligation or the weak arguments of those who would keep him away from the polls slow his step. To sell his vote for a dollar is to bring Judas up-to-date. To say that "things can get along without my vote" is to express a thought which, if followed by others, could mean the complete breakdown in the American way of life. To complain that the time taken to vote means a loss of considerable business or time or energy is to lay the groundwork for a "going over" by "mugs" in high places who would leave you little in business or in money to boast about.

When we surrender our right to vote to apathy, to unconcern, anger, disappointment or to a spirit of petty retaliation, then we sin against our citizenship and against our fellow men. Tyranny in government is spawned by the neglect of those who hold legitimate power. In many American communities a real tyranny has been effected through a citizenry which failed to recognize that freedom lies only in the vigilance of the ballot box. Freedom and the vote walk hand in hand. Corruption is civic slavery sired by our neglect to vote.

What of the corrupt Catholic politician? In the true sense of the words, he is neither Catholic nor a politician. Speaking bluntly, he is a cheap crook who uses the faith as another gimmick to help him get into the lush field of easy pickings. If he had followed the moral injunction of his faith, he would never have been stained with the filth that makes him so obnoxious. If he understood the real mission of politics, he would be a servant of the people rather than a devourer of their substance. He is what he is precisely because he is not a real Catholic nor a true public servant. A good Catholic in office must, by the necessity of the Catholic principles he professes, be a real politician. And a dedicated politician must be a man of God. How otherwise could he fulfill the mission of politics which is the application of the principles of morality and religion to the government of the State?

Very often these pseudo-Catholic politicians are most charming in manner, benevolent in attitude and generous in giving — other people's money. Too often the eyes of the electorate are blinded by the little tricks of the dishonest political bosses such as giving baskets of food to the poor, jobs to the unemployed, picnics for kids, special favors to the important, free beer to the corner boys. If this be benevolence, then what do you call that whereby these same benefactors grow fat on the mismanagement and diversion of funds placed into their hands as a trust by the taxpayers?

Kickbacks, padded contracts, unauthorized fees, service

costs for the unserviced, diversion of repair funds, community service funds, recreation funds to private pockets are nothing but a robbing of the people in a manner that makes their own little handouts look like peanuts. For every picnic given for the kids, what about the recreational centers, the playgrounds, the slum elimination projects that don't exist and which would really constitute a year-round contribution to the best interests of youth! Where are these needed improvements? In the pockets of the "big shots" as so much cold cash.

Again, if these picnics for the kids be benevolence, then what of the gambling joints beckoning to the youngsters in the lure of pinball machines, punchboards, and numbers? What of the houses of prostitution flourishing to pander to young passion? What of the taverns and illegal joints that violate the law with impunity by selling liquor to minors? Benevolence! This is really the kind of a pat on the head that knocks a child's teeth out. As for the baskets of food for the poor, why are conditions such that the poor need handouts? Why not better employment opportunities, why not a community that is run so efficiently and fairly that industry would be attracted to settle there?

Recently in a survey made by the Upper Ohio Valley Development Council the industrialists themselves, when asked, stated that they did not want to move their industries into communities disordered by immoral conditions. No wonder the baskets of food and jobs for the unemployed have to be doled out to the needy. It is really a confession by those in power that they have failed in their responsibility. Remember, for every penny these political quacks hand out in the form of free drinks and favors for votes, they take it and much more out of the pockets of those who had their hands outstretched for a dole. As long as the mind of the electorate is closed to these stupid tricks perpetrated by political spongers on the civic life, so long will men suffer the effects of their stupidity.

Of course these Catholic politicians of ill repute justify their conduct on the theory that politics has its own rules. If those rules are immoral, against the law of God, then they can be justified only by the philosophy of hell. Politics cannot be divorced from God. There is no field in which man can defy God and morally get away with it. A crook is a crook no matter where he carries on his trade. And any Catholic who maintains otherwise, steals from the faith a name he has no right.

Then again, these so-called Catholic politicians appeal to a double standard of morality. They live what appears to be exemplary lives. They let everyone know that they are faithful husbands and good fathers. They contribute to the church and appear in the front pews in their Sunday best. But no matter how exemplary their conduct may be in private, if in public and official life they stoop to graft, trade in vice, defile the public trust by dishonest dealings, then they are immoral men no better than the panderer they allow to walk the streets unmolested or the cheap mug they commission to carry out their dirty work. The scandal they cause good people is enough to show how low they have fallen in character and deed. There is no double morality for politicians; there is none for anyone. Nor is schizophrenia an "out" for these civic plunderers. The only split in their personality is that by which they separate themselves from their God. And this makes them totally unfit for and dangerous to the political good of the community.

America's future lies in the quality of its citizenship. That quality must have spiritual value in which a people realize that nothing matters save the accomplishment of the will of God in their own lives. Freedom means the right to work out the Divine Will without interference. Freedom has no meaning outside of God. That is why, in our American conception of life, the idea of God and of freedom are inseparably linked. America guarantees us the liberty whereby we can walk in the ways of God. As long as we vote, so long do we, in the exercise of our citizenship, tell God that we love freedom and the America which breathes its life.

TO ALL ITS PEOPLE

BY MARTIN GLEASON

ONE hundred and sixty-five years ago the Bill
of Rights became part of the Constitution. So successful
has it been in protecting the majority of Americans from
unjust and repressive governmental action that this majority
has often forgotten that the Bill of Rights applies to *all*
Americans. If these rights are not the constitutional guarantee of all Americans, then which of us can claim them
as his very own? Today we are aware that many Americans
are being deprived, both individually and collectively, of
the liberty and opportunity that a free and bountiful
America should offer to all its people. The Negro is not
alone in our history in his struggle to secure those rights
which under law are his due. Others have fallen victim
to officially sanctioned bigotry and have sought constitutional relief in vain. One such group is the Americans of
Japanese ancestry. The rupture of the principle of equality
under law portrayed in their case is a short but tragic footnote to contemporary American history.

The treatment of persons of Japanese ancestry who reside
on the West Coast has for over fifty years been a matter of
particular concern for those interested in the vagaries of
that reality known as the American Way. Over the years
the Japanese Americans have been shamefully denied their
fair share of those intangibles known as Brotherhood, Fair
Play, and Americanism. Brought here to be exploited as

cheap labor, their thrift and industry made them in later years substantial middle class members of the coastal community. For this and a multitude of other reasons less logical but more vicious, they were resented.

In 1941 there were 112,985 persons of Japanese ancestry living in the four western states of Oregon, Washington, California, and Arizona. Of this number 41,089 were foreign born and aliens. Most of this group were alien not because of choice but because United States immigration laws forbade their naturalization. The remainder of the West Coast Japanese, numbering 71,896 were American born and therefore endowed with full and complete American citizenship. The great majority of these people were engaged in domestic service, farming, and small shopkeeping in their own communities. In the area of farming they achieved their greatest degree of economic success. Hired originally as "stoop labor," they had risen to a position where they had near control of the West Coast produce and fresh vegetable market.

The original Japanese settlers were regarded as a convenient scapegoat for unscrupulous politicians and irresponsible journalists. Anti-Japanese sentiment had become an integral part of the political and social fabric of the West Coast. Indeed, it has been said that this regional anti-Japanese policy has been powerful enough to set national policy, and on the international level, to determine the climate of relations between the governments of the United States and Japan. Considered in this context of hatred and bigotry, it is not surprising that the crisis precipitated by the disastrous attack on Pearl Harbor should bring about a new low in the treatment of Japanese-Americans.

On December 7, 1941, carrier-based planes of the Imperial Japanese Navy rained death and destruction on the United States Naval Station at Pearl Harbor in the Hawaiian Islands. The nation was justifiably shocked to learn that

3303 American lives had been lost and our Pacific Fleet nearly destroyed. Most Americans were frightened and confused by the suddenness with which their nation had been plunged into war. Surprisingly enough, most of the West Coast reacted calmly to the news. But the "professional" race baiters saw the attack as the opportunity they had been waiting for — an excuse to rid the West Coast of the Japanese. The racists set out to prove that citizen Hearst had been right all along about the "yellow peril." But not all West Coasters were ready to prejudge their Japanese neighbors on the question of loyalty. This was the time for responsible officials to inform the American people that, as far as was known, the great majority of Japanese Americans were loyal to the U. S. This reassurance was not forthcoming; instead all that was heard were the cries of the White Supremacy advocates.

True to form the traditional anti-Japanese groups closed ranks and began to shriek that the "enemy" was among them, conveniently forgetting the fact that two thirds of this "enemy" group were American citizens. Some of those who led the movement had economic interests in getting rid of such good competitors as the Japanese. Others mistakenly cast themselves as "superpatriots," proving that they had never learned the first principles of Americanism. Barroom commandos assembled to take up arms against their neighbors. Whatever the group — Growers Association, American Legion, West Coast Congressional Delegation, Dies Committee, Native Sons of the Golden West, or the Los Angeles Chamber of Commerce — it received ample space to voice its ravings in West Coast papers. But public opinion on the Coast was more fair-minded than the bigots had anticipated. It has been said that "It took a great deal of false publicity and over three months time to produce the public sentiment for evacuation."

On December 11, the West Coast was declared to be a Theater of War, and the Western Defense Command was established under Lt. Gen. John L. DeWitt. As soon as it became known that Gen. DeWitt was responsible for the defense of the area, the racists directed a clamor toward him which proved to be as effective as it was out of proportion to their number. The General was quite willing to accept the anti-Japanese advice that came in great quantities, once again affirming that "It is necessary for the triumph of evil only that good men do nothing."

The goal of the racists was to get the Japanese off the West Coast, whether it be accomplished by voluntary or forced evacuation. The charges and accusations which supposedly proved the need for removing the Japanese came from the above-mentioned groups, plus several *ad hoc* groups formed for the exclusive purpose of driving off the Japanese-Americans. These groups were adamant in their insistence on removal. The legal implications of removing from their homes 112,000 people, two thirds of them citizens, presented a difficulty. Obviously, some kind of case would have to be made for taking such an unprecedented step.

Charges were hurled about which had absolutely no basis in fact or even in sanely written fiction. The notorious Dies Committee handed out daily press releases concerning its "findings" on the question of Japanese-American loyalties. The House Select Committee on National Defense Migration under the chairmanship of the Hon. John M. Tolan was dispatched to the West Coast, where it conducted a series of hearings which became monopolized by the "professional" anti-Japanese groups. With the aid of the Hearst press and newspapers of like caliber, the Tolan Committee became the official sounding board for those favoring evacuation. The appeals presented before this committee ran the gamut from the crudely vicious, through the sophisticated arguments of the White Supremacy advocates, to the "humanitarian" appeals of those who wished to "protect" the Japanese. It was charged that the West Coast Japanese had no loyalty to the U. S. and would surely commit sabotage. It was said that they were a strange, inscrutable group who were not, and never could be, assimilated. It was pointed out that they were concentrated around "strategic areas" and that they would surely form a "fifth column" to aid an invading enemy; that even then they were injecting poison into the produce they grew for West Coast markets.

No doubt there were some among the West Coast Japanese who were loyal to Japan rather than to the United States. But even granting this, the charges made before the Tolan Committee were so ridiculous and unfounded that they were readily identifiable as the stock arguments the racists had been using, war or no war, for the past fifty years. It was to be hoped that such a hearing would also bring out at least some facts to cancel out frankly anti-Japanese testimony. The people of the West Coast had a right to know that by December 8, "all Japanese and other enemy aliens previously ticketed by the Federal Bureau of Investigation as potentially dangerous were in custody." During the hearings the charge was constantly made and allowed to stand that the Japanese would commit acts of sabotage "Just as they did on Hawaii on December 7." Yet it was officially known that not one act of sabotage had been committed on Hawaii on December 7. Supposedly responsible officials, such as the Attorney General of California, Earl Warren (now Chief Justice of the United States Supreme Court), testified that the Japanese minority was concentrated about strategic points; that they were the worst possible "fifth column" danger; that an "invisible deadline," when the Nisei fifth column would strike, was fast approaching. Mr. Warren, probably the most forceful and convincing advocate of mass evacuation, argued that the Japanese were inscrutable and that it had been his observation that it was "more than mere coincidence" that so many Japanese were concentrated about "vital installations." Needless to say, Mr. Warren should have known that one would have to live near a vital installation or any other community if one was to supply it daily with fresh vegetables. A statement from Washington at this time would have allayed fears and suspicions about the Japanese and negated the local racists' arguments. Yet, except for the Attorney General of the United States, Francis Biddle, no high government official challenged the racists' contention that all persons of Japanese descent were treacherous, sly, dangerous, and prepared to sell out the U. S. at the first opportunity.

Gen. DeWitt had ample time to exercise his military judgment on the subject of what should be done with a group of citizens and aliens who to him constituted a "large unassimilated tightly knit racial group, bound to the enemy by strong ties of race, culture, custom, and religion. . . ." On February 14, 1942, he forwarded to the Secretary of War his final recommendation which he titled *Evacuation of Japanese and Other Subversive Persons from the Pacific Coast.* In this report he asked that "by reason of military necessity" he be given permission to exclude from designated areas "*all* Japanese, all alien enemies, *and all other persons suspected for any reason* by the administering military authorities of being actual or potential saboteurs, espionage agents, or fifth columnists." On the basis of preconceived conclusions and unfounded allegations, the general asked for a grant of powers seldom given to the military except under martial law. It is not difficult for one to conclude to the need for such drastic measures if one grants the General's major premise that "The Japanese race is an enemy race. . . ." The general also reported to his superior this observation:

"The very fact that no sabotage has taken place to date is a disturbing and confirming indication that such action will be taken." This and other information like it was sufficient to convince Washington that the Japanese must be removed from the Coast. On February 19, 1942, President Roosevelt signed Executive Order No. 9066, having been advised by three of his legal aides that it was within his wartime power to do so. This order authorized the Secretary of War "and the Military Commanders whom he may from time to time designate . . . to prescribe military areas in such places and of such extent as he or the appropriate Military Commander may determine from which any or all persons may be excluded." Such an order was of obviously doubtful constitutionality and many legal authorities, including the U. S. Attorney General, advised against its issuance. In order to bolster the legality of the measure, the War Department succeeded in pushing through Congress a bill which provided federal criminal penalties for violating the exclusion orders. By these actions Gen. DeWitt was given what he interpreted to be the power to exclude, forcibly evacuate, and detain those whom he deemed dangerous. No doubt the racism exhibited by the General and his staff was unmistakable, but those who placed him in such a powerful position and those who accepted his recommendations as to an "enemy race" must share with him the responsibility for the action taken. According to Dorothy S. Thomas, the best authority on the subject, "the evacuation was a policy proposed by the Western Defense Command," as a matter of military necessity, "accepted by the War Department, and sanctioned by the President of the United States."

Once begun, the Army's policy of evacuating the Japanese was taken, in lieu of any other official explanation, as proof of their disloyalty. Thus voluntary evacuation was impossible because no community would accept the evacuees; what had

begun as "exclusion" became evacuation in earnest, and
what was proposed as temporary refuge became confinement
in centers designed to last for the duration of the war.
On a record which, according to one constitutional authority, "would not support a conviction for stealing a dog,"
112,000 persons, two thirds of them American citizens, were
torn from their roots in the community. They were exiled
without charge, hearing, or defense, and held for two and
one-half years in concentration camps. Living under guard
and behind barbed wire, they experienced "conditions in
major respects as degrading as those of a penitentiary."

Abruptly driven from their homes and businesses, the
Japanese sustained heavy property losses. "Faced with the
decision of storing or selling in a few days the accumulated
property of a lifetime, they often ended by giving away or
leaving behind what they could not take." According to
Bradford Smith, the Japanese, in addition to being misled
and defrauded, "suffered from a wave of vandalism unprecedented in any nation unencumbered by invasion or
famine and allegedly existing under a regime of law."
Congress in 1948 finally passed an Evacuation Claims Act
recognizing the monetary losses sustained by the Japanese-
Americans. We are told that the adjudication of evacuee
claims was quite slow and that many of the evacuees died
before receiving any compensation.

More important than the material losses sustained was
the damage done to the evacuees themselves. Forced to live
under almost primitive conditions, they endured straw mat-
tresses, whitewashed stalls, and desert sandstorms. In many
cases family relationships disintegrated; older people became
bitter and indolent, youngsters wild and unruly. There was
no place to call home, nowhere where one could find privacy
or solitude. One evacuee, Mine Okubo, relates: "The incomplete partitions in the stalls and barracks made a single

symphony of yours and your neighbor's loves, hates, and joys." With the summer's heat the stench of manure returned to the former race tracks, which were utilized as Assembly Centers while the more permanent inland desert camps were being built.

The agency established to care for the internees, the War Relocation Authority, was under continuous attack for "coddling" them. Irresponsible columnists on the West Coast fabricated stories about camp life designed to keep alive the fires of hatred. The newspapers made much of the fact that some 20,000 evacuees voiced a desire to be sent to Japan. Yet, considered in the light of the fact that 112,000 were deprived of whatever benefits this country has to offer, it is amazing that 92,000 of them chose to remain here. Here were Americans who in their own country were being treated, for all practical purposes, as prisoners of war! The WRA says that internees were given treatment which as far as possible was in accord with the Geneva Convention on Prisoners of War. But, lest we congratulate ourselves on being so humanitarian, we must note that this was done "only to avoid giving the Japanese Government any pretext for reprisal in the treatment of American citizens in the hands of the Japanese."

On December 17, 1944, the Western Defense Command revoked the West Coast general exclusion order for persons of Japanese ancestry which had been in effect since March, 1942. When it was learned that some of the evacuees planned on returning to their old homes, the forces of racism regrouped and demanded that the Japanese never be allowed to return. "Those who had benefited from the economic ruination of the Japanese were going to see to it that their victory was complete." Businessmen and truck farmers protested against the return of competition, and American Legion posts removed the names of Nisei soldiers from their honor rolls. The first to return generally received an unfriendly and sometimes a violent reception. Where it was violent, law enforcement officers closed their eyes and failed to act. When asked what he thought about allowing the victims of his earlier decision to return home, Gen. DeWitt characteristically replied: ". . . a Jap's a Jap. . . . It makes no difference whether he is an American citizen, he is still a Japanese."

Thus a dangerously un-American policy had been adopted by the Executive and Legislative branches of the government and carried out by the military. The 112,000 people who had suffered the awful injustices of this policy had a right to seek justice in the courts of the land. They were to seek this justice in vain.

The United States Supreme Court had, on three occasions, ample opportunity to pass upon the constitutionality of the Japanese-American episode. The occasions were three because the court apparently chose to follow a course of divide and conquer in considering the legality of: (1) the *curfew* imposed prior to evacuation on persons of Japanese descent; (2) the *evacuation* of these people from the West Coast; (3) their *detention* in WRA camps. Involved in any or all of these cases was the question of fundamental rights under the Constitution — of the meaning of Due Process of Law and of Equal Protection under the Law. None of the litigants questioned the fact that civil rights must yield to the demands of defense and the prosecution of war. But it is an established rule of American law that an individual or class is to be deprived of his or their rights only under certain circumstances and according to certain tests. According to Professor Jacobus tenBroek, who has made an extensive study of the issues involved, if an individual or group is to be deprived of equal protection under the law:

1. No discriminatory purpose can be involved.
2. The classification must be neither overinclusive nor underinclusive.
3. There must be an emergency justification for such action.
4. There must be an absence of any adequate alternatives.

Applying these standards to the evacuation, we need hardly point out the obvious discrimination and lack of objectivity on the part of those wishing to rid the West Coast of Japanese. Also to be noted is the fact that the classification of Japanese-Americans was overinclusive in that it deprived all of their rights because some were suspected to be disloyal; it was underinclusive in that it failed to recognize the fact that if persons of Japanese descent were dangerous, so were persons of Italian or German descent whose ancestral lands were also at war with the United States. There was no emergency justification for such action as proved by the fact that the evacuation was not begun until four months after Pearl Harbor and not completed until November, 1942. The FBI, Naval Intelligence, and special agents of the State and Justice Departments had all decided in advance that evacuation was unnecessary. There were quite adequate alternatives for evacuation as had been demonstrated by the British when they individually screened 74,000 enemy aliens for loyalty in a period of six months.

The crux of the government's argument for mass evacuation was the alleged fact of "military necessity." The government contended that Gen. DeWitt had made a reasonable and honest judgment in finding that conditions on the West Coast warranted the evacuation of all persons of Japanese ancestry. Government attorneys asked the Court to decide ". . . not whether it would have ordered evacuation, but whether the facts available were such that the

Commander could, in an honest and reasonable judgment, conclude that evacuation was a military necessity." These "facts available" were shown to be the very same "findings" and "beliefs" expressed before the Tolan Committee. Briefs filed for the Japanese-Americans pointed out that there were no facts to support the conclusion that there was a military necessity for the evacuation. Gen. DeWitt's motivation could only have been a sincere but misguided patriotism rooted in an ignorant racial prejudice.

In three historic decisions the Supreme Court of the United States chose to whitewash the Japanese-American episode and, in effect, to write racism into the Constitution. In the first of these cases, *Hirabayashi* v. *United States* (1943), the Court unanimously upheld the legality of the curfew imposed upon West Coast Japanese. In the second case, *Korematsu* v. *United States* (1944), the Court accepted the contention of the military that evacuation was a "military necessity" and a permissible exercise of military authority. In the third of these cases, *Ex parte Endo* (1944), the Court rendered a decision that no admittedly loyal evacuee could be compelled to remain in the relocation centers. This decision has been widely misinterpreted as a condemnation of the program by the Supreme Court. Here the Court merely ruled that provision three ("community acceptance") of the WRA's Leave Clearance Program could not be applied to persons whose loyalty was unquestioned. The paramount issue of the constitutionality of interning anyone, citizen or alien, on the mere suspicion of "disloyalty" was conveniently avoided. These three cases leave the constitutional issue involved in the evacuation exactly where it stood before the Court spoke. The decisions refused to examine the constitutionality of the program and did not touch what Justice Murphy referred to in a dissenting opinion as ". . . the unconstitutional resort to racism in the entire evacuation program." In refusing to invalidate the evacuation, the Court gave credence to the malicious doctrines on which it was based.

Thus the Supreme Court of the United States upheld a discriminatory curfew, evacuation and imprisonment carried out on racial and ancestral lines because it accepted the view that such a program was "reasonably related to the war effort." Such an opinion was based largely on the unquestioned acceptance of a "finding" by a man who thought the United States was at war with "an enemy race." In taking such a course of action, the Court "accepted and gave the prestige of its support to dangerous racial myths about a minority group. . . ." Out of what appeared to be undue respect and awe for the military in time of war, the Court declined to ascertain whether the military was motivated by a genuine military peril. On matters of grave importance it accepted the judgment of a professional soldier who spoke with the certitude of a chemist upon matters of a sociological nature. This soldier, the arm of government that he represented, and the policy it had adopted were given an extraconstitutional status in determining the fate of the Japanese-Americans. Professor tenBroek charges that the Court ". . . carried judicial self-restraint to the point of judicial abdication in sustaining a drastic act of the military without inquiring into the factual justification for such an act."

That the evacuation, the detention, and the hardship and humiliation that went with them were not condemned by the Supreme Court is indeed shocking. Even more shocking and more dangerous are the implications for all Americans of such a miscarriage of justice. The dangerous precedents established by the evacuation and the detention, and the menace they create, have been aptly summarized by constitutional authority Eugene V. Rostow:

1. Protective custody is a permitted form of imprisonment in the United States.
2. Political opinions may justify such imprisonment.
3. A racial or other group can be *presumed* to possess ideas requiring their imprisonment.
4. In time of war the military can decide what opinions require imprisonment and who holds them.
5. Decisions of the military can be carried out without regard to the safeguards of the Bill of Rights.

The evacuation policy and its justification by the Court is less important as an historical incident than as a legal precedent. Edward S. Corwin has stated that the decisions in the *Hirabayashi, Korematsu,* and *Endo* cases "expose the constitutional rights of the individual in time of emergency to dangers without precedent." The decisions constitute a radical departure from the American ideal of equal protection and nondiscriminatory treatment for all the people. Furthermore, they ignore those maxims of American legal and political practice which hold that guilt is individual; that an individual is innocent until his guilt is proved in a court of law where he is allowed to defend himself; and that the military is at all times subordinate to the civil authority. There is no question but that this was "an outstanding perversion of American legal practice." We can only hope that what was a perversion does not long stand as a precedent.

So it was that the United States, "a nation conceived in liberty, and dedicated to the proposition that all men are created equal," was found guilty of a striking loss of faith in itself. Our treatment of the Japanese-Americans shows such a glaring disparity between creed and practice that the word hypocrisy scarcely describes it. Speaking of racial discrimination in a nation which professes liberty and justice for all, Justice Murphy said: "It is unattractive in any setting but utterly revolting among a free people who have embraced the principles set forth in the Constitution of the United States."

The Japanese-Americans are not, and never have been, a problem. Racial prejudice in the American democracy has been, and continues to be, a serious problem. In a world engaged in a struggle for men's minds, we can little afford to practice discrimination while preaching equality. The new nations of the world are watching and listening to the United States; they will take sharp notice of hypocrisy if we as a nation practice it. The record of our treatment of Japanese-Americans is emblazoned forever in American Legion resolutions, Hearst headlines, Congressional Committee reports, and Supreme Court archives. It is written in the lives of 112,000 human beings. It can't be erased, but it can serve as a reminder of our own fallibility.

Against an atheistic materialistic system which considers men equal but equally worthless, we uphold the natural dignity and worth of each man as a creature of God. To judge a man according to any lesser criterion is to do him a grave injustice. Where laws permit such an injustice, they ought to be altered or abolished. Where, as in our country, laws prohibit that injustice, it is imperative that they be applied.

SOME THINGS ARE CAESAR'S

BY JOHN COGLEY

THE first Christians were a small, despised sect huddled together in a tiny corner of the globe. For them, I suppose, the problem of the Christian in the world was mostly a question of survival. The great pagan Empire had its own beliefs and values, its sources of power and influence tightly controlled, and for the Christians there were the catacombs, the inevitable feeling of being cut off from the society they lived in, the ever present possibility of being tossed to the lions, and only that hope which is sister to faith and charity. There may have been some who dreamed boldly of a day when millions of men and women would glory in the name Christian, but I suspect that, to most, except in rare moments of burning faith and high hope, the probability of whole societies calling themselves Christian seemed wholly remote.

Later there were the generations who lived out their days in something called Christendom, when the word really meant something. In medieval society being a Christian must have seemed as natural as being a man. It must have been hard for the medievals to imagine any kind of world other than the one they knew, where belief in God, in the Incarnation, in the Church and the sacraments came as easy as breath.

The Church hovered over their world like a mother. The

institutions of society were consciously shaped to conform to the Christian idea of man.

In the first days of the Church not all were willing to face persecution and death; many fell into apostasy. But in the Middle Ages it wasn't that the Church had so little influence but that she had so much. Survival was no longer a problem. It took more courage to deny Christ then than to confess Him. Not belief in Christianity but disbelief was the great crime. Christians were no longer tossed to the lions, but heretics might well fear the Hounds of the Lord who governed the Inquisition. It was a time of great saints but also of corrupt clergymen, pompous prelates, and the so-called "bad popes." It still took stamina to be a Christian even in that consciously Christian world, but the problems a man faced were not the same as those of the catacombs.

The Christendom we call medieval collapsed in time. It will never return. "You can't go home again," the novelist wrote. That is as true for mankind as for individual men. Too much has happened for any return to the medieval past. Not all that happened has been bad, by any means. The Holy Ghost did not cease to brood over the bent world; history has not moved without God for 400 years. There were numerous influences, changes for good and evil. Now the Christian in the West lives in a world that has gone through the great schisms, the Reformation, the rise of nationalism, rationalism, industrialism, popular democracy, Nazism, and Communism. In America today, he lives in a world not atheistic or irreligious but largely permeated with the spirit of secularism, even though churches dot the landscape and, statistically, religious life flourishes.

No one who reads this magazine regularly need be told what secularism is. It has often been defined, described, and detailed in these pages. It has long been a perennial

pulpit theme. A few years ago the assembled hierarchy of
the United States described it as more dangerous, because
more prevalent and subtle, than Communism. The word
occurs frequently in papal documents. The philosophy has
properly been called the father of Marxism.

Even with all this, the present article is another on the
general subject of secularism. The author makes no apologies,
since this time he wishes to say something *for* secularism,
or at least for something that might be called secularism
without torturing etymology if present usage didn't confine
the meaning of the term to a hateful exclusion of religion
and God from the practical concerns of man.

As a writer, in this magazine and elsewhere, and on the
lecture platform and in the classroom, I think I have done
as much as most laymen and journalists to make Catholics
aware of the dangers of secularism. I have not changed
my opinion that it is the predominant moral disease in
our world. But I do want to stand behind the idea that what
we now call secularism is a good idea gone wrong. The
time has come, it seems to me, to dissociate these efforts
from every tendency that would blur the distinction between the things of Caesar and those of God — to use an
honorable phrase — or destroy the autonomy of the secular
aspects of life, in the name of "fighting secularism."

Extremes beget extremes. As a reaction against the exaggeration of secularism, there is a temptation to fall into
another that has been called "integralism." *By "integralism"*
I mean the tendency to reject, or despise, secular values and
natural truths — especially those reached by scientific meth-
ods — because they are of "the world" and to replace them
with values from the supernatural order.

This is very abstract language, I know, and it is difficult
to frame my meaning without risking the danger of being
misunderstood. Concretely, what I have in mind can be

illustrated by examples of two extremes in several different fields.

Politics: The *secularist* finds no place for religious or moral concepts to come into play. If a thing works, regardless of its moral nature or its effect on religious life, it is desirable. Religion and politics, the secularist tells you, simply don't mix. The Church and all it stands for belong in the sacristy and should be confined there. For the secularist it is not a question of making a distinction between politics and religion so much as erecting a wall of separation. Adolf Hitler was such a secularist, almost the perfect example.

The *integralist,* on the other hand, tends to long for a "sacral" political society in which the state would again become an arm of the Church. He may not propose outright religious coercion but still gives vigorous approval to the idea of the state's backing up the Church with all the police power at its disposal. Let a "sacrilegious" movie or book appear, and the "integralist" immediately thinks of having the authorities close the doors of the theater or raid the library shelves. The problem of preserving Christian truth is more efficiently handled by policemen than by priests in a case like this, the *integralist* reasons. A certain "integrity" is achieved when the two work hand in hand for the greater good of society.

Literature: The *secularist* finds no tension between art and prudence worth bothering about. The artist should be a completely free agent untrammeled by moral considerations. He is free to write as he pleases whatever the effect on himself or his readers. Censorship of all kinds is a monstrosity.

The *integralist,* on the other hand, is concerned almost wholly with the moral effect of books. If the "message" which a novel, a play, or a poem conveys is good, he is likely to overlook or play down its artistic failings. He properly abhors the art-for-art's-sake theory, but endorses art-for-the-message's-sake. Literary standards are denigrated; cultural values, except those with an ecclesiastical or clearly religious inspiration, are despised. A pitiful bit of religious doggerel is regarded with more approval than an excellent poem on a secular subject.

The *integralist* anxiously awaits a "revival" of Catholic literature that would reach the heights in both matter and form and be both edifying and clearly conducive to the good life. But in the meantime, literary values as such have little or no claim on him, though he is rarely hesitant to set himself up as critic. He is ever ready, almost eager, to circumscribe the artist's choice of subject matter, excluding the scandalous, the disedifying and what he considers "dangerous." He puts far more stress on the author's role as moral teacher (which should at most be indirect) than as artist. The role of censor, which one might think would be among the least attractive and most hesitantly undertaken of clerical responsibilities, he assumes cheerfully — and with a suspicious zest.

In a classroom under the *integralist's* tutelage it is quite possible to get an "A" in "Modern Lit" without ever having read a line of such writers as James Joyce, William Faulkner, or Ernest Hemingway. It was not greatly surprising a few months ago when a Catholic publication vigorously denounced Faulkner under the mistaken impression that he was the author of *God's Little Acre* (actually written by Erskine Caldwell), though its staff was not a bit averse to editorializing on "integrating" modern literature. Literature in the hands of the *integralists* becomes primarily a "guide to Christian living" rather than a value in itself. For this reason such writers as Joyce Kilmer, Lucille Papin Borden, and Owen Francis Dudley may loom larger on the literary horizon and in the Catholic anthologies than, say, the three gentlemen mentioned above.

Science: The *secularist* thinks that science has not only the last word but the only word. The scientific method, to him, is the sole way to reach the truth. What cannot be submitted to the measure of the test tube has no logical claim on the belief of men. The truths reached by induction, by Revelation or tradition he finds almost meaningless. He may agree that they help some men lead richer lives, but their value is measured as a relative one, in the area of opinion, not as objective reality. The secularist — here his philosophy is called scientism — lives in a world which is just as big as a laboratory. He denies that anyone can see beyond the limits of the largest telescope.

The *integralist* often reacts to scientific bigotry by going to the opposite extreme. He consciously belittles the methods and aims of the scientist and makes serious attempts to "theologize" areas of endeavor which belong properly to science. He is, for instance, quick to pounce on the similarity between the psychiatrist and the confessor and often ends up confusing the two, turning the psychiatrist into a secularist substitute for the confessor, and the confessor into an ill-equipped psychiatrist for the believer. He is inclined to such radically "supernatural" programs as proposing the sacraments as sufficient therapeutic for psychic ills. Again, you may hear him talking wishfully of an ideal Catholic mental sanatarium where the first and immediate diagnosis would be diabolic possession and the chief remedy exorcism.

But every truth is God's truth. There is a very real sense in which the fact of subconscious motivation or the formula H_2SO_4, to cite two scientific examples, are profoundly religious truths. It is one thing to debunk the pretensions of certain scientists; it is another to debunk the truths they have discovered. It is one thing to reject the notion that all truths are reached by the scientific method; it is practically the same thing again to apply philosophical and theological methods and principles to problems clearly in the scientist's province. To do so in the name of "integrating" science is particularly mischievous. It does violence to both disciplines.

World Peace: The *secularist* rejects the use of supernatural means entirely. Peace, he believes, if it is to be achieved at all, is the result of diplomatic and political agreement. It is hardly necessary to belabor the secularists' dismissal of prayer.

The *integralist* seems to reject everything *but* prayer. Sin and sin alone, according to him, explains things; prayer and prayer alone will set everything right. The efforts of good men in the world's councils (men whose vocation is political) are ridiculed and derided. A supernatural formula is triumphantly offered and the futility of human effort stressed. Not only is the work of political leaders derided, it is even sabotaged — and in the name of prayer crusades! We know nothing of how much or little these men themselves pray, but it is not at all rare that their attempts to wrestle with concrete political problems, according to their proper competence, go unappreciated; they are even condemned out of hand as "irreligious" in some quarters because, so it is said, prayer is the only answer to world peace, while their efforts are prosaically political and diplomatic, hence "worldly."

The political responsibilities of the citizen in a democracy are played down, even ignored, with the result that the temporal, you might say "secular," wisdom and experience of the Church goes unapplied. An unreal dichotomy between prayer and political action is set up.

Now I don't think it's necessary to reaffirm the fact that prayer and penance are primary means. But they simply do not negate necessary diplomatic, political, and military efforts. St. Ignatius wrote: "Act as if everything depended on you; pray as if everything depended on God."

* * *

These are only random examples of a tendency to answer secularism with a kind of "integralism" which would cause almost as much mischief as it cured. What has been called *integralism* seems to be pervaded with a kind of exaggerated supernaturalism which belittles all but specifically religious values. Merely to limit the examples to the fields of action cited here, I think would destroy the hard-come-by autonomy of science and limit the artist to the role of preacher and teacher. In the long run, it would restore the dangerous concept of the state as the secular arm of the Church and reintroduce the hopeless hodgepodge of science and theology that confounded even such a great medieval thinker as St. Thomas Aquinas.

In the name of *integration* it pretends, or deludes itself into thinking, it enjoys a competence to which no man can lay claim — to give the supernatural significance of news happenings, for instance (who but God sees what that is?), to know the supernatural causes for specific political and historical events and the exact measurings of the divine economy, the heavenly ordered fate awaiting the world and the precise extent of diabolic influence on contemporary history.

This has been merely a surface treatment of the phenomenon. I know I have not dealt with it adequately. But I do know that it is draining off energy that might go into a genuine effort toward the victory over secularism. That is the saddest thing that can be said of it.

True integration must begin with the joyous recognition of all values, not only those specifically religious, and acceptance of their divine meaning. It must take for a starting

point the stupendous idea that God is the author of all
truth, no matter how it is reached, however secular its uses.
It must rigorously preserve the distinction between the
natural and supernatural orders while stressing their inter-
dependence and common source. It must beware of the scien-
tist-theologian as well as the theologian-scientist. Happily,
both these types are far less common than they used to be.
Now we must watch out for the *integralist* who is neither
scientist nor theologian.

It must do all in its power to keep Church and State
free from the mutual entanglements that history has shown
enslave the Church and rob the State of its specific autonomy.
Finally, it must be content to leave many things mysterious
and not pretend to know infallibly the mind of God. To
say this may, in a sense, be called "secularism" — as opposed
to such concepts as clericalism and "supernaturalism" — but
it is not the secularism that has been condemned. To exalt
true secular values and preserve the distinction between the
two worlds man lives in, without negating the temporal,
however inferior its claim to those of the spiritual, is not
to deny God's rights but to recognize the diversity of His
creation.

The true integralist must show a generation how to claim
for God whatever is good or true or beautiful in the world.
St. Paul wrote: "And now, brethren, all that rings true, all
that commands reverence, and all that makes for right; all
that is pure, all that is lovely, all that is gracious in the
telling; virtue and merit, wherever virtue and merit are
found — let this be the argument of your thoughts."

I doubt that such a movement will proceed by blueprints,
simply because there are none, nor can there be any. "Go
into the city," the Gospel says. Go into the city not to
conquer it, but to redeem it; rather, to bring it the good
news that it has been redeemed.

HOPE FOR TOMORROW

BY CHARLES LUCEY

A GOOD deal has been written recently about the low intellectual prestige of American Catholicism, and of the failure of American Catholic colleges and universities to produce leaders in thought, writing, and the arts generally such as have come up in England, France, and elsewhere. Learned men say so on the basis of much study and research. There seems scarcely a choice but to agree.

Yet, drawing solely on personal observation, without attempt to generalize from a narrow range or to suggest a different conclusion from the authorities, it seems to this reporter a little early to be impatient, or despairing, and that there is bright hope for tomorrow.

Comparison so often is made with the men English Catholicism has produced, especially among the converts. So often one looks for an Arnold Lunn or Ronald Knox or someone with the impact of a G. K. Chesterton or Hilaire Belloc.

Yet, the advance over here since the waves of immigration of the 1840's, 1850's, and 1860's and on into the early nineteenth century — the Irish, the Germans, Italians, and Poles around whom the Catholic Church in America was so largely built — has been tremendous.

Consider for a moment the Irish, who have had such vast influence on the American church. The bulk of the millions of young Irish men and women who came through the old Castle Garden and later Ellis Island immigration station, came with only the most meager education — often barely able to read or write.

For centuries an Ireland under foreign domination had been kept unlettered and ignorant. Trinity College in Dublin flowered as an Oxford or Cambridge for a non-Catholic elite which ruled Ireland from Dublin Castle. In the glens and mountains young Irishmen knew only the hedgerow school, conducted secretly and surreptitiously, at a time when young Englishmen carried their arts and letters to bright fruition at Baliol and the Magdalen. The Irish writers of stature who were produced, the Dean Swifts who saw the tragic injustice of what was happening in Ireland, came mostly out of a background of English culture.

The proposition is this: millions of Irishmen came here in the late nineteenth and early twentieth centuries able only to take the labor-class jobs. Ditchdigging was almost a synonym for Irishmen at one time. The sweat of men from Mayo and Clare and Kerry and Limerick drove the first railroad and telegraph lines across the country, dripped on the docks and on the hods of bricks hoisted aloft for the first skyscrapers. Young Irish women by the thousands became serving maids in Boston, New York, San Francisco because lack of education meant they were not equipped for anything else.

Some of the sons and daughters of these first-generation Irish in America attended elementary school as far as the eighth grade — roughly, eight more grades than their parents ever knew. Some of the sons and daughters of this second generation began to make high school, as did the children of first-generation Irish who came a few decades after the first wave of immigration. Economic barriers against them were not as formidable as in the mid-nineteenth century.

So the years pass and a third or fourth generation of young Americans of Irish extraction goes to university. Some be-

came teachers and lawyers and journalists and physicians —
often the first to know higher education in all the coursing
of their families down through generations and centuries.
Behind most of them, even today, there is not the economic
freedom which permits study for study's sake. Once they
are finished with undergraduate work, the first drive is to
make a living and rear a family and build a home.

There was another difference, of course. A tradition of
culture and learning, which drives thoughtful and original
men beyond accepted boundaries of knowledge for the sake
of knowledge itself, scarcely is to be developed overnight.
In England the history is one of centuries of devotion to
scholarship and learning. Measured against such a background results here may seem meager; but is this true
measured against the advance of a people who came to
these shores in their first generation with no more than
stout hearts and strong hands?

Anyone can think of Catholics who have gone out of the
universities here to medicine or law or teaching or business
and whose intellectual curiosity and growth stopped the
day they hung out their shingles.

But I personally can name bright, young sons and daughters of Catholic friends and acquaintances who are beginning to bring good minds to the arts and sciences as their
parents and grandparents before them never could have
brought.

None can say whether there is among them even one
who has the spark of intellectual greatness. But I know one
or two young scientists and engineers already with real accomplishments. I think I see a fine young writer coming up.
And I'd almost wager I've got my eye on a young man who
will be a senator some day.

The day is young yet, really.

5 POINT SOCIAL
PROGRAM

BY REYNOLD HILLENBRAND

IF SOMEONE were to ask you, "what is the most acute problem in the world," what would you answer? You might say: "the breakdown of the family"; you might say, "the breakdown of peace"; you might say, "the breakdown of racial justice and charity — the incredible treatment that our Negroes receive in this country." This last is a most acute problem for us in the United States, and yet I submit for your thinking that the most acute problem in the world (with one exception, the parochial problem) is the economic problem — the social problem construed in the most restricted sense of the economic problem.

Why has Communism grown in this country? Why has it attracted followers as it has? Why has it appealed to so many intellectuals who had nothing whatever to gain from it? Surely not because Communism denies God, although atheism has been one of its beliefs from the very beginning; not because Communism hates Christ as it does; not because it invokes violence and deception; not because it uses government autocratically, despotically. No, Communism has had its appeal for one reason: because it presents itself as a solution to the economic problem, the industrial problem, the problem of employer and worker; because it sets itself to right injustice in the field of labor. As Pius XI says there is something messianic about Communism. It is redemptive.

It proposes to redeem those who are economically distraught. This is the reason why it has grown.

It was born in the mind of a man over a hundred years ago, living in a garret in Brussels. It has grown until it has become a massive political and military power in the world, and enslaved much of the globe. It has grown to the point where we have to fight subversion among our fellow Americans. It has grown to the point where we all live under the shadow of nuclear extermination. And why has it grown to this point? (And this is what so many Catholics overlook.) It has grown to this point because it offers itself as the solution to the economic problem — of the world-wide economic problem. We are inclined to forget this fact, because we live in the richest country in the world at the time of its greatest prosperity.

The economic problem began a long time ago, almost at the same time as the American Revolution. It had a very simple beginning. A man who was seeking a method of spinning more threads of cotton invented a machine which could spin seven. He called that little machine after his wife, whose name happened to be Jenny — the spinning jenny. That was the source of much of the economic problem, because from that simple machine, machines multiplied. Later power was applied to machines — first steam power, then electrical power.

But at the outset, with the multiplication of machinery, the first traces of the disorders that are still with us began to manifest themselves. The machine created factories. It created the city, such as we know it now. It created an enormous increase in wealth from the sale of things which were manufactured. Right at the beginning, therefore, there was the problem of how that income was to be divided between the people who owned the machines and the people who worked on them. Right at the beginning we had the problem which the popes have pointed out: income was concentrated too narrowly in the hands of a few.

Also (and this is most important), at that time — roughly from 1776 to about 1815 — everything in the nature of a labor union in Europe was destroyed. The laws which protected them had been inspired by the Church. Those laws were abolished, and after the space of forty years not a single labor organization remained in Europe.

There appeared at the beginning, too, a new phenomenon — unemployment. The laborers were infuriated. They erroneously blamed the machine for their trouble, and they organized into bands to destroy machinery. And we have the horrendous spectacle, the ghastly sight of a dozen men being hanged on the gallows of the city of York because they had destroyed machines. Almost at the beginning, there were the outlines, the lineaments of the problem that we know today.

The Church came to grips with this problem through a great Pope — Leo XIII, who entitled his monumental document *Rerum Novarum,* i.e., "Of New Things." What were these "new things"? They were the industrial things, the new things that had come into the world with the industrial revolution. From the many things that Leo XIII wrote let me select just three points. His document is distinguished because it insists that there must be a conscience in economic life — that wherever human beings deal with situations there must be the play of conscience upon these situations. We, in the apostolate are very familiar with this idea, yet it sounded very strange when the Pope first wrote it. And it still strikes the ear as an alien thing even of a good many Catholics — that the same kind of sensitivity of conscience they have in matters of purity, for example, or of family relations, must also mark their relations in economic life.

The second point that Leo XIII made was that each human person has great dignity. This was, of course, the whole basis of the Church's solution to the economic problem.

The final thing is what he himself says is the worst element in the whole picture — and what he scores mercilessly — the destruction of the labor organizations. Years later Pius XI, in singling out three great achievements which the Church had accomplished in the economic field, chose from the long, long range of the Church's history these: the abolitions of slavery in the Empire, the building of an organized, democratic economic life in the Middle Ages, and the defense of labor unions by Leo XIII.

This great encyclical of Leo written in 1891 was mostly unheeded, although some conditions grew better. Then just as the world was spiraling to the lowest depth of the depression, in 1931, Pius XI wrote the greatest of all the documents dealing with the economic problem — his encyclical on "The Reconstruction of Economic Society."

In this encyclical Pius XI reviews the four economic systems which existed in the more recent centuries. The first was the great system which the Church inspired centuries ago, an organic, democratic economic life, which disappeared when the labor organizations were destroyed. The second, which succeeded it, was a system of unlimited free competition. The third system is the one we have now, the characteristic note of which is the concentration of income into a few hands. (The Pope did not except our own great industrial country) and the concentration of economic power into a few hands (which Pius XI says is even more ominous). The fourth system is the one that Pius XI outlined. It is still unachieved. It is the system of the future. It is the necessary object of all our efforts. It is an economic society that will be well organized and much more democratic than the one that we have today. It is the system of the "industry councils."

In the same encyclical Pius XI deals with the matter of free enterprise. He declares that while we have to have free competition, it cannot be the ruling principle of economic life, and where necessary must be curbed by government. How many Americans know that this is the teaching of the Church?

We have a great pope now, Pius XII, who has returned to this theme of economic reform. Frequently each year he talks to groups stressing how little has been done, how much needs to be done. In 1950 Pius XII said a very important thing: that the doctrine of the Church which is enshrined in an encyclical, whether it is on matters economic or any other matter, may not be challenged by a Catholic, even if he is a trained theologian. If you ever read an encyclical (and I hope that you do read the two great social encyclicals), you must bear in mind these wonderfully clarifying sentences of Pius XII. "Nor is it to be supposed that a position advanced in an encyclical does not . . . claim assent. In writing them, it is true, the Popes do not exercise their teaching authority to the full. But such statements come under the day-to-day teaching of the Church which is covered by the promise, 'he who listens to you listens to Me' . . . and when the Roman Pontiffs go out of their way to pronounce on some subject which has hitherto been controverted, it must be clear to everybody that in the mind and intention of the Pontiff concerned, this subject can no longer be regarded as a matter of free debate among the theologians." When we hear the pope, we hear Christ. We don't have two heads of the Church. We have only one head — Christ. And the pope forms one head with Christ — to articulate Christ.

What do the popes speaking with such compelling authority have to say about economic life? First of all they say the purpose of economic life is to supply enough for all the people in the world and (mind you this is important) for each person in the world. Pius XI was a genius, in the sense that he was a great teacher on economic life. He was the first in the history of economic thought who defined clearly and satisfyingly the words that we hear so often — "social justice." There used to be a lot of controversy as to what social justice was. Pius XI said that the keyword in social justice is the word "each." Economic life must not only provide for all humankind but for each person as well. It is not satisfied until each person receives what he should from the resources of this world. You see what an emphasis the Church puts upon the dignity of a person. Why that emphasis upon "each"? Because each person is so wonderful: a wonderful soul, the depths of which we are only beginning to see now, a wonderful human body. But more than that, each person is intended to share the very life of God — not only a creature, but a divinized creature: not only having his own nature of body and soul, but sharing the nature of God. The price of Christ's blood upon each one, and each one destined for the close unity of the Mystical Body in which Christ feeds them with His own flesh and gives them His own blood to drink. (Why in heaven's name aren't we more interested in feeding human bodies the world over, if Christ thinks so much of them as to feed them with His flesh and to give them His blood to drink? In the Mystical Body there is no distance that separates us from the other members, no matter how remote geographically we might be.)

There are five simple points from the encyclicals which are the basis of the Church's social doctrine.

The first is that the Church wants every person to be an owner — wants every person to own something, unless the person voluntarily renounces ownership for purposes of his

own soul or the kingdom of God. It is important to point
out that the Church defends ownership not only as we
ordinarily suppose against the encroachments of socialism
and communism, which oppose private ownership of the
means of production — the factories and the machinery.
Many people think this is why the Church is against socialism. She is against it for that reason, but that is not her
main reason. Her main reason is because she wants every
person to be an owner. She is thinking of all the people
and of each person, because ownership is that important. She
does not want a proletariat in the world. (And that's a good
Catholic word found in the encyclical.) A proletarian is
one who doesn't own anything, whether he is a share cropper
in our south, a rural worker who makes only a pittance, or
an underpaid servant in a home. People who earn a salary,
but because of their necessities are never able to lay anything aside, are proletarians. Such people would react with
horror if anyone suggested that they were among the pro-
letriat. Yet they are! A man should own, the Church says,
so that he will be safer and more secure against the vicissi-
tudes of life. And also because he should have a stake in
the world. Ownership makes for his full development, for
the development of his sense of responsibility. Ownership
helps to bring out the best in human nature. No one in
this world should be economically cut adrift, should be
economically without roots. Ownership, therefore, is one
of the great basic points in the social doctrine of the Church.

The second point is the matter of income, the matter of
wages, the matter of salary. The Church's teaching about
wages is that every man should earn enough so that his
wage will constitute a living wage, a family wage, and more
recently in the teaching of the Church, a wage sufficient
to permit him to lay something aside for the future. Pius
XI said this should be "an ample sufficiency" — not just a

sufficiency, but an ample sufficiency, enough to supply cultural advantages, recreational advantages, educational expenses, medical expenses. All these things must be included in our thinking about the matter.

If you will bear with just a few statistics: In 1952, 42 per cent of the families in this country who were wage earners earned less that $3,000 a year. The figure hasn't changed much since that time. That adds up to about $60 a week. You can make your own deductions about it. If we sometimes think the prosperous times that we have in this country make the social encyclicals less of a necessity here, we must remember that although it is true in a sense, there is, nonetheless, a driving necessity to increase the income of these families. In 1952 only 9 per cent of our people earned over $7,500. If you earn more than $7,500, a year, you know in which fortunate group of American citizens you are. You are surely not in the 42 per cent who are earning under $3,000 a year. We have a long way to go on this matter — even here in the richest country in the world at its most prosperous time.

In 1955 there were debates in Congress whether the federal minimum wage law should raise the minimum from 75 cents an hour either to 90 cents or to a dollar. What did that mean? It meant that the debate was whether a man would earn $36 a week or $40 a week. Surely neither of these fulfills the teaching of the Church about wages. And I should think that if a man was earning only $36 a week he could well use the additional $4. I hold it against President Eisenhower that before the vote was taken in Congress he said he thought 90 cents was sufficient.

And do you know how many violations of that law there were in one year recently, in 1953? Twenty-four thousand violations of the law in all its features. There would have been many more, if more spot checks of payrolls could

have been made by the Department of Labor. And this
doesn't include, of course, the thousands and thousands of
workers who aren't covered by that federal law, who need
the protection of some state law because their particular
business does not cross state lines. In Illinois, which is one
of the largest industrial states in the Union (Cook County
in which Chicago is, is the largest industrial county in the
country), we have a law on the books. Do you know what
the highest minimum wage guaranteed by that law is? The
highest minimum wage guarantee is 28 cents an hour to
laundry workers. So outmoded as to be fantastic. And we
have only six classifications of workers, including the spa-
ghetti manufacturers, who are covered by that law.

We have been citing statistics for the United States. When
you consider the rest of the world (and this is what we must
do) you find things frightening. I will cite you just one
instance — in the country of Haiti. I use this example because the enterprises down there are often American owned
and controlled. In Haiti, for the most part, the people
only work half a year, and when they do work their daily
wage is $1.25. That is for the semiskilled. For the unskilled
it is $1.06 a day — not $1.06 an hour but a day. When the
popes write about wages they are thinking about all these
people — these thousands of millions of people the world
over who are underpaid and underfed. The Church has
them in mind when she says that this world must provide
enough for each person to enable him to live in accordance
with his dignity as a human being, let alone as a being
graced with the life of God.

The next point about wages comes not from the pope,
but from our American bishops. They said that wages take
a priority over any claim to profit. That does not mean
that people who are working in a concern should not be
remunerated for the work they put in, but it does mean

that no one is to receive a dividend on his stock unless the workers have been adequately remunerated. Why should wages take priority over any claim to profit? Because wages are a basic human need. The workers are contributing not money to the enterprise but themselves, their labor to support the human lives depending on them. Business may not make a profit at the expense of human beings.

Pius XI, like Leo XIII, descends to details and takes up the case in which a business cannot pay wages that are adequate. What should be done in such a case? The pope says, first of all, let management and labor get together and see what they can do. And then in this worthy enterprise, he says, let them enlist the aid of government if they can secure it, to keep the business alive. But, he says, if ultimately the business cannot pay adequate wages, "then let counsel be taken whether this business should not be dissolved and other provisions be made for the workers." This conclusion is based again upon the unassailable moral premise that a marginal firm like that should not continue indefinitely because it cannot satisfy the first charge upon industry, which is the payment of adequate wages to its workers.

The third point in the papal teaching on the economic question is the matter of organization. The Church wants people to organize — employers into trade associations, employees into labor unions. Both are necessary. And both are indispensable for what the Church has in mind. Without labor organizations, workers are weak. With them they have some power — the power of negotiation, the power of striking if necessary. Leo XIII pointed out (and Pius XI praised him for it) that the right to organize is a natural right — something that people are born with, as natural as any other right which a person possesses. A man has a right to his life, a right to a wage, a right to vote in a democracy, the right to marry, a right to have children, a right to worship God. All these are natural rights, and among this group of sacred rights is the right to organize. This right to organize is, by the way, the same right which people use to form a government. Pius XI pointed out that when a government obstructs the right of workers to organize, it is contradicting the very principle on which it itself is founded, the right of free association.

This is the teaching of the Church, and yet it took us from 1776 to 1935 to enact the law which guaranteed to our American citizens the right to organize in labor unions. And it is ghastly to think that now when we are trying to oppose Communism on every front, not only at home but abroad as well, our Congress has enacted the Taft-Hartley law, a law which makes the vindication and implementation of that human right, so strongly defended by the Church, much more difficult. And what is even more astonishing (and these evil things stem from the Taft-Hartley law), we now have in 17 states "right-to-work laws." It is immensely consoling to reflect that when it comes down to a basic right of the working people we find the core of the Church rising to defend that right, as the bishops have in dioceses where these laws have been proposed. We have seen in our times an extraordinary exhibition in which men in New Orleans took advertising in a paper to contradict their bishop who spoke out against the "right-to-work" law. These men had not only no sense of the social doctrine but no sense of the Church. Why did the bishop speak? Not because he is a management-labor expert, but because there is a moral issue here. These laws are designed to make organizing difficult and to impede it and thereby keep wages low. And all the scholars who write on this subject — Monsignor Higgins, Father Toner, Father Cronin, Father Donnelly, Father Kelly — all have said these laws are wrong. The job of organizing is not even a fourth completed. Of the 65,000,000 people who are working in this country, only 15,000,000 are organized.

The fourth point — a more complex point — is the role of government in economic life. The principle is very simple. It was enunciated by Leo XIII, Pius XI, and Pius XII that the government should do the least possible in economic life. The popes have insisted, however, that the principle holds true only where there are no injustices, no inequities to remedy. If there are injustices and inequities, the government must take measures. The Church does not, therefore, envision a government which is overladen with economic responsibilities. (Why, for instance, do we have to have a law describing the amount of washing and toilet facilities in places of work. It degrades the majesty of the government to have to descend to such small details. And yet the government has to do it, because sometimes no one else will see to it.) Nor does the Church want too little government, a government which does not step in with the laws that ought to prevail. The government must have a special regard for the poor according to the papal teaching. The main thing, however, as Pius XI said, which the government has to do in this field, is to give help toward establishing the system which he proposes for our economic life. This leads to the fifth point.

What the Church proposes for lay people to do, is to take our economic life, which has been so rife with injustice and uncharitableness, and rebuild it. Nothing short of a rebuilding will do. A new structure must be formed. What does that mean? This is the reason why the Church is so intensely interested in organization. Suppose a worker had very good wages, much in excess even of what he needed. Suppose he had nothing to complain about; had a good contract, good grievance machinery, good fringe benefits. Some people would say that such a worker would not need a labor union. But this conclusion is wrong; he does need one. The chief reason for joining a labor union (or for an employer to join his trade association) is not to secure the things that we need. The chief reason is to reconstruct our economic life, to build a structure in which everybody will be playing his part in an organized way. Therefore, even if all the conditions were good, the paramount reason for joining a labor organization or a trade association would still prevail. This is the teaching of the Church.

Such a reconstructed economic society would be an organized economic society, and it would be a much more democratic organized economic society, one in which all feasible problems would be met at the lower levels. We do not know just how it will look, but in order that we might get at least a hazy idea of what such a society would be, let me illustrate. Take, for instance, the Ford Motor Company. In such a society, all the workers in the company would be organized, the management would be organized, and the two groups would deal with one another. It would require also that on an industry-wide level the management of the automobile corporations be organized and the workers, too, be organized, and that both groups would deal with one another about problems that affect the whole industry. Such organization is necessary because the problems of any industry are common problems and cannot all be solved at the lower level. Finally, it would mean that the nation itself would co-operate on an economic level: all the professions and industries and the rural group. This is necessary because our economy is one thing, completely interlaced and interdependent; the problems are mutual problems. This is the industry-council system which Pius XI had in mind.

Such an idea should not seem strange to us. Isn't it, rather more strange that while we could not tolerate a lack of structure in any other phase of life, we do not expect structure in economic life? In religious life Christ gave us the structure of the Mystical Body. In political life we have all kinds of structures: Congress, legislature, and city council; federal courts, state courts, and local courts; president, governor, and mayor. On the world scene we have the United Nations: the security council, the general assembly, and the commissions. But when someone proposes that we should have structure in economic life people find it incomprehensible. Pius XI, however, says that it is natural to economic life, quite as natural for people working in an area to set up the industry council system as for people living in a geographical area to set up a government.

The Church is committed to a monarchy in the religious sphere because Christ is King, the head of the Mystical Body. And with Christ the pope is our ruler. The Church deems political democracy the best government for people. But the Church also wants economic democracy, and toward this we must work. It will end class warfare, all this bitter contention that we know now. It will eliminate the government's doing more or less than it should. And it will result in an economic society, which, as Pius XI said, would resemble the Mystical Body — all members, organically united, doing their share for the common good.

The people in the lay apostolate are committed to a change of institutions. This means that men must help to bring Christ's redemptive influence to things as well as to people, to do what He did when He hung on the cross (and when He renews His sacrifice in the Mass) — to draw all of human relations, all human beings to Himself. This includes the economic order. It, too, must be renewed in Christ, and working for that renewal is one of the things to which the lay apostolate is dedicated.

But there must also be a change of people, and this means a change of ideas. The economic thinking which is at variance with the Church's doctrine is very, very deep-rooted and widespread, derived to a large degree from the newspapers which people read. Here, then is an opportunity to change people's ideas. But we cannot change ideas if we resist the necessary changes in our own thinking. And don't ever let the women in the lay apostolate say "well, this is mostly the concern of men." It may be mostly the concern of men, but it is still a very great concern of the women. Why? Twenty million women are working in this country; eleven million of these are married. Even in the case of women who are not working — their husbands are working, and they have a stake in what their husbands do and what their husbands think. But an even more important point is that the right social thinking of mothers be transmitted to their children. This is a great part of the solution. It is not my thought, it is the thought of sociologists. Who are the real builders of a culture? It is not the men who lead the enterprises; it is the women who rear the children. The economic problem is as important for the women, therefore, as it is for the men.

The job is an immense one, and we in the United States have to do more than any other nation on the face of the globe. We have the organizations to help Christ with that job — the organizations of the specialized lay apostolate.

CATHOLIC "SEPARATISM" AND ANTI-CATHOLIC TENSIONS

BY GORDON C. ZAHN

Most Americans are so accustomed to the presence in their country of a great variety of religious beliefs, all coexisting in an apparent harmony of tolerance and mutual respect, that any discussion of religious "tensions" or "conflicts" seems somehow lacking in good taste. In one respect, this state of mind is a distinct contribution to social peace and stability. Certainly, as a norm governing association between citizens of diverse faiths, it is far preferable to one which would erect inflexible religious barriers to social interaction or poison the social climate with mutually antagonistic suspicions.

Nevertheless, the appearance may offer more grounds for optimism than reality. Recent works, especially the excellent analyses developed by John Kane (*Catholic-Protestant Conflicts in America*, 1955) and Will Herberg (*Protestant-Catholic-Jew*, 1955) have made it quite clear that religious differences have significant social effects even in America. There are other evidences as well that these differences may also involve currents or animosity that run strong and deep beneath the seemingly placid surface. This is most easily seen, perhaps, in Christian-Jewish relationships; for the scandal of anti-Semitism is never entirely absent from the national scene.

Less obvious, but none the less real, is the fact that Catholic-Protestant relations may also carry undertones which represent a threat to the social unity so essential to the preservation of a democratic order.

From time to time, this hidden animosity finds its way out into the open, though usually in a somewhat guarded manner. The success of books "exposing" some facet of Catholicism or the "threat" Catholicism presents to "the American heritage"; the heat generated on political issues which even remotely involve Church-State relationships; the canons of political prudence which seek to match the religious persuasion of candidates for office with the religious composition of the electorate to which they must appeal — all these may be taken as indices of continuing religious tensions, a potential source of open and socially harmful conflict.

That these tensions can reach almost unbelievable excesses of intensity was borne out by the reading of approximately 4000 letters written to Paul Blanshard and the Beacon Press following publication of their phenomenal best seller, *American Freedom and Catholic Power* (1949). The overwhelming majority were written by individuals who revealed themselves as antagonistic to Catholicism and, therefore, most enthusiastic over Mr. Blanshard's efforts to unmask what one writer called the "Spiritual Cancerous and Diabolical Power" which "dominates the four corners of the world."

For the most part, these letters were written by extremely "tense" Protestants. Indeed, some contained inescapable internal evidence of unrestrained bigotry. Nevertheless, the letters do give some idea of the major areas of potential tension as well as occasional clues as to how these tensions could be produced, increased, or diminished by the behavior of American Catholics. Though we may assume with confidence that these extremes of opinion are not representative of the great bulk of American Protestantism, we should also realize that they may be reflective of more moderate opinions that *are* generally prevalent but which are carried, in these letters, to their ultimate extreme.

Many of the letters dealt with traumatic experiences suffered by their authors at the hands of Catholic parents, spouses, neighbors, or civic officials. Others voiced fears of political domination by Catholics and the religious persecution they felt would be a certain outcome of such domination. The Catholic hierarchy emerges rather consistently as "the villain of the piece," not only because of the supposed treachery of its operations but also by virtue of the absolute power it is believed to wield over a helpless laity. As one man had it:

> Here's the situation: you have a Catholic neighbor — he's a swell fellow — he'd never think of harming you or cheating you but if he is told to cut your throat, he's got to do it or they'll cut his. And what'll he do — it's too late for him to denounce — he will naturally defend himself. It's a sleepy Government that lets any organization get that dangerous.

Doctrinal and dogmatic differences are involved in some of the letters, but these are in the minority — except, of course, for the Church's claim to being "the one, true Church," which is challenged in many of the letters not otherwise concerned with specific religious teachings.

The importance of the evidence of extreme tensions presented by letters such as these should not be underestimated. Admittedly, some allowance must be made for delusional content, some of which approaches a neurotic or even psychotic quality in at least the more extreme cases. These opinions could be taken as gross exaggerations of more moderate fears, beliefs, and objections held by other Protestants who did not bother to write (but who did buy an astonishing total of Blanshard's books). It might be well, in that case, to use them as a frame of reference for evaluating Catholic behavior, so that we may be able to predict when and where and to what extent we approach these sore spots and risk activating these subsurface tensions in actual social situations.

To be sure, Catholic behavior is not alone responsible for the existence of anti-Catholic tensions. We have already mentioned the possibility that neurotic or psychotic influences make for hypersensitivity to the imagined Catholic "menace to our democracy and our Christian way of life." Indeed, one woman provided internal evidence of this possibility by relaying to Mr. Blanshard her psychiatrist's prophecies concerning the Church!

Other factors supporting these tensions lie in real social changes. Catholics in America *are* advancing, both in number and — even more significant in this context — in social and economic status. People, therefore, who are convinced that malicious designs emanate from Rome to be carried out by an all-powerful U. S. Catholic hierarchy need only to observe these changes to feel that the situation is getting more "desperate" by the hour. Still another factor to be taken into account is the traditional attachment to "liberalism" as the democratic ideal; the "medievalistic totalitarianism" of the Church almost automatically brings it under suspicion by those in whom this value is operative.

It is against this background that Catholic behavior is judged and often found wanting by these "tense" Protestants. Certain Catholics in their behavior may give substance to these fears and lend support to the distorted stereotype of Catholics and Catholicism upon which these fears rest. To this extent such Catholics may actually be endangering the well-being of the Church in America and impeding its efforts to win converts to the faith.

Catholic "pressure groups" may well succeed in banning an offensive movie or silencing an anti-Catholic speaker or removing a book from the shelves of the public library or even the local bookstores. But are such "victories" really worth winning if they are obtained at the price of confirming the belief of many observers that the Catholic Church in America is seeking to regiment tastes, block democratic processes, and establish thought control?

The minister-teacher who described the activity of Catholicism in the following manner would certainly be "confirmed" in his beliefs, extreme though they may sometimes be:

> Like a cancer its arms are stealthily, sometimes arrogantly, reaching into our Protestant homes, institutions and government to drag us all down to the level of primitive magic and ignorant, helpless subservience to a ruthlessly priestly system. . . . In a short time our Protestant voices will be throttled by Catholic-made laws ruthlessly enforced by Catholic officials.

True, we may make allowance for the fact that this is an unusually "tense" Protestant. But how many others will he be able to win to his point of view by pointing to the "confirmation" afforded him by the successful show of Catholic strength?

Pressure-group activity and similar manifestations of that type of Catholic "separatism" (or, as some refer to it, the Catholic "ghetto complex") presents a dual challenge to the Catholic aware of its inherent dangers. First, definite steps must be taken to counteract the baleful influences of such "separatism." Second, its adherents must be brought to a fuller understanding of the proper role of Catholicism in America, thereby preventing further manifestations of such separatist behavior by shutting off its source. Both objectives will take some doing. Both will involve serious risk of suffering personal unpleasantness, if only to the extent of

having one's "orthodoxy" or "sincerity" called in question.
For the separatist influences are not found only among
the "general run" of America's Catholic laity, but at times
may reach even higher. They are in evidence, if only by
implication, in some Catholic publications or in the official
statements issued by prominent Catholic organizations. In
addition, political figures can wax strong upon this separatism, and more than a few Catholic businessmen may be
only too ready to appeal to and exploit the advantageous
position they hold with respect to "the Catholic trade."

To say this, however, is to repeat what has been said
before. It leaves much of crucial importance unsaid. For
there is another kind of "Catholic separatism" to reflect on,
one that is not only permissible but could actually become
a matter of obligation. To state this another way: anti-
Catholic tensions will always be present as long as Catholics
live and behave as Catholics. Not only will they be present,
but it may very well be true that they *should be more in
evidence* from time to time, that a period of relative freedom from anti-Catholic tensions might be a period marked
by a dormant or ebbing Catholicism.

It has already been noted that the letters to Mr. Blanshard placed major stress on nondoctrinal and nondogmatic
objections and fears. Because of this, those doctrinal or
dogmatic matters which were mentioned take on added
significance. Exception, often strongly worded, was taken
to the claim to being "the one, true Church" of Christ, to
Catholic opposition to birth control and therapeutic abortion, to the marriage promises of the non-Catholic partner
in a mixed marriage, to the belief in papal infallibility, to
the veneration accorded to the saints and the Virgin Mother,
etc.

Another minister, for example, wrote: "As long as Rome
can flourish as a church and get away with the claim of

being the only true Church, she will have enormous power." This same claim was denounced by one writer as "a subversive and despicable doctrine" before he turned to an attack on the "naked barbarity" of the Catholic position on therapeutic abortion, which implies "equality of mother and fetus." (At that, he fell short of the opinion voiced by a lady minister who saw this position as merely an attempt "to add another member to their church roll.") The mixed-marriage problem is summarized by a man who complained:

> My own daughter, a Protestant, married a Catholic. Her freedom to be married in the Church of her choice and by her own minister was taken away from her. But what was far worse, she had to agree to leave her children (she now has three) be brought up in the Catholic faith, and I can see that is being done every time I visit in their home. I am very fond of her husband as a man. I concede to him the right to believe as he pleases. I would not fall out with my next-door neighbor if he kept venomous snakes, so long as he did not let them slip through the fence and come over on my side and endanger the lives of my family. That is how I feel about Roman Catholicism intruding upon the rights of others. Personally, I think their growing power is more of a menace than communism.

Other examples abound, but they would merely reinforce the point already made: even if Catholics abandoned all of their *unnecessarily* "separatist" attitudes and behavior patterns, sources of anti-Catholic tension would remain in the mere fact that they continued to adhere to beliefs and practices that *are* demanded by their faith. This is a fact which must be faced.

And these legitimate sources of tension will be exaggerated by the selective perception common to all forms of prejudice, so that "tense" Protestants will continue to misinterpret or distort Catholic behavior and intentions. A classic example may be taken from a brief article entitled "So This Is

Heresy," published in the July, 1949, issue of *World Outlook*. It opened with the statement: "No person can be
saved who is not in the Roman Catholic Church. Those
who teach otherwise are heretics." From there the article
went on to discuss the now celebrated action of Archbishop
Richard J. Cushing of Boston in regard to the ex-Jesuit
Leonard Feeney:

> The archbishop confirmed the action of Boston College in
> firing three teachers and unfrocked a Jesuit priest for teach-
> ing that there is salvation outside the Catholic Church. He
> also said that persons who frequented the center where the
> priest taught that heresy would forfeit the right to receive
> the sacraments of penance and Holy Eucharist.

This is an exact reversal of the facts, which were common
knowledge.

Only if Catholics were prepared to hide, compromise, or
abandon even the essential doctrinal core of Catholicism
would it be possible to eliminate anti-Catholic tensions altogether — and even in such case, some "tense" Protestants
would probably suspect a ruse. Obviously, such Catholic
behavior would be an utterly unacceptable "solution" to
the problem of religious tensions. The aim of Catholics
should be so to conduct themselves that any tensions which
do arise are clearly linked to real doctrinal distinctions or
can be traced in their entirety to misinterpretations and dis-
tortions on the part of those evidencing such tensions.

If this principle were followed, it might well be that new
tensions might emerge — indeed, *should* emerge. For Catholics would then be committed to new patterns of tension-
producing "separatism." The courageous and forthright statements and actions of Archbishop Joseph F. Rummel of
New Orleans in regard to racism have undoubtedly produced anti-Catholic tensions among racist Protestants
throughout the South. Such tensions will increase to the

extent that the Catholics of his archdiocese follow him. For a judgment has been passed on secular practices, a judgment clearly set in terms of Catholic moral principles. By the same token, the Catholic in the North who refuses to join in efforts to exclude Negroes from his neighborhood will be likely to stir up some anti-Catholic tension because of his adherence to the "separatist" behavior demanded by his moral code.

Catholic teaching on the morality of war, with its concern for the protection of noncombatants and innocent neutrals, might well require increased active opposition to a military establishment that becomes more and more dependent upon weapons that might not meet these requirements. One would certainly have hoped that the Pope's Christmas message of 1955, calling for steps to bring about the cessation of atomic-weapons tests, would be echoed by Catholic leaders and theologians in this country. Unfortunately, it seems that we can stir far more righteous indignation over attempts to exhibit a film depicting the life of Luther than we can over the application of the virtues of justice and charity to interracial or international relations.

To the degree that Catholics are prepared to follow the logical implications of their beliefs, they will be obliged to stand apart from accepted secular norms of behavior, to "separate" themselves from certain practices generally regarded as right, proper, or "normal."

We reach a point in this discussion, then, when we may conclude that, first, there are certain times when Catholics must be "separatist" in their behavior. This may involve adherence to the formal teachings of the Church or ways of acting derived from a prudent application of such teachings to the actual social order. Second, such "separatism" will most certainly stir anti-Catholic tensions in those non-Catholics who reject or do not understand these teachings and, consequently, oppose or misunderstand the derived behavior. Any attempt to reduce or eliminate these tensions by "watering down" Catholic teaching or modifying the derived behavior in such a way that prudence becomes a cover for expediency would be nothing less than a denial of the faith. The only way to avoid or mitigate the harmful effects of such tensions would be to state our case clearly and honestly, placing full reliance in the enlightened understanding of men of good will.

It is all the more important, then, that we take careful account of where we stand right now; and here the letters to Mr. Blanshard may give us some helpful hints. "Catholic separatism" of the wrong type, the type that measures its accomplishments in terms of pressure-group objectives and the number (rather than the character) of Catholics elected to public office, can only weaken our position if we want to challenge anti-Catholic tensions.

Our aim is the greater perfection of society through the perfection of its members. It is therefore essential that we bring the light of that objective to bear on the selection of our intermediate goals and the means by which they will be gained. Our non-Catholic friends may not always agree with what we try to do or the way we go about doing it, and their disagreement may give rise to a certain amount of anti-Catholic tension. This must not deter us from the goal; rather, we must take this for granted, as part of the price of being a Catholic. But there is no use in inflating that cost needlessly by initiating or supporting actions which serve to give substance to the totally irrational fears, suspicions, and resentments held by obviously bigoted or hopelessly deluded enemies of the Church.

THE MASS AND INTERNATIONAL ORDER

BY MOST REV. JOHN J. WRIGHT

AT FIRST statement our subject, "The Mass and International Order," may seem forced and factitious. Even to some Catholics, certainly to many of their neighbors, there is probably scant connection between what appears to be the almost casual devotion that is daily Mass and the titanic problem that is international order — or rather, disorder.

And yet the briefest reflection reveals the propriety and pertinence of our subject. One can certainly speak of "the Church and international order," for the Church is the soul of society; it holds together, more than could any purely natural bonds, those parts of the international community which are subject to its beneficent influence.

Now the Mass is the Church at prayer, the Church achieving that which she was instituted to do. The Church is never more surely and more perfectly herself than she is in the Mass. Wherefore, since we may speak of the Church and international order, we may equally speak of the Mass and international order, for it is in the Mass that the Church does supremely and sublimely that by which in other and lesser ways she reconciles men with one another and mankind with God, thus creating the spiritual climate in which alone an international order can have enduring growth.

So, too, we can assuredly speak of "Christ and interna-

tional order." Christians everywhere, whatever their understanding of Christ, are talking more and more of Christ as
the hope of the world. In their ecumenical gatherings non-
Catholic Christians have been debating whether Christ is
the hope of the world only in an eschatological sense or
whether He is also the source and center of a social gospel
by which He is the hope of the here and now and the here-
below.

Alas, sometimes one might fear that the Christ of the
social gospel has replaced among many Christians Christ the
Father of the world to come, so that men find it more easy
to speak of Christ and international order than to speak
of Christ and eternal life.

Catholics understand that Christ is the hope of our lives
both considered in their total and eternal sense and considered in their temporal and social aspects. They understand
that it is by the Gospel and the redemptive action of Christ,
by His very word and work, that individuals are saved for
eternity and that nations are pacified in time. Christ is at
once the Lord of time and of eternity; it is by Him that
we are both redeemed from sin and ransomed from its
social consequences. Reconciling each one of us with the
Father, He is our hope for the world to come; reconciling
us with one another, breaking down the walls of division
that were between us, He is the hope, by prerequisition,
so to say, of the international order of the world in which
we now live.

It is in the Mass that Christ is still at work among us in
His ministry of reconciliation and redemption. It is from
the Mass that His Gospel derives in each generation the
energies by which it renews the face of the earth.

Even were we to think of the Mass merely as a prayer
and without reference to its deeper theological realities,
its role in creating a spiritual atmosphere indispensable for

the right ordering of international society would still be incomparable. Pope Pius XI, preoccupied at all times with the achievement of a truly humane world order, frequently wrote of the manner in which prayer acts as a bond of the human community and as a counteractive to the forces which divide mankind.

Men who in every nation pray to the same God, he argued, will not fall victims to the cult of their own nation or allow the exclusive interests of their own race or tribe to separate them from the children of God wherever these may be. He spoke of prayer as the common language of the spiritual family which comprises all the children of God, a language which expresses a "common family feeling" and constitutes a bond transcending all regional or national divisions.

Prayer, indeed, is the bond of that even deeper human solidarity which rises above not merely regional and local but even temporal divisions: the communion of saints.

The social implications of this admirable doctrine of the mysterious but real solidarity which prevails among the sons of God, living and dead, have been frequently explored by the thoughtful. These have pointed out how, in the communion of saints, even the most cloistered contemplatives make their contribution to the social order through their prayers. Pope Pius XI reflected on how even the blessed dead, still at one with their fellow citizens here below in the communion of saints, continue even in heaven to influence by their suffrages the destinies of the nations to which they belonged (as in the case, he said, of St. Thomas More) and the humane common good of which they were the devout servants.

It is, then, chiefly through prayer that religion serves to create the spiritual solidarity which must be the prelude to any hoped-for orderly unity in international society.

Cardinal Suhard reminds us of the special excellence in this regard of the prayer life of Christians as contrasted with that of even the most refined pagans of old. He quotes from Fustel de Coulanges how, in the ancient city, worship was local and divisive. "Each city had its corps of priests independent of any foreign authority. There was no link between the priests of two cities . . . no exchange of teaching or rites. . . . Religion was quite localized and quite civic in the original sense, i.e., proper to each city."

What the pagan religion lacked, modern society has within its reach. Before Christ there was certainly an infinitely adorable God, but no infinite adorer. Now, on the other hand, thanks to the Incarnation, our Lord and Saviour Jesus Christ serves as the *universal man* who renders by His prayer all the honor God the Father should receive from creation and serves, in His capacity as the New Adam and the High Priest of the New Law, as the living link between all altars and all cities.

If this be true on every level of prayer, it is pre-eminently true of the prayer that is the Mass. Again the late Cardinal Archbishop of Paris may well be our guide in appreciating the pertinence of the Mass in our divided society and the manner in which the Mass, even as a prayer but most particularly as the renewal of Christ's universal sacrifice, serves as the bond of mankind.

The French Cardinal's analysis of the destiny of the Catholic intellectual in terms of the Mass is worth quoting entire.

> The Catholic intellectual of today has an exceptional mission. He must replace under God's dominion culture, cut off piece-meal for so many centuries from theology. The Catholic must reply with Christian realism to positivist theories seeking to possess the world without offering it to God, or to jansenist moral theories which condemn the temporal order

and humanism as sinful and are content at Mass to offer without possessing. The Catholic's motto will be to possess in order to offer, to conquer everything — matter, without which there would be no bread, no wine, no host; and spirit, intellect, the basis and instrument of faith and love — in order to return everything to God. The universe is like an unexplored continent, going to the first occupant. Christian thinkers will have to be able to get there first to plant the cross in every corner of it. The extension of the boundaries of the known world is an enlargement of the material of the offertory and so of the Redemption.

At the same time, while our modern task means primarily the "recapitulation" of a universe in childbirth, it has thereby no call to be exclusive. Human distress and defeat, sin and error, moral corruption and sickness, social oppression, political and international hatred cry out for deliverance, for purification, for consoling and healing. Flesh and blood humanity, full of its faults and sorrows, is what the offertory has to gather together, and what the Mass has to lead to the heart of God. Yet here, even more than a dedication to God of the known universe, there is needed a consecration and a redemption, involving something extra: offering is not enough, for a sacrifice is necessary. And for this it is not sufficient to be baptized; a priest is needed.

That priest is, of course, Christ. He, at once priest and victim, is present in the Mass as the New Adam speaking and acting for all the race and as the universal victim, uniquely adequate to atone for the sins of all mankind. Of each Mass, as of Calvary, the fruits are such that we may acclaim Christ, present at the one as at the other, in the words of the introit to the Mass of the Most Precious Blood: *"Redemisti nos, Domine, in sanguine tuo, ex omni tribu, et lingua, et populo, et natione: et fecisti nos Deo nostro regnum.* Thou hast redeemed us, O Lord, in Thy blood, out of every tribe and tongue and people and nation, and hast made us a kingdom for our God."

Who shall deny that the *regnum Dei,* the City of God

thus called together out of every tribe and tongue and nation, powerfully disposes the wills of men to the more universal loyalties which are needed to build a truly humane world-wide City of Man? Each of us who is privileged to stand at the altar as vicar for Christ in the exercise of His priesthood, makes his contribution, strictly spiritual and without partisanship of any kind, to the realization of a world order which, while it includes political aspects, is primarily moral and religious in its postulates. The meanest and the least of us who are priests take on something at least of the universality, dignity, and majesty of Christ for the hour that we stand at the altar for Mass.

Whatever his personal limitations or individual defects, then at least the priest speaks to God for all mankind as does Christ. What he does "for our salvation and that of the whole world," to quote the Canon of the Mass, he does as the ambassador of all humanity, the agent of the new Adam. Again Cardinal Suhard gives modern expression to the ancient truth concerning the universal and unifying role of the priest at the altar when he writes:

> He re-unites (human society) completely and offers it with the Host in his outstretched hands in tne name of the Church, to the Father, by the Son, and in the Holy Spirit; the priest is in the world, but also the whole world is in the priest. It is he who lifts it up to God. He introduces and accredits it to Him, not through his own power or by delegation from the people, but by the enabling power of Christ, the unique mediator, with whom he is identified more truly at the altar than anywhere else.

A function, so sublime, so universal, necessarily transcends considerations of social class, national background, racial origin or political preference in the priest who stands at the altar. All this is what Gertrud von Le Fort meant when she wrote: "The priest at the altar has no face. . . ." He has no color, no comeliness, no purely personal qualities good or bad. He has no virtues nor vices, nothing individual which commends or discredits him. He takes on all his priestly significance from Christ, the Son of Man, the Universal Redeemer, the sole Priest of the New Law.

Everything about him emphasizes how impersonal is the priest's individual part and how universal is his sacerdotal function. He wears liturgical vestments which disassociate him — or should! — from the fads and the modes of his place and period. He speaks a liturgical language — like that which, please God, will continue to be the universal language of a civilization still *Latin* in its healthiest roots — and he conforms, or should, by rubric and rite to liturgical requirements which again emphasize the universality of his function and the relative insignificance of himself and of his personal impulses and preferences.

Thus in the liturgy the Church contributes uniquely and mightily to the organic vitality of a truly humane world organization. This was the theme of our present Holy Father in his broadcast to the recent international eucharistic congress in Brazil. The Holy Father was quick to point out the social implications of the spiritual dogmas he enunciated. He spoke of the unitive power and function of the Eucharist. He said:

> The earth is but a speck in the immensity of the universe! However, the eucharistic Sacrifice transforms it into an immense thurible that moves through space and exhales spirals of infinite glory to the Creator. . . . This mystery of unity, by incorporating and almost identifying the faithful with Christ, tends to unite them into one single family and one sole body in which beats one heart alone, one soul alone, and in which each member is as zealous of the well-being of others as of his own and even more so. . . . Thus (the Redeemer and King) will establish in each His kingdom of peace and love, of justice and sanctity, according to the divine promises, and

even in that which is temporal there shall be a kingdom of
order and progress, one of tranquility, harmony, and of true
prosperity.

It is well to underscore the phrase "even in that which
is temporal." For here is the assertion by the Holy Father of
that optimism concerning the power of grace to transform
even the secular order which is so often absent from the
thinking of the "angelists," those of the faithful who too
patly isolate the supernatural, the Gospel, and the action of
the Church from the everyday concerns of the temporal
and political order. Here the Holy Father provides the
ground for our discussing the relationship of the Mass to
international order.

In his message to the eucharistic congress in Brazil the
Holy Father spoke in a tradition already eloquently de-
veloped by his predecessors Pope Benedict XV and Pope
Pius XI.

The Christian reconciliation of nations is achieved more
securely by international eucharistic congresses than by any
other spiritual means, Pope Benedict XV wrote, since thus
the members of the several nations are brought together in
common worship of the Way, the Truth, and the Life for
societies as well as for individuals. Pope Pius XI frequently
spoke of the social rule of the Eucharist as the most dynamic
and effective of the forces by which the Church makes her
contribution to international order among the divided
nations.

No living voice speaking on the lofty levels of international leadership has more consistently argued for the need
of an organized international community than has that of
the reigning Holy Father. Compared with his clear and
unqualified assertions of the necessity and nature of a world
society, the declarations of even those political chieftains
with reputations for clarity and outspokenness have been

hedging and cautious indeed whenever there has been question of the extension of Federalism, frank limitations on national sovereignty, disarmament or any other points which arouse controversy but which must be faced before a decent human community can be brought together out of the divided and antagonistic nations.

The Holy Father has sometimes clearly offended the ultranationalistic and isolationist spirit of many of his own people, not only in this country, but wherever else the sensitive spirit of undisciplined nationalism dies hard. He is confident, no doubt, that in the final issue all superficial commitments of a narrowly partisan and purely political character will yield to the higher and more universal loyalties of those in every land who share the solidarity of one Lord, one faith, and one baptism; who are made one Body because nourished by one Bread; and who, at their several altars, are quickened and united by the life-giving energies of one sacrifice, the holy sacrifice of the Mass.

Chateaubriand recognized how the Eucharist announces the reunion of mankind into one great family, inculcating the cessation of enmities and the commencement of a new law which makes no distinction between Jew and Gentile, but invites all the children of Adam to sit down at the same table. Catholics of our day who are genuine in their desire to follow the dogmatic and moral instructions of the Holy See will meditate at one and the same time on what are two sides of the same problem: the pronouncements of the Holy See concerning the special responsibility of Catholics toward the achievement of an international community and its pronouncements concerning the place of the Mass in the lives of individuals and nations.

The Holy Father has said that there is no other group of human beings so favorably predisposed, in breadth and in depth, for international understanding as Catholics should be. He has said that they, above all, must realize that they are called upon to overcome every vestige of nationalistic narrowness and to seek a genuine fraternal encounter of people with people. He has reminded them that Christian peoples must be conscious of the brotherly ties that bind them to each other and that they must not await the threshold of death and the dawn of eternity before realizing the practical corollaries of their spiritual fraternity.

The kingdom of God comes to its perfection in the world to come, but it has already begun on this earth in the Holy Catholic Church, which, though it is spiritual and divine, has many and important effects on human social order and on the peaceful unity of the political order. Dante understood this in terms of his day; Catholic citizens of the age of democracy must understand it in terms of their modern world.

Accordingly, whatever occasional Catholic Christians may say from campaign platforms in political tussles or from editorial chairs when partisanship may dominate their thinking, at least at Mass the will of Christ to restore the unity that was in the beginning should stir nostalgic desires in their own narrow hearts for that same unity.

Whether it be at the offertory where the solidarity of the Church is so explicitly proclaimed; or at the *Nobis quoque peccatoribus* where our solidarity in the need for redemption is humbly acknowledged; or at the *Agnus Dei* where our prayers for peace, shorn of all individuality, are made collective in the true spirit of the liturgy — everything about the Mass recalls the unity that was in the beginning and that must be in the end. Whether the liturgy be offered in the solemnity of the papal Mass where the unity in fact of the Church and in intent of the race is almost photographically evident, or whether it be offered in the hidden Mass of a Father Henri Perrin in his concentration camp, where the unity of the race was flatly contradicted and even that of the Church was sadly obscured, the fact remains the same. Fr. Perrin expresses it unforgettably:

> I offered to our Father from the bottom of my heart all the suffering of the prison, and the gloom of all the poor wretches sleeping under its roof; I offered it through Christ, for the forgiveness of all the omissions and sins of men, for the salvation of the world. . . . I was alone in this "communion," but through the body of Christ I was in communion with the whole Church and with all my brethren in this room, in this prison, in all our growing Christian communities. . . .

See, then, how the Mass must never be a priest's mere private devotion or something which the faithful attend once a week so as to remain in the good books of the parish priest. See how it is not so much a prayer as it is a principle of divine action, a force in the shaping of life, individual and collective; an instrument, the greatest, for the achievement of what Christ came on earth to do. See how superficial are questions like, "Should I use a missal or say my beads?" And how the basic question is "How far does my Mass make me one with Jesus Christ, and through Him with all mankind and with God?" For He, the priest and victim of our Mass, is the Son of Man, not of any one nation alone; the hero of all our race, not of any people alone; the King of kings here below and the Prince of Peace; the Father of the world to come; He is our Redeemer for eternity; our teacher, and our hope in attaining personal peace as well as the international order for which the clear of head and clean of heart so ardently pray.

THOUGH THE HEAVENS FALL

BY THOMAS E. MURRAY

WHEN the first man fell from grace because of an act of prideful disobedience, his whole relationship with nature changed. The garden of Eden, wherein all things had been instantly subservient to man's purposes, became a wilderness. Dark, untamed forces resisted the will of man and even threatened his very life. Over the millennia the gradual development of human arts and sciences has restored to man some small part of his original dominance over his earthly environment.

Then, on what seems yesterday, a gigantic stride was made. Man stumbled upon atomic energy. This scientific discovery has resulted in the greatest alteration in man's relations with nature since the spiritual upheaval of the garden of Eden. This is sober fact. Man now has at his disposal what someone has dramatically, though perhaps presumptuously, called "Nature's last secret." Possessed of this secret, man has succeeded in making weapons of mass destruction powerful enough to reverse history and to reduce the world to the primitive conditions of the time of Cain and Abel.

Our hope at the moment is that human reason will find some way of securing mankind against the abuse of this new destructive power. The devising of effective methods of international control is a primary task for statesmen and scientists. But I wish to emphasize today the fact that statesmen and scientists cannot and will not succeed in their task unless the peoples of the world themselves come to realize that a fundamental change has occurred in man's relations to nature. This fact has placed before mankind a unique challenge. The challenge demands an immense response — a tremendous collective effort — a marshaling of all man's spiritual and moral and even physical energies. This response and this effort will not be forthcoming unless you and I and millions like us in all the nations of the world come to understand the crucial nature and the dizzying magnitude of the challenge.

Nowhere in the world today do I see sufficient evidence of this necessary understanding. Nowhere do I see the beginnings of an adequate response to the challenge. Tradition and habit and inertia combine to make our international thinking much less bold than the nearness and the size of the new threat that looms over us. A gigantic race for armaments, unprecedented in history, is going on. It will not do to think of it in the old-fashioned framework of a threat of war. It would be a mistake to think that it may possibly be solved by conventional diplomatic negotiations. Rather, we have to force our imaginations to face our situation after the fashion of men who face a great catastrophe of nature.

If this world were threatened with an invasion of beings from another planet, we would have little trouble in agreeing even with the Soviets on a plan for joint defense. If a universal plague swept down upon the earth, the differences between capitalist and communist would not stand in the way of a pooling of information and a union of effort to stave off the menace. Why then are the prospects so dim for finding some measure of common ground with the Kremlin? The matter at hand is hardly less urgent. Rational means

must be found to avert the danger of universal destruction
by the fire — the blast — the radiation and atmospheric con-
tamination — all resulting from nuclear explosions. Natural
catastrophes — earthquakes, floods, plagues — cannot be prevented by human industry. But man should be able to
prevent catastrophes of which he alone is the cause. If men
throughout the world today are not setting their brains and
hands more strongly to the work of preventing the human
catastrophe of atomic war, the reason is a simple one: men
do not yet understand or appreciate their own danger.

This common appreciation of a common danger is the
necessary condition of any fruitful negotiations between the
Western world and the U.S.S.R. Behind the chronic intran-
sigeance there has recently been some slight suggestion that
the Soviet mind is at last beginning to catch the glimpse
of the common peril that lurks in man's possession of the
ultimate weapons of universal destruction. In our own country, in consequence of the unscheduled and unexpected publicity given to the hydrogen bomb tests, more and more
men are realizing that every possible effort must be employed with all possible vigor to avert the coming of an
all-out atomic war. Perhaps the time is at hand when the
thought of total destruction should make men see national
sovereignty in a new light. It should induce them to consent
to those limitations of this treasured right which are essential
for effective international control of atomic weapons. For
years America has shown its willingness in this respect. The
world again looks to the Soviet Union. Will its response
to the hydrogen threat be as negative, as disappointing, as
alarming, as was its earlier response to the A-bomb threat?
I think not. I pray not.

We look therefore to the Kremlin. But we Americans must
also examine ourselves — examine our own state of mind.
Suppose the Kremlin does conclude that it is to its own

interest to recede somewhat from its past obduracy; would our problem be therefore ended? By no means. There would still remain the problem of educating our own people to the mentality, to the attitudes, to the habits of thought required in this atomic age. In our efforts toward peace, we are still thinking in terms of power, in terms of our assumed superiority of force. At best we are thinking in terms of "collective security," which is at bottom a power concept. We shall undoubtedly have to go on thinking in these realistic terms for some time. God knows how long. Nonetheless, we must begin to think in terms of a higher realism — the realism of reason — the realism of law — international law, stated in agreements on the control and use of atomic power.

These agreements must have their safeguard and sanction in force, for every law must have behind it a power which will insure its enforcement. But we cannot go on indefinitely putting our highest trust in power or in a sheer balance of power. Our highest national responsibility is somehow to bring the new and awesome power we now possess under the reign of law. In order that this responsibility may be fulfilled, there is need of a long process of education — education of statesmen and scientists indeed, but also the education of the people, the training of the public mind.

The first necessary step in this process of education — a step that has not yet been taken firmly enough — must be to impress upon the public mind the immediacy and the proportions of the threat that exist today and that will increase as each day passes. I am not speaking of a course of propaganda that will scare the public out of its wits. I put little trust in sheer fright; I put no trust at all in men who are out of their wits. I am speaking of understanding the thing that confronts us. I am proposing that we gather up all our wits. I am proposing that we bring the collective power of human reason to bear on our own fears and on the fears of other peoples. We should likewise bring this mighty power of reason to bear on the dreadful force that inspires our fear and theirs, in order that we may subject this fearsome force to the reign of law.

I think that our traditional national sense of responsibility for furthering the reign of law in the world needs new impetus if it is to be kept abreast of the colossal and continuing increase in our weapons power. In April, 1816, Stephen Decatur gave his famous toast to the United States: "Our country! In her intercourse with foreign nations may she always be in the right; but our country, right or wrong." But in the world of today there can be no place for a United States — or for any other country — which acts wrongly, because today a country in the wrong will have in its service the power of atomic weapons. Therefore, in pain of fearful retribution, our policy today can only be that of Abraham Lincoln: "Firmness in the right, as God gives us to see the right."

We Catholics must assume our proper share of the responsibility. We have led the field in pointing out the threat of international Communism. Even among those who do not share our religious faith there are many who are frank to admit that the Catholic Church is the strongest international bulwark against the appeals of Communism. But our task is not yet done. We still must join in the further lengthy task of alerting the world to the need of sacrificing some of its conventional habits of political and emotional conduct. In this sacrifice of outworn habits we can only hope that the Russian people will join us.

The same genius of this nation must now be harnessed to the unprecedented job of keeping under rational control the forces of the atom, and of bringing these forces to serve the constructive purposes of mankind. God the Creator of all things brought these natural forces into being in order that they might serve and not destroy the human race. If in this hour of opportunity we fail in our task of making these forces obey the purposes of their Creator and ours, there may be no further work for us to do on earth.

We Catholics understand the necessity and therefore the justification for our present effort at rapidly building up our atomic weapons potential. But the problem of the use of these weapons is much more complex than the problem of their possession.

New looks and new styles in military affairs may come and go. But there can be no new look in what concerns moral principles. The vast ever increasing destructive atomic power in our stockpiles should not be used save in defense of our vital interests — in defense of that most vital interest of ours which is the cause of justice. National conscience demands that even in our defense of ourselves and of the order of justice, only as much of this force should be used as is necessary. An ungoverned, wanton use of force is as immoral in the atomic age as it ever was.

I think that this kind of caution may be particularly in order for us for a reason that may sound strange at first. We believe in the reality of Satan. We think that Satan must be the patron of atheistic Communism. We might therefore be tempted to think that any means of destroying this greatest of all historical menaces would find favor with God. Some men have even indulged in the thought of preventive war. This, I have insisted on other occasions, and I again insist, is nothing but spiritual bankruptcy. It cannot be said too often that every person in the Soviet Union is a human being, compounded of mortal body and immortal soul. Each is dear to God its Creator as we too, men and women of the Western world, are dear to Him. If all-out atomic war is to come, it must come only as the last of all last possible resorts. And in the course of its waging, we shall have to remember that the outlaw nature of the enemy does not justify outlaw methods of warfare.

I have another suggestion which I think is valid in our present emergency. Science has shown us that a disease can be prevented by vaccination. Infecting people with the germ of a disease enables the human system to develop antibodies which will destroy the disease if it should later strike. Cannot a lesson be learned from this scientific technique which will teach us something about the way to prevent that recurrent disease of mankind which is war — a disease that today would be more virulent and fatal than ever? This is my suggestion: Let the peoples of the world, especially their leaders, witness a special atomic demonstration — witness modern war in a capsule — in an explosion of a large scale hydrogen bomb. Let them thus experience in a way that will leave them undamaged, save in their illusions, what modern war really means in all its horror, in all its shocking destructiveness. I feel sure that such a special demonstration could be arranged without damage to security. It would make the political leaders and the peoples of the world realize what the word "war" means in terms of the 1954 models of atomic weapons. God alone knows what atomic war will mean in a comparatively few years if some sane solutions to the atomic arms race are not soon found. If the present meaning of the word "war" were universally realized, there would rise in the world a reasoned horror of war, and a rational opposition to all policies that might lead to all-out atomic war. This horror and opposition might make even the leaders of a totalitarian dictatorship so unpopular that they would eventually be displaced.

It seems to me that we cannot rely merely on a vaguely hopeful assumption that the terrific destructiveness of hydrogen bombs will deter nations from their use. The new meaning of war should be demonstrated. General Sherman's remark "War is Hell" is no longer a figure of speech. It can now be taken almost literally. If this fact were ever universally grasped, the search for peace would take on a new and needed sense of urgency.

Even the Russians must now realize that man's relations with nature have been radically altered. They must realize, too, that this fact must inevitably make a change in the relations between nations. Even now they may be wondering if this new, apparently limitless force demands any adjustment of their dogmatic belief that destiny is on their side. America must quickly capitalize on this turn of affairs — on this possibility of a birth of receptivity in Moscow — in order to avoid a likely doomsday caused by man's disagreement with man.

As Christians we must hope that there can be sowed in the Kremlin's mind even some small measure of skepticism as to the value of the barren earth which the victors in a future war might ultimately inherit. If this can be done there may well develop in the Soviet that minimum of willingness to compromise which is essential to real negotiations looking to disarmament and to the control of atomic weapons by international agreements and laws.

After the awesome tests in the Pacific, man can no longer plead that he knows not what the experts do. All of us, educators and students, government officials and voters, priests and people now have a firsthand, personal responsibility in this ultimate matter of atomic weapons policy. Our recent experiences in the Pacific have brought the problem of this responsibility into the light for all to see and ponder — and, I would add, to pray over.

The words, "Thy will be done," must also take on new meaning in this age of peril. You have heard the reply of St. Francis to the question put to him while hoeing in his garden — he was asked, "If an angel appeared to tell you,

Francis, that tonight you are to die, what would you do?"
"Keep on hoeing the garden," he replied. Similarly, today we
have no alternative but that of keeping on doing, that is,
we must go on strengthening our defense with the best
weapons we can devise. At the same time, it as all-important
that we should vigorously strengthen our resolution to find
peaceful solutions to the issues that seem so insoluble now.
God alone knows what is going to happen. All we can do
is to try our very best to realize in fact the prayer we make,
"Thy will be done." His will is peace, not war.

And so we must not forget the urgency inherent in our
present situation, created by the radical alteration of man's
relation to the forces of nature. The response to the emergency is not that of fear, unless it be a holy fear, not a
slavish fear. We are not frightened by the forces we have
discovered and unleashed. They are in a sense our own creation; we are their master. They cannot destroy us against
our will. Nevertheless, we must stand in fear, not of these
blind forces, but of our own blindness and apathy, our own
failure to rise to the heights of the emergency that confronts
us. This holy fear will make us pray more earnestly, "Thy
will is peace; Thy will be done; we will do it."

The emergency is also an opportunity. The power we
now hold in our hands is not evil in itself. On the contrary,
the energies of nature are of God's creation. They are good,
and it is good for us to have unlocked the secret of their
use. Everything now depends on the way in which we use
them. We can use these new energies to lead us forward,
not indeed into some new garden of Eden, but at least into
a more tranquil, human, prosperous, ordered world. Or we
can use them to drive us backwards into the primeval chaos.
It is for us to choose.

The responsibility for the choice rests upon all of us.
Ours is a government by consent of the governed; in that

sense, therefore, the makers of atomic policy are not only a small group of men in Washington. We, the people, are policy makers, too. We shall not consent to any policy that is not in accord with the norms of justice; for we know that peace can only be the work of justice. "Let justice be done, though the heavens fall." Moreover, we will not consent to any policy that does not strongly tend toward the establishment of the reign of law over the possible brutalities of sheer power. In order that there may be peace, we must presently have power, as much power as we can recruit from nature's atomic storehouse. We trust our power, but we do not put our ultimate trust in it. Our ultimate trust is in the forces that alone in the end can control power — the spiritual and moral forces of reason, justice, and law.

Finally, I think the United States might well unveil the new face of war — war's new look in this atomic age. This would help us in America, and help all the peoples of the earth, to realize more fully our common situation, and our common responsibilities. If this display were made, I think the peoples of the world and their leaders would cry out with a great voice: We reject war! We choose peace! We refuse methods of violence as the way out of our conflicts of ideas and interests. We choose the methods of argument and agreement — arguments honestly made and agreements slowly reached. We choose the methods of reason, not of wreckage. Lest the heavens fall, let justice be done.

CATHOLIC CHURCH AND AMERICAN DEMOCRACY

BY ROBERT J. WELCH

THE more or less educated Catholic today often feels that he has a rather adequate grasp of the answers to most of the important questions which sincere inquirers or unfriendly critics may hurl his way. At least he feels that answers are available, even if they are not always in the front of his mind when the questions are asked.

There is one question, however, which of all inquiries posed for the American Catholic today, seems the most embarrassing, the least easy to dispose of with a sense of satisfaction. At the same time it is precisely the question which most needs clear answers for the contemporary American. It is the whole question of "The Church and Democracy," of "Tolerance and the Catholic."

In the practical order it is a thoroughly alive question today — and not all credit is due to Paul Blanshard for this. In fact, in one way or another it has always been a question — or a taunt — that American Catholics have had tossed their way. It is, indeed, several questions, although basically it is pretty much one question — the question of the compatibility of Catholic thought with American democratic thought and life.

To pose the question, or questions:

What in general must be the attitude of Catholics toward men of other philosophies and religions?

What especially should be the treatment of non-Catholics in a state that is predominantly Catholic — the fearful question which comes to the mind of many a sincere non-Catholic in our midst today?

Do Catholics claim (as Montalambert once quoted a Catholic) that "when I am the weaker, I claim freedom from you since that is your principle; when I am the stronger, I take it from you since that is my principle"?

To get directly to our question: If America were to become a Catholic State, would that Catholic State put an end to the American tradition of separation of Church and State? Would it deprive non-Catholic religions and non-Catholic persons of religious liberty, freedom of conscience, freedom to profess their religion and openly proselytize in its favor? Is there in Catholic teaching something which *requires* intolerance by a Catholic State in relation to those not of the Faith?

What are we to answer to all of this?

"The first thing is that the question needs to be faced honestly. It is no good merely to say that no American non-Catholic has reasonable grounds for being concerned . . ." (Dunne, "Religion and American Democracy," 42).

Blanshard can quote a writer from the *Civilta Cattolica,* and *Time* can quote some remarks by Alfredo Cardinal Ottaviani, and *Christian Century* can lift a few lines from Ryan and Boland's "Catholic Principles of Politics."

And everybody who has a finger and reads the papers occasionally can point that finger at some features of modern Spain, a so-called "Catholic State."

The fear of which we speak is less a fear of the present than of the future. That is not the same as saying the fear is entirely well based, or that Catholic teaching actually demands such fear. As Heinrich Rommen remarks:

"Much misunderstanding and the fear that the Church

and Catholics do not sincerely recognize the freedom of religion, of conscience, of speech and of the press, stem . . . from a lack of judicious information for which . . . not a few Catholic writers may be involuntarily responsible" ("The Church and Human Rights," in *The Church in World Affairs,* 148).

The topic, then, is timely and important. It swarms with many corollary and related questions which are themselves important but with which we cannot deal here. Is the Church constitutionally opposed to democracy and in favor of monarchy because she is a monarchy? What is the origin and ultimate meaning of political authority in a democracy? In a Catholic State, would the Pope dictate domestic policy, etc.?

We confine ourselves in this discussion to two matters only. If the United States were, in the future, to become "a Catholic State."

1. What would be the condition relative to union of Church and State?

2. What would be the condition relative to religious liberty and toleration in such a state?

There are two matters which particularly irritate today's American Catholic when the above questions are asked.

First, there is the implication that as a Catholic he is somehow potentially a dangerous character on the American scene and thus a currently questionable citizen, when the fact is that the Catholic record has been so good. Catholics have served in wars and shed their blood out of all proportion to their numbers; their loyalty record is practically unblemished in peace and war.

Second, if he knows a little of the history of America, the Catholic is aware that factually (rather than in terms of some future theoretical situation) the Catholic record on the questions posed is a clean one. At the same time he is aware that the ones who so often pose the questions and accuse the Catholic are members of religions which in the past have both espoused union of Church and State in America and denied religious liberty to those who did not profess their particular religion!

In passing, one might observe that there is a measure of impertinence in the seemingly superior and holier-than-thou attitude of certain Protestant organizations, publications, and persons in dealing with this question which amounts to a practical blackout of the well-known facts of history. There is clearly no room for this air of superiority and it throws both the question and the answer out of focus by presuming that this is just "a Catholic problem."

A glance into our American past will show that the only Church-State unions in our history have been Protestant Church-State unions. Although these were principally in the colonies — nine out of the 13 colonies had Church-State unions at the time of the Revolution — the situation continued even into the nineteenth century. Connecticut had such a union until 1818, Massachusetts until 1824.

It is important to mention also that in predominantly Protestant America in Colonial days the laws which denied religious and political rights to Catholic and Jew were numerous and of Protestant origin.

Section 32 of the North Carolina Constitution, drafted during the Revolution, stated: "No person who shall deny . . . the truths of the Protestant religion . . . shall be capable of holding any office or place of trust or profit within the civil department of this state" (Maynard, "The Catholic Church and the American Idea," 30).

The early history of American public education through the nineteenth century also reveals the interesting story of what Protestantism did on this question when they had the power and as long as they had the power to control. These

are matters which for some reason are absent from Blanshard's "American Freedom and Catholic Power" (cf. Cur-
ran, *The Churches and the Schools*).

These matters are not alluded to in any spirit of bitterness
nor as an attempt to divert attention from the Catholic question at hand, but to suggest that perhaps the thing we are
dealing with here is not an exclusively Catholic question at
all but rather a human problem which with Catholics becomes a Catholic problem.

It is evident that there is a need of perspective and a
knowledge of and advertence to history in order to deal in
any sensible fashion with this question.

Christ did not deliver to the Church a revelation on
Church-State matters other than to indicate that we were
to render to Caesar the things that are Caesar's and to God
the things that are God's.

Whence, then, comes the Church's doctrine on Church
and State and their mutual relationships?

It comes first of all from Revelation, then from a consideration over the centuries of the nature of man, society,
the State, largely from the use of human reason, i.e., from
natural law considerations. Since these things were not
there from the beginning of the Church as a developed tract
on Church-State relations, it is evident that they have developed out of the Church's mind through the centuries
and thus have become a part of her teaching. The process
of that thought, ever more detailed and explicit and clear,
goes on even in our own day.

That thought, as found in Pope Leo XIII's encyclical,
"The Christian Constitution of States," emphasizes certain
points of Catholic teaching, valid in every age and not subject to change. Let us mention just three of these basic
notions in Catholic teaching.

First, the right to rule is not necessarily bound up with

any special mode of government. It may take this or that form, provided only that it be of a nature to secure and insure the Common Good, the general temporal welfare of the citizens, for that is its purpose.

Second, "the Almighty has given the charge of the human race to two powers, the ecclesiastical and the civil . . . each in its kind is supreme, each has fixed limits within which it is contained, limits which are defined by the nature and special object of the province of each . . ."

Third, "there must, accordingly, exist between these two powers a certain orderly connection . . . the nature and scope of that connection can be determined only . . . by having regard to the nature of each power. One of the two has for its proximate and chief object the well-being of this mortal life; the other the everlasting joys of heaven."

It is evident from these remarks of Leo XIII — and from numerous other expressions of the Church and of her theologians — that the Church teaches that there should be a relationship between Church and State. This is often termed "union" but Leo XIII speaks simply of "a certain orderly connection."

At various times and places in history that relationship has taken different forms and human judgment is inclined to consider some of these as more desirable than others. But there is not in the Church's teaching any stipulation as to what this relation should be, precisely and in a given case.

Father John Courtney Murray, S.J., remarks that "for all the divinely established character of the Church itself, the actual relationship between Church and State, especially in its legal forms, is a matter of human institutions. And all human institutions, even those which embody some permanent idea, are in some sense historically conditioned.

"To this law of historical development and change the institutional expressions of the Church-State relation constitute, on the evidence of history, no exception" ("On the Structure of the Church-State Problem," in *The Church in World Affairs*, 18).

The question at hand (whether in a Catholic America there would be a union of Church and State) is complicated by two lines of thought current in some circles in America today.

First is the misconception — found at times even in Catholic thinkers — that there is but one, unique pattern of Church-State relationship or connection. That is the traditional picture of union which was brought into being as much by the forces of royal absolutism as by any ideas which are a part of traditional Catholic thought (Murray, *op. cit.*, 23). This is the union of the days of the *ancien regime* of early modern times, in France and Spain, a union which was more a manifestation of *caesaro-papism*, serving the state but not necessarily serving the best interests of the Church. It was, one might add, the union which characterized Church-State relations in Protestant countries as well as Catholic countries.

It is that sort of union which haunts and disturbs so many Americans who think that the relationship of Church and State must be that sort of union. The Church never has said so. That type of union was the product (we might say the unhappy product) of an age that is past, an age which bears precious little similarity to our own.

In the course of defending what the Church does teach about the need for "a certain orderly connection" between Church and State, it is worse than folly to presume to have to defend any particular Church-State relationship as the necessary type as if it were as unchanging as the idea that real *concordia* should exist.

Second, American thinking on this subject is complicated in our days by the rise of purely secularist thought which presumes to define the American reality in terms of "a total or complete wall of separation" between Church and State. This is not only alien to Catholic thought; it is even alien to the Anglo-Saxon tradition from which so much of our thought has come.

Actually it is the view of continental liberalism of an extreme sort against which the Church in the nineteenth century had to contend continuously. Its basis is a secularist notion of man and society that is alien to Christian thought.

The question of the intention of American Catholics on the matter of union in a possible, future Catholic America, has arisen at various times in our past. It has always been answered in the same way, whether in the words of Al Smith answering Marshall's attack on his Americanism, or in the words of James Cardinal Gibbons in his famous essay on "Catholicism and Americanism," or the 1948 statement of the Catholic bishops of the United States.

In an NCWC release of January 26, 1948, Archbishop John T. McNicholas, O.P., made this statement:

> We deny absolutely and without any qualification that the Catholic Bishops are seeking a union of Church and State by any endeavors whatsoever, either proximate or remote. If tomorrow Catholics constituted a majority in our country they would not seek a union of Church and State. They would then, as now, uphold the Constitution and all its amendments, recognizing the moral obligation imposed upon all Catholics to observe and defend the Constitution and its amendments.

We will return to this statement of Archbishop McNicholas in our concluding remarks because they are important and in need of comment.

At various times in the past century papal statements relative to the American situation have been made. For the most part they have simply praised the American arrangement.

However, in 1895, Leo XIII, in a letter to the American hierarchy, called *Longinque Oceani,* wrote these words, often quoted:

> It would be very erroneous to draw the conclusion that in America is to be found the type of the most desirable status of the Church, or that it would be universally lawful or expedient for State and Church to be, as in America, dissevered and divorced . . . but she (i.e., the Church) would bring forth more abundant fruits if, in addition to liberty, She enjoyed the favor of the laws and the patronage of public authority.

What is one to make of such a statement? As John Cogley has remarked, "the best answer is simply that the statements are true — as general statements." And Cogley goes on to say:

> But given the historical memory of religious strife, the development of the lay state, the well-beloved tradition of the U. S., the temperament of its people, would the *de facto* relationship in a Catholic America be one which fitted our scene and temperament and history, or some imported version which would be alien to the United States? (John Cogley, "Catholics and American Democracy," in *Catholicism in America,* 81.)

Cogley further remarks that John Courtney Murray, speaking of Leo XIII, has written:

> He made it clear that the Church-State relationship is not an end in itself; it is importantly a matter of *vivendi disciplina,* which looks to the temporal and eternal welfare of man, who is both Christian and citizen (*op. cit.,* 82).

In speaking of the question of Church-State union in a possible future Catholic America, this much would seem evident enough. There is no requirement in Catholic teaching that what the average American thinks of as Church-State union would have to be a part of the picture.

Certainly, also, a Catholic America would differ in many

ways from other nations whose backgrounds are not the same, for example, those whose roots are more directly in the medieval age.

A Catholic America would, naturally, imply certain changes. That would always be true of any country which would become a land of almost one religious mind, whether that mind be Catholic or Lutheran or Unitarian. To think there would be no changes would be a foolish flying in the face of both history and human nature.

If America were to become "a Catholic State" it is safe to say that there would be some changes of orientation and laws. It happens when we change from Republican administration to Democratic, or vice versa! It would be safe to say it would happen if America were to become Lutheran or Unitarian.

One can suggest that in "a Catholic America" there would be a change in divorce laws, perhaps changes in the educational system, perhaps greater public recognition of religion.

That is not only a common-sense observation which rests on a knowledge of history and human nature; it also follows the normal laws of democratic procedure, as long as it serves the common good and does not infringe upon the true rights of others.

A United States turned Catholic so as to fit the designation "a Catholic State" would still be America. It would not be England or Italy or Spain.

"Every country," says Sheed, "has its national memory, conditioning its here-and-now decisions" (*Society and Sanity*, 201). American memory, American history, American experiences would condition the institutions of "a Catholic America."

If America were to become overwhelmingly Catholic, what would happen to that condition of general toleration we call "religious liberty"?

Many questions are involved in this one question and we shall not try to touch them all but to concentrate on one; namely, the question of Catholic doctrine and civil toleration and religious liberty in a Catholic state.

Here we are face to face with certain unchangeable Catholic views with reference to non-Catholic religion which must be placed at the very head of the consideration.

The Church can never and will never approach this question of religious liberty from the viewpoint of religious indifference. The Catholic Church teaches that God has revealed through Christ, who established a Church to preserve and teach that true Revelation. It can never be a Catholic statement that one religion is as good as another — one Church as true as another.

Much as our separated brethren would like to have us abandon that position concerning the unique truth of Catholicism, the Church continues to teach it in the face of modern criticism. From that teaching of the Church it follows logically that the Catholic Church considers that all non-Catholic religions, by that very fact, are false religions, whatever may be the elements of truth in each of them. No discussion of the question at hand can ever be attempted without mutual understanding that this is the viewpoint of the Church and will continue to be so until the end of time.

This means that toleration, as an attitude of the Catholic Church toward non-Catholic religions, will always be (what toleration of any kind will always be) the recognition of something as false, or in some way at odds with one's own views.

We do not tolerate those who agree with us — we agree with them!

"Thus, tolerance is a practical maxim, not a metaphysical absolute truth" (Rommen, "The Church and Human Rights," in *The Catholic Church in World Affairs*, 143). It is rather a practical prudential judgment which must, however, as Rommen adds, "take into account the inviolability of conscience, the common good, and the interests of religion and public morality" (*ibid*).

To say that is to state that there is no such a thing as absolute tolerance on the part of any State. It would be simply anarchy if a State attempted to operate on the principle of absolute tolerance. The State, by its very nature, is committed to the promotion and preservation of the common good. It could not fulfill that function with absolute tolerance.

The United States does not practice such tolerance, and we do not have to restrict ourselves to the case of the U. S. *vs*. the Mormons to demonstrate it. The practical views on the limits of toleration on the part of the State in all things, including religious and moral questions, will be based upon "the judgment of prudence that tolerance is more favorable for the common good than is enforced conformity."

The Catholic Church has no final, set practice, made obligatory by her doctrine in the matter of toleration and the Catholic State, which could possibly be unrelated to, or independent of, the question of the common good and the inviolability of individual conscience. It is clear enough in Catholic teaching that the Faith cannot be forced upon anyone.

It is likewise clear, from the statements of Catholic teaching, that a Catholic State can permit the existence and exercise and profession of non-Catholic religion and worship.

Leo XIII, in his encyclical on Human Liberty, states that "while not conceding any right to anything save what is true and honest, she (i.e., the Church) does not forbid public authority to tolerate what is at variance with truth and justice, for the sake of avoiding some greater evil or of obtaining or preserving some greater good."

The Pope added that "God, Himself, in His Providence, though infinitely good and powerful, permits evil to exist in the world, partly that greater good may not be impeded, and partly that greater evil may not ensue. In the government of States it is not forbidden to imitate the Ruler of the World."

This Catholic doctrine was repeated substantially by Pope Pius XII in his allocution to Catholic Jurists in November, 1953:

"The duty to repress religious and moral deviation cannot . . . be an ultimate norm for action. It must be subordinated to higher and more general norms which, in some circumstances, permit and even make it appear as perhaps the better part not to impede error in order to promote a greater good."

Theoretically, in a vacuum, with no consideration for the common good (which, we repeat, is the domain of the State), it might be argued from a basis of Catholic teaching that a Catholic State could and should repress the religious liberty of non-Catholics, as long as it was not a violation of their consciences.

Many a theory, reasonable in a vacuum instead of in human society, reasonable in the speculative order as a theory, reveals its incompleteness when applied to the human order.

Communism in its merely economic aspects might be said to be an example of this, and St. John Chrysostom (as Sheed somewhere remarks) had some nice things to say about the benefit to a society where "that word mine and thine is unknown." But applied to the *de facto* world of man the same theory is seen to be impossible.

As Sheed has remarked also, "so many things would obviously be for the Common Good, which yet it would be against the Common Good to command by law. . . . It would obviously be for the Common Good if all the citizens had the same religion — but only if they accepted it for themselves, not if the State forced it upon them" (*Society and Sanity*, 212–213).

To attempt to translate into policy what may seem reasonable in the abstract is folly if one ignores the human factor, the common good, and history.

It would be less than correct to say that among Catholic thinkers at the present there is total unanimity about what a Catholic State can and ought to do in this matter of toleration and religious liberty. The contemporary discussion finds the division of antagonists into what we usually label Conservatives and Liberals.

The Conservatives, starting from absolute and unchangeable Catholic views, consider the Catholic State to have the obligation to restrict non-Catholic religious activity, sometimes even drastically.

The Liberal group of theologians has concentrated more and more on certain emphases: a more rigid distinction between the functions of State and Church so as to emphasize more strongly the State-function of the Common Good; a greater interest in the man as citizen, with a correspondingly greater consideration for the validity of what are called "civil rights": perhaps a greater awareness of history and how history shows the failure of restricted toleration to actually serve the common good.

Theirs is not really new thinking, by any means, but a further elaboration of ideas which the medieval theologians had already expressed, although incompletely and not, of course, in the light of later developments of human society.

In their thinking, the political order belongs to nature. So does political authority "which derives its competency from the people whose temporal common good it serves . . . the temporal common good was considered a genuinely independent, though natural, value" (Rommen, *op. cit.*, 129).

So, it is argued, "it is not the function of the State to establish the moral law or to be its interpreter, to teach all nations . . . its function is the common good. The field of its proper exercise is the temporal order. . . . In the doctrine of the two perfect societies (Church and State) it seems clear that the personal rights of all, especially the freedom of conscience, have to be protected" (*ibid.*, 146–157).

There is, they argue, such a thing as the equality of citizens before the law and this is an idea drawn from and related to the notion of the State as an independent society. Further, there has evolved, through political evolution, a concept of civil liberty which seems necessary to the common good. For the State to make exception to these civil liberties would not be just because it would imply some violation of that political equality which all citizens can claim as a basic civic right.

The fact that the question with which the two camps busy themselves is a question is proof enough that it has not yet been settled conclusively so that one can say that this or that is the unique Catholic view.

The Church has always had, among its theologians, the Conservatives and the Liberals, and we are grateful for them both, for each has its precious function. The Conservative is the watchdog of the Church's teaching, who functions at his best when he is calling the rash mind back to the established teaching of the Church, and the theological development of the Church would be poor without him.

But without the Liberal the theology would have drifted always toward a "traditionalism" which would have seriously handicapped that marvelous development of doctrine which is the crowning achievement of Catholic theology.

The Church has needed at all times the courage of the Liberal and his willingness to stress the idea that the Church is "a Learning Church" and that theology has not reached the end of the road on any subject.

On the questions we have before us, it seems to this Catholic that the difference between the Conservative and the Liberal is not the great gulf that it may, at first glance, seem to be. It is to be noted that this is in no wise a difference as to the Church's doctrine of the Church and the role of the State.

Rather, the differences seem often enough to lie in that field of prudential judgment. The difference is perhaps, in the application of principles concerning which there is no disagreement. Both camps know that the domain of the State is the common temporal good of society.

The disagreement, it seems to me, is on the question of the means by which a Catholic State would act in fulfilling its agreed function in relation to those not of the Catholic Faith.

The Liberal quite clearly considers that the whole range of civil liberties in the developed society of our day is a part of that common good and the State must preserve and protect them, even if (as in a Catholic State) that may involve tolerating what one personally *considers* to be error. The Conservatives seem not to consider that these considerations are of such importance as the Liberal would conceive them to be.

There is an analogy in the everyday political life of the average American which may be helpful here in throwing light upon the theological question at hand. It is agreed quite universally by our citizens that the State exists to promote the Common Good — to do for the citizens what they cannot do for themselves, or what they cannot do well enough for themselves to ensure both the private and the common good. On that a man and his neighbor are thoroughly in agreement.

Yet, while agreeing on this basic doctrine of the State, they may differ in the most extreme fashion on the prudential judgment by which they apply the doctrine to the realities of American life. And so Americans will, in their views of what the State ought to do, range all the way from left of Left to right of Right.

By way of conclusion, we wish to say a few things in summary and in comment. It is clear that the questions under consideration are not finished questions in the thought of the Church's theologians and in the teaching of the Church.

If St. Thomas Aquinas were alive today, I am confident he would be scandalized to be told that the questions of Church and State are closed questions.

What goes on today is no new phenomenon in Catholic history. It is the age-old system by which the Church herself has learned, become more perceptive as she drew more and more from the twin fonts of Revelation and natural law. There is need of more study and the need is being met in many quarters.

In dealing with these questions which so often seem to push the Catholic into positions which might be interpreted as not quite good "Americanism," it is important that the Catholic, in seeking a solution, avoid the danger inherent in linking Catholicism and Democracy as a solution to the problem.

Have we forgotten the lamentable blindness of the French Right in attempting to ally the Church with Monarchy?

There is a temptation, in arguing against the current myth of the incompatibility of Catholicism and Democracy, to attempt to settle matters by trying to show some "native kinship" between the two.

This is the fashion of Liberal American Protestantism which seeks to climb on the band wagon by claiming that Democracy is the political expression of the Protestant Faith.

The Church and her official teaching transcend all particular political forms, and thus are truly *catholic*. She cannot ally herself with any of the particular form of political society as the one and only form of the State — even though in a given age she may consider one or the other to fit the needs of that age best. The answer to the problem at hand is not to commit the Church to an alliance she has always shunned, doctrinally speaking.

One might observe in passing that the danger which is suggested in the questions considered is not so much a danger from Catholicism or Protestantism but from a secularism stripped of the Christian premises on which all rights rest.

One need not read very far into the works of Paul Blanshard to conclude what he would do with Catholics if there were some way of doing it under the label of "Americanism" and in the name of the State.

But what is the answer to the questions initially proposed — the questions of union of Church and State, and of religious liberty, in a possible future Catholic America.

I must confess my inability to read the future on both questions. How can anyone say what would necessarily happen in any kind of projected future America. How can a Lutheran today give you any guarantees as to what a Lutheran America would be in terms of the union of Church and State and religious liberty? Or a Unitarian or a Mormon? Neither can a Catholic give any final and conclusive answer when these questions are asked.

Earlier we quoted Archbishop McNicholas as saying:

"If tomorrow Catholics constituted a majority in our country they would not seek a union of Church and State. They would then, as now, uphold the Constitution and all its amendments, recognizing the moral obligation imposed upon all Catholics to observe and defend the Constitution and its amendments."

With all my reverence for so fine a churchman as the late Archbishop McNicholas, I cannot see how he could have made so unequivocal a promise for the future.

Of course, the American Catholic respects the Constitution and its amendments. He is taught to do so by his Church, in terms of positive virtue. But the Constitution has been amended many times in the course of our history and, in a Catholic State, it would probably be amended some more. Why not? It would, understandably, reflect the citizenry of the country.

And how can anyone today know what kind of Catholics would populate this future "Catholic State"? On the answer to that would depend, to some great extent, what kind of a Catholic State it would be — and not all Catholic States are the same.

This much I think we can say: There is nothing in Catholic teaching that requires that any certain type of Church-State union must characterize even an ideal Catholic State, least of all a union of the historical type so generally abhorred by Americans, Catholics as well as non-Catholics. That there should, in such a state, be some kind of "orderly connection" is good Catholic teaching and no Catholic needs to shrink from it in the name of "Americanism."

Again there is nothing in official Catholic teaching which definitely requires that a Catholic State tamper with the religious liberties of those not of the Catholic Faith — and much that serves as a clear warning that the Common Good may demand that such tampering must not take place.

There are indications, too, that the whole concept of Church-State relations in practice is undergoing a healthy study and development which (if any guarantees are possible) would at least suggest that the chances are rather remote that in "a Catholic America" the current fears of some Americans would be realized.

INDUSTRY COUNCILS

BY MOST REV. KARL J. ALTER

THE strikes in vital areas of our economy have arrested the attention of all thoughtful people. The question which is universally asked is: what can be done about it? There seems to be no satisfactory answer arising out of the existing economic system: not at least if we desire peaceful relations, the common good, and protection against the disastrous consequences of inflation. There is an inherent conflict of interests which today meet at the bargaining table. Both sides are arguing over a contingent future — namely, what will be the future profits of a particular business, and therefore what wages are to be paid out or what welfare benefits distributed? The conflict arises in large part because neither side can be clairvoyant as to the future. Costs cannot be estimated without knowing how much production the market will absorb, and hence no one knows what profits will accrue from future operations.

The solution offered by some is national planning with public ownership, on the model of the British Socialist Labor Party. Others propose a managed economy along the lines of continental social legislation. Some are content with a further development of the Social Security Program of the "New Deal" or "Fair Deal." Of course, there are some blind and stubborn reactionaries who will not learn the lesson of history and therefore think that we can return to the "laissez-faire" economy of the nineteenth century.

There are others still, small in number, who reject the

idea of further interference and control by the state and propose instead a democratic and functional system along the lines of the papal encyclicals.

This vision of a new order which derives from natural law and Christian ethics is called by common consent and for the sake of a uniform terminology the "Industry Council System." It is hoped that it will engage the interest of a much wider group and take on definite form and a concrete program of action.

In the first place, it is highly desirable that we have a clear understanding of the characteristic elements of the present economic system so that we do not start from a false premise. In the second place, we should have a comprehensive grasp not only of the abstract principles involved in a new economic order conforming to principles of social justice, but also of a concrete workable plan or program.

It is not quite correct to describe the present situation as one of individualist capitalism according to nineteenth century notions. Change and modifications have taken place in current economic thinking, so that a quite different picture is presented from the one which was portrayed by classical economists of the past. The legal encouragement and protection provided by the New Deal Government have outmoded much of the economic theory of individualism, particularly in respect to the determination of wages, hours, and working conditions.

Our economy is no longer dominated exclusively by big business or finance capitalism. National and international unions have in the past two decades attained a position of power and prestige unlike anything which existed in the past. In the present historical juncture, it is not so much the domination of management and ownership over labor and the public which we have to face, as it is the domination over the public interest and the common good by the class or group interests of highly organized business and highly organized unions.

The recent victories for labor in the steel, coal, and automotive industries have been gained partly at the expense of owners, but more particularly at the expense of the public. The unorganized forty million workers with their dependents are obliged to pay the increased prices for steel and coal without any concomitant advantages in terms of higher wages for themselves and without the substantial security and welfare benefits secured by the union members.

It is an utter illusion to assume that the increased benefits for the organized workers can be derived from profits alone. The corporate profits which were substantial in the past few years have in large measure been plowed back into new plant and better tools and equipment. The owners did not secure the chief benefits of this improved productivity. Dividends were only moderately increased and the market values of common stocks have fluctuated in accordance with dividends paid out or reasonably anticipated. Wages, by contrast, together with hours and working conditions in the manufacturing industries, have greatly improved.

So far so good. There is no intent whatsoever to find fault with this better distribution of income, but nevertheless it is a fact and should not be suppressed since it is a direct result of substantial changes in our economic thinking and economic processes.

Management and ownership cannot honestly be regarded as supreme in those sectors of our economy where strong union organization exists. It can be readily granted that the spirit of individualism still carries over from the past and colors our current thoughts and actions. But this spirit is found in the ranks of labor as well as ownership; and in the final analysis it is the spirit of human selfishness which we must combat.

It is not beside the point to call attention to the fact that it is easy to mistake the means for the end. The end is social justice and social charity. The papal encyclicals lay great stress upon this moral renovation of society as a supreme objective. Without the spiritual and moral reconstruction, it is hopeless to expect any great improvement no matter what sort of an economic system is adopted. This does not mean that we should depend solely upon supernatural means for the improvement of moral conditions, but rather that we should act on the individual conscience and simultaneously exert every effort to create a social environment in which the individual can achieve his spiritual destiny and practice justice and charity with the largest measure of success.

A Christian order of society can be as helpful in the economic field in achieving spiritual objectives, as it is in the political field. No one, however, would say that the democratic political order is essential to the achievement of social justice. It may be the most desirable and effective, as our Catholic authorities in political science maintain. The same holds true for the economic order. Here, also, a democratic form of organization may be most helpful; but, again, it is not essential. Hence, it seems to be an exaggeration to compare our Christian concept of an economic order with our precise and dogmatic teaching in respect to marriage and the family. In the latter case, our teaching is clear and unmistakable in its application. There is no uncertainty between the abstract principles and the concrete situations to which they apply.

A body of principles is not in itself a plan nor a program. The principles must be reduced to concrete proposals before a program can be advocated. Furthermore, there will be of necessity a variety of plans even though the principles stay the same — for the concrete economic conditions vary greatly from one part of the world to another. What applies to Indonesia or the Near East will not apply to the U. S. A. Pope Pius XI makes this pertinent observation: "Thus, even in the sphere of social economics, although the Church has never proposed a definite technical system, since this is not her field, she has, nevertheless, clearly outlined the guiding principles which, while susceptible of varied concrete applications according to the diversified conditions of times and places and peoples, indicate the safe way of securing the happy progress of society" (Par. 34. *Div. Red.*). It is precisely when we come to a consideration of the concrete plan that we find ourselves in difficulties. These difficulties are not merely the result of faintheartedness nor an unwillingness to face problems, but are due rather to the obscurity of the concrete proposals and the resistances to social change found in human nature itself.

Pius XI, in *Quadragesimo Anno* and *Divini Redemptoris*, lays great stress on the fact that it should be the aim and the chief function of the state in its social legislation to restore or recreate the vocational or functional groups as integral elements in a sound economic order. This emphasis on the state's duty evidently assumes that direction and stimulation in the reconstruction of the social order must come from government by way of new laws. Furthermore, it is not sufficient that they be merely laws of social reform in the sense that they correct certain individual problems, but rather that they correct the fundamental conflicts and evils of the system itself. New laws, moreover, will not come into existence by themselves. They presuppose an open mind and readiness to accept the new ideas on the part of legislators, and they require also the presentation of a definite program to the legislature by those who understand and energetically urge the new order or ethical approach to an improved economic system.

If we speak of a new social economic order, then logically there must come into being an authority vested with power to make and enforce decisions. There can be no order without authority. Sanctions require, moreover, an exercise of police power. Hence, a new system cannot come into existence merely by voluntary effort but requires also government action.

Now, what are the difficulties which stand in the way of further progress? The chief difficulty is the disagreement among the proponents of the new order concerning the function of the Industry Councils. Some Catholic social scientists hold that the function must include the determination not only of the processes of production and distribution, but also decisions concerning profits, prices, wages, hours, and the expansion and location of industry. Others vehemently reject such a definition of function, especially in respect to profits, prices, and capital investment. They hold that here is a legitimate field for the operation of the principles of competition under social control in an open market. This disagreement must be resolved before any notable progress can be made.

A second difficulty arises in respect to union activities. Shall they continue the process of collective bargaining between themselves and management as at present over wages, hours, and working conditions? If so, how shall we reconcile these activities with the function of Industry Councils? Either the latter must be limited in their functions or else the unions must be limited. They cannot both be the determining authority.

Pius XI, in *Quadragesimo Anno,* makes a statement which cannot be interpreted in any other way than as a reference to this situation: "The demand and supply of labor divides men on the labor market into two classes, as into two camps, and the bargaining between these two parties transforms the labor market into an arena where the two armies are engaged in combat. To this grave disorder, which is leading society to ruin, a remedy must be applied as speedily as possible. But there cannot be question of any perfect cure, except this opposition be done away with and well-ordered members of the social body come into being anew, vocational groups namely, binding men together not according to the position they occupy on the labor market, but according to the diverse functions which they exercise in society."

A third difficulty arises in respect to the area in which Industry Councils shall operate. Shall they extend to retail trade or only to wide-flung wholesale trade? Shall they include small business or only big business, and how big is big? Shall they apply only to interstate commerce or to local commerce within the states?

Since the three elements which have to be harmonized are the public, the owners, and the workers, how shall we create a common denominator of interest? Obviously, the particular interests do not change merely because they are expressed through an Industry Council. Shall all three elements have equal representation in the Councils, and shall decisions be made by majority vote? Shall the government delegates have a veto power only when the public interest is adversely affected, or shall it vote equally on all questions raised? It is obvious that, even if the Industry Councils were organized with broad powers and possessed with authority to enforce decisions, there would still be need of management or an executive authority on the individual plant level. How shall management personnel be selected, and to whom shall it be responsible? Moreover, what functions shall be performed by the boards of trustees if the Industry Councils take over the determination of profits, prices, wages, investment policies, etc.?

It is manifest that a great deal of spade work still remains to be done. It would be easy if we were to follow the pattern of the socialist-labor government of England. There the government merely passes the necessary legislation defining function, powers, and structure of the various boards or councils which it considers necessary to regulate economic life. It is a planned economy; but the planning is in the hands of one political party and represents the will of government. It is radically distinct, therefore, from the papal doctrine which does not approve of extensive nationalization of productive property, but which insists on the maintenance of private property and demands that the three elements, viz., public, owners, and workers, be organized on a voluntary basis even though authorized by the government.

In the logical order structure must follow function. Hence, it will be impossible to create the structure of the Industry Councils in actual practice until there exists a clear pattern respecting functions: it need not be a complete blueprint. The type or form of organization will depend on the rights, duties, and over-all responsibilities which shall be delegated to the Industry Councils, as distinct from those retained by the state, the owners, and the workers in their respective areas. We recognize the truth of what the famous Belgian commentator, Father Muller, states on the encyclicals in his book entitled, *La Politique Corporative:* "Corporative organization is not assembled like a machine; it is born; it grows and flourishes from the impulse of internal and spontaneous forces which the legislator can certainly 'direct, watch, stimulate, restrain' but on which it is useless for him to impose his will."

There are two particular countries which have attempted to put in effect a corporative system in their national economy. They are Italy under Mussolini and Portugal under Salazar. We can hear almost immediately the cry "Fascism."

But wait! We are not recommending the adoption of either system. Pius XI paid his respects to the Italian system in *Quadragesimo Anno,* and no one can forget his criticism of it. Nevertheless, he did not condemn it entirely, but only its excesses. There is moreover a fundamental distinction between a corporative political state and a corporative social economy. Mussolini adopted the former, Salazar the latter.

It would be very helpful if some of our social scientists would contrast both systems and spell out their specific differences. It would be better still if they would point out features of the Portuguese system and of the more recent legislation in Belgium which could be accepted by us in the U. S. and those which should be rejected. It is, in fact, necessary to come down out of the realm of the abstract and grapple with such concrete problems as the following: Shall government initiate the Industry Council System, or shall it come about by voluntary action? If so, by whom? Shall there be collective bargaining as now between labor unions and management? Shall strikes be allowed or forbidden, with recourse only to labor courts? What rights shall owners retain as distinct from those of the Industry Councils? Will labor unions be sanctioned by the state if they are in competition in the same industry with one another as the C.I.O. and the A.F. of L.? Will labor unions be allowed to continue to include in the same organization workers in such diverse functions as metal trades, textile, leather, plastics, and enamel manufacturing? If so, how can they be classified as functional groups? The only common denominator is the class conflict interest. These are practical questions which disturb students, executives, and also labor leaders. We know that there is far more to the Industry Council System than this, but we shall make more rapid progress if we remove the obscurity surrounding some of these questions.

While we are waiting to clarify the function and structure

of an Industry Council System, we might give some thought to that other section of the papal recommendations which concerns a modification of the present wage system. The Holy Father says that a wage contract is not unjust, but it should be modified by a participation in profits, management, and ownership. Such a modification by means of a real partnership would at least create on the individual plant or corporation level a real mutuality of interest between owners and workers. It would be a departure from the existing wage system and would be a real adventure into a form of co-operation which could give to workers a new status in the economic order.

Just as in the political order each citizen has a voice in government by reason of the fact that he can vote for government officials and stand for election to public office, so also it would be possible for him to have a similar voice in economic life. Two things would be required. Since economic policies are determined by the boards of trustees of business, and since these also elect or appoint the responsible executives in the field of management, why should it not be possible for workers to elect some of the representatives to the boards just as owners or stockholders do now. There would be real partnership of capital and labor, if they would jointly choose the management and outline policies. Labor, however, should be content with a minority position at first and until such time as it has developed experience and by means of its dividends purchased the right to a larger representation through ownership of stock.

The second requirement, in order to develop a common interest with owners, would be for labor to share in the profits of the business for which it works. The term profits should be defined not as surplus or reserves, but as dividends which accrue to owners and workers according to a predetermined formula. Surplus and reserves at the present time really belong to the business and are for the benefit of both owners and workers. Only dividends paid out have value for ownership; for even the value of their stock is appraised by the ratio of dividends received. The present demands for pensions and welfare benefits in coal, steel, automotive industry, glass, etc., are predicated on the fact that surplus and reserves belong not to the owners but to the business and hence are to be made the basis for funded pension plans rather than pay as you go plans.

The first charge against industry is a living wage. Unfortunately, the living wage is not an exact measuring rod, but rather a goal to be sought after. In a real partnership the wages would be defined as the going rate in comparable areas of business or employment. The charge against industry over and beyond material and management costs is, or should be, a rental charge paid to the owners for the use of plant, tools, and equipment. This rental charge should be equal to the current rate of interest paid by government on its long-term bonds. At present this rate is between two and one half and three per cent. The third charge against industry or business is the formation of a reserve or contingency fund. This is an absolute necessity in modern business, if the latter is to be prepared to finance promptly technological changes, plant expansion when needed, obsolescence, and other emergencies. It should be set up at a fixed ratio of the capital investment, say between 15 and 20 per cent. When drawn upon, it should be immediately replaced out of earnings.

Only after the above needs of business have been cared for out of income is it proper to consider the residue of earnings as profits. Owners and workers would share in this residue, if there is to be a true partnership. Moreover, the constantly recurring conflicts which precipitate strikes would, if not altogether, at least in large part be eliminated. The present conflict revolves around the question as to how to divide equitably the profits of business or industry between owners and workers. If there were a fixed formula of participation, then the question would be automatically solved.

This formula for the division of profits would be established by the board of trustees on which both owners and workers are represented. It would provide, moreover, a sliding scale of distribution of dividends between capital and labor. The bigger the profit, the bigger the share of the workers; the smaller the profit, the smaller their share. To illustrate: if a business earned 5 per cent profit (as defined) on capital invested, then the formula might provide 75 per cent of dividends to owners and 25 per cent to workers. If the profits paid out were 25 per cent or better, the reverse might be reasonable, viz., 50 per cent to workers and 50 per cent to owners. The formula should be flexible so as to permit a graduated distribution between these extremes according to the percentage of profit paid out. In this way, owners would be protected against the risk of capital invested and workers would be guaranteed that the bigger profits, the bigger would be their share. Surely, such an arrangement ought to meet the legitimate claims of a partnership between capital and labor. It would also satisfy the requirements of the papal encyclicals.

The only danger foreseeable is that the public interest might not be protected. This would be true if the business in question were a monopoly with administered prices, or if the principle of competition were for some reason ineffective. In that event, government would have to step in with a veto or a public hearing and decision as in public utility rates at present. Increased productivity and a reduction in prices is the best protection of the public interest.

In a brief outline such as this, it should be needless to state that exact figures, ratios, and formulae are tentative and should be subjected to further refinement by discussion and compromise. At least this much can be said for the plan that it is not altogether visionary, for the liberal party in England has adopted this idea of management participation and also some idea of profit sharing. In this area of human relations, the Liberal Party seems to be far out in front of the Socialist-Labor Party with its sole emphasis on nationalization and a government-managed economy.

We readily grant the Industry Council Plan has a wider vision of economic planning than the limited approach here presented. We are not suggesting it as a substitute for the larger objective, but as something which by its very nature is complementary to the broader outlook. We might well devote a considerable part of our attention to the lesser objective, which can be achieved by an approach to individual businessmen and union leaders who have both good will and an intelligent grasp of the particular problem which causes so much bitter conflict.

ORDER AND APATHY

BY WILLIS D. NUTTING

IT MUST always be a cause of dismayed wonderment that Catholics, who have been born into Christ's Mystical Body and thus raised up into a supernatural life, should act so much like other people; and that the Church, which has been a conquering thing, should now be chiefly concerned in a vast holding operation to keep its members from hell at any cost.

To say that faith has cooled is no answer. It is merely another way of stating the fact to be explained. Neither can we say Christ's Church is wearing out, and that the great outburst of energy evident at the beginning cannot be expected to last forever.

Because of the power of God's grace which raises fallen man, it is *normal* for a Catholic to live ever in the presence of God. It is *normal* for him to have a realization of the obligations entailed by being a member of Christ and to carry out these obligations with joy, to perform the works of mercy and to work for the extension of God's kingdom. We dare not fall into the treason of assuming a standard of normality lower than that revealed in God's Word.

For Catholics to have to be pushed and herded is a shocking abnormality. Since it is only by being pushed and herded that most of them now move at all, contemporary Catholic life is abnormal. It is then the duty of those who see the anomaly of the situation to search for its cause. What is there in the present-day Catholic environment — in our popular beliefs, in our way of doing things, in our devotion, in the relation of clergy to laity, etc. — which might put a damper on fraternal love, creative thinking, willing work and joyous sacrifice? What is it that has clogged up the springs of life among us?

Perhaps we might approach the problem with the Catholic Action technique: observe, judge, act.

Observation will show that in the public relations between clergy and people the following pattern occurs most frequently. A plan to be acted upon is proposed to the people — a plan for spiritual development, for education, for carrying out the works of mercy, for raising money. They are urged to carry it out, reminded that the sacrifice involved on their part is comparatively little and that the benefits accruing to them are great. The response is lukewarm, and this brings reproaches for the people's lack of interest in their own welfare, and often a very unfavorable comparison of them with the communists or the Jehovah Witnesses.

Anyone who is the parent of children will sympathize with the pastor in this tendency to reproach; but anyone who has had experience with life will be compelled to observe that neither with children nor with parishioners does the reproaching accomplish much. Frustration is its cause and further frustration is its result. Nagging makes mere apathy into sullen opposition.

Behind this relationship of reproaches, nagging, apathy, and opposition one can detect a conception of order in the Church which can claim the venerableness of age. It may have come from disheartening experience long ago. It may be the result of the classical aristocratic tradition. It certainly did not come from the New Testament.

This conception of order regards all life and initiative as

coming from the top down in the Christian society, so that the laity at the bottom is a religiously inert mass whose only distinctive quality is obduracy, like Plato's *matter*. The function of the clergy is to try to give this mass some Christian form, by dint of ceaseless, arduous and devoted striving, for the mass not only resists being formed but is ever inclined to fall back into its native formlessness. The pastor succeeds with any individual of the mass if that individual does not fall back permanently.

That this conception of order exists can be observed in a thousand instances: in the priest who understands thoroughly the penitent alcoholic but is flabbergasted by the man who wants spiritual direction in making the best possible decisions; in the educators who show kindly sympathy for the students who have violent temptations against the sixth commandment but who shrug off the boys who long for Christian perfection; in the myriads of laymen who know that they are good Catholics if they do not happen to be in mortal sin at the time.

It has, we must admit, its beautiful side in the shepherd and lost sheep relationship which is embodied in the lives of thousands of saintly priests. It has its ugly side in the pastor who is cynically "realistic" and will allow his enthusiastic young assistant to go no farther with the people than bingo and basketball.

Our observation can thus show us that a state of apathy among the laity exists widely, is recognized as something to be expected, and is even justified by a certain conception of order. Now we must judge this situation.

In the first place we can say that the apathy of the laity is so utterly at odds with the theology of the sacraments that we must say that either this apathy is wrong and abnormal or that the theology is not true. *For this apathetic, obdurate mass upon which the clergy work so devotedly is made up of baptized people,* people who have died to sin, people who have put on Christ. Most of them are also confirmed people, "strong and perfect Christians." Just what do words mean, anyhow? How are we to reconcile these words and this teaching with the reality?

The situation is clearly wrong. How did it get so wrong?

If we look at the Church as it came into the light of history we find in it an order much different from that order mentioned above. We find some classes subordinate to others, it is true, but no class which is merely matter to be worked upon. The first status or class was that of the clergy: the pope, the bishops, and the lower orders. Then there were the virgins and widows, people for whom the Church had a special care and on whom it put a special value.

Then came the faithful, the great body of baptized and confirmed Christians. They were God's holy people (*plebs sancta*), the ones standing around the altar (*circumstantes*), who assisted the clergy in offering the holy Sacrifice after the penitents and catechumens were dismissed. They supported the Church with their goods; they showed to the world the corporal and spiritual works of mercy. The famous "see how they love one another" was said of them. Together with the clergy they supplied the martyrs and missionaries that converted the Graeco-Roman world. Articulate and religiously intelligent, they were the audience to which an Augustine, a Leo, and a Gregory could direct sermons on a high theological level.

Then there were the penitents, a temporary status containing those who had fallen from the class of the faithful by the abnormality of mortal sin, and were undergoing penance before being received back. Finally there were the catechumens, who were to enter the class of the faithful through baptism and confirmation.

This was the class structure of the ancient Church. These classes, with the proper subordination that existed between them and within them, formed an order in the true sense, each group having not only its relation to the others, but also its own proper function and dignity. And apathy, or the mere capacity to be formed (or to resist formation), was not the function of any of them.

Now when we compare the modern Church with this ancient order we make an astounding discovery. *The class of the faithful, as a recognized status of great dignity and great responsibility, has to all intents and purposes ceased to exist.* Undoubtedly there are very many individuals who are faithful, but they are faithful *individuals*. Neither in their own minds nor in anyone else's do they constitute a distinct status in the parish, let alone one of great dignity and responsibility. They may even be regarded with tolerant amusement by clergy and laity, both anxious to get back to planning the parish festival.

In the mind of the priest and in the mind of the people the layman, even when he has received five sacraments, is a perpetual catechumen and an almost perpetual penitent. He is treated as such and he acts the part. Always being taught the rudiments of the faith, he never even imagines that he can go beyond them. The mission that we hold this year is directed toward getting the layman out of the habit of sinning that he fell into again after having been lifted out of it for a moment by the mission we held three years ago; and we know that three years hence he will need another mission.

Balancing forever on the doorstep is not easy, and when there is no known place to move into, when the doorstep is all there is to the room, the only direction one can fall is out. And thus we climb to the doorstep, fall back, climb up again, and so on until death catches us either on it or off it. When a person is treated by everybody as a perpetual catechumen the initial religious zeal he may have had is almost certain to disappear, so that he will have to be prodded even to keep trying to stay on the doorstep. Certainly he cannot be expected to show forth such fruits of a full Christian life as an appreciation of Christian education, an eagerness to support the clergy, a longing for perfection, or a willingness to participate in the apostolate. These are manifestations natural only to a state of life to which he has had no real opportunity to become acclimated.

Here is perhaps an explanation of that futility that so often pervades parish life. The lines of activity carried on in a parish — the education of youth, the C.Y.O., the convert classes, the mission, the Holy Name Society, the Saturday confessions, the house to house visiting — these all have their meaning in leading people into the circle of strong and perfect Christians or bringing them back if they have fallen away. But if this circle of strong and perfect Christians does not exist in the parish, if neither the leaders nor the led have any idea that it could or should exist, what is the goal of the activity? It becomes meaningless — a monotony, a grind, in which tempers are lost and in which people are always falling away.

But if all these lines of activity should converge in an actually existing class of strong and perfect Christians, then the whole process becomes meaningful. Our school system's function is to give the light which must accompany the sacramental life of those who are strong and perfect Christians. The convert classes do the same for adults who come in from outside. The missions bring the good news to the world. Once people have been brought into the class of the faithful (if it should come into existence) they will be secure enough so that the shepherd can leave them for a while and go off in search of the one lost sheep. He will not have to fear that the minute his back is turned the whole ninety-nine will get themselves lost.

These faithful will be the ones to whom the pastor can appeal for help in what needs to be done. They will love God as much as he does and will do God's work with no urging. No prodding, no scolding, no bingo will be needed to maintain the necessary things. No frustration, no discouragement, no cynicism need fill the pastor's mind with regard to them. And the world could see that we Catholics really are God's holy people.

For when the actual *class* of the faithful is restored it will be more than a number of holy individuals. It will be a *people,* a body having a corporate life which is the life of Christ in His members, the life of the Vine in the branches. This life will produce in the individual Christian a sense of belonging and fellowship, a strength and a supernatural joy which will make his belonging the most precious thing in the world for him. The supernatural life strengthening the brotherly love of member for member will give a steadiness in perseverance, a fullness of dedication and a willingness to sacrifice which will make real the language by which we describe the sacraments. It would bring us back to the standard of Christian normality which we find in the New Testament.

To explain why, as a matter of historical fact, the class of the faithful evaporated out of the Christian order would demand a greater knowledge of the early Middle Ages than we possess, but there are at least some elements in the situation of this period that make it somewhat understandable.

The overpowering influx of barbarian people, the ignorance of these same people, the linguistic difficulties, the unsettled condition of Europe — all these would make it almost impossible for a layman to receive the same Christian training that he received in earlier times. He would have less knowledge, and this in turn would lead to less being expected of him. It would have been very easy in this way to fall into a descending spiral in which lower expectations were met with lower standards which in turn would drive the expectations still lower until a minimum Christianity was reached, which then came to be regarded as normal Christianity.

In this process of degeneration there is one line of retrogression which is of particular importance. This is the disappearance of any effective conception of the priesthood of the laity. The class of the faithful, by virtue of their baptism and confirmation, were a chosen race, a royal priesthood, as St. Peter calls them. They were in a very privileged relationship to God. *"Divina institutione formati audemus dicere 'Pater noster' "* — no pagan could rightly say that. The most privileged, the most significant, the most distinctive act of this royal priesthood was the corporate participation, under the leadership of the ordained priest, in the offering of Christ in the Mass. This act showed forth what the faithful were and also made them what they were in the sense that their whole Christian life flowed from their exercise of that act.

Now if a priest, from the time of his ordination, should never offer the Mass, we would say that something was wrong, that he was not exercising the distinctive act of his status. We would not be surprised if we found him neglecting the other acts of a priestly life and losing the virtues that should accompany that life. Since there was such a glaring lack at the center we should expect to find lacks everywhere, and we would explain these lesser lacks by the greater one.

Is it not the same with a member of the lay priesthood? If such a one does not exercise his supreme privilege — if

he does not participate with articulateness and awareness in
his function at the holy Sacrifice, how can he fail to lack
in other duties and virtues of his status? The failure of the
lay Christians to exercise their lay priesthood to the full in
the worship of God may very well be the chief cause of the
disintegration of the class of faithful and thus for the dis-
ruption of right order in the Church.

Having observed the existing situation and judged its
unsatisfactoriness, we come to what is to be done about it.

The chief task before us today is the restoration of a right
order by reconstituting the class of the faithful. Only when
this class exists will there be a fit instrument for the conversion of the world and for the reform of the social order,
for this is the class by which the Spirit acts on the world.

It would seem also that the Spirit is giving us opportunity
for this restoration, for there is clearly in progress an awaken-
ing of men to the seriousness of the Christian calling. At the
university one sees freshmen coming up from high schools
with the mark of the apostolate already on them, and upper
classmen eager to learn that a more than minimal Christianity exists. One sees young married couples wishing to
know how to dedicate their married lives completely to
God. This was by no means so true fifteen years ago.

We are being presented, then, with the elements from
which a definite status in the Church can be constituted —
a status of lay people whose serious intention it is to live
their lives in a wholly Christian manner. But we are also
being presented with a very serious problem, for the techniques of parochial and educational practice by which minimal Catholics are handled are utterly inadequate in dealing
with people who are striving for a complete dedication of
their lives to God.

What must be done is to cherish these people who regard
lay Christianity as a real vocation, to hold them as most

precious treasures of the Church, to discover a type of spiritual direction fitting for them, and to weld them into a recognized status which has its recognized set of functions centered in the exercise of the lay priesthood in the offering of the holy Sacrifice. This means that they must no longer be regarded as exceptional individuals, to be left outside the main stream of parish life and pastoral consideration because of the smallness of their number. They *are* the main stream of parish life by any worthwhile standard of measurement. All the activities of the parish become meaningful only in so far as they direct people into this stream.

The Christian fellowship of the faithful, culminating in the corporate worship of God, must be considered the most important thing in the parish, and that no matter how small that fellowship may be numerically, and how few may at first be interested in participating in the corporate worship of God. To put anything else first is a disorder.

It is of course not easy to adopt a scale of valuation which places chief importance on activities that involve neither big numbers nor big money, but it is a move in the direction of order, and it may be a move that in the future will change the character of the great numbers. For an actually existing fellowship of one hundred per cent Christians in a parish will be the best possible instrument for converting the multitude.

In the restoration of the class of the faithful the schools, particularly the high schools and colleges, can be either a great help or a great hindrance. The opportunity is there, for it is in adolescence that the young person is capable and even desirous of beginning a life of serious dedication to something. If the school offers him a minimal Catholicism he will make his dedication elsewhere. Therefore if the school is to help students to be faithful Christians it must be so constituted in its faculty, in its way of teaching, and in its student life that it constantly sets forth the ideal of an actually functioning community of Christians. Perhaps a new kind of school is needed to accomplish this.

A great opportunity can be either seized or lost. We now have the opportunity to do something to remedy the deplorable apathy of lay Catholics. God is raising up for us a multitude of apostolically minded laymen. How are we going to treat them?

It may well be that the triumph of the Church in our century will depend, not on her understanding of the labor problem, nor on her reconciliation with democracy, nor on her diplomacy in the Church-State relationship, but on the wisdom of her leaders in understanding and dealing with the people who love God as much as they themselves do.

CHRISTIANITY AND
THE NEGRO

BY JOHN LA FARGE, S.J.

THE American Negro knows no country but the United States. His entire past over two centuries is inexorably bound up with our country's history in peace and in war, and there is no conflict of our nation from the Revolution of 1776 to Korea in which Negroes have not shed their blood for our freedom. Like the Indian, the Negro is in a peculiar and special sense that much-talked-about being, the one hundred per cent American.

In the New World American Negro slaves were completely cut off from their ancient tribal heritage, language, and customs. It was not until the beginning of the eighteenth century that some attempt was made by the Protestant church bodies to teach them about Christianity. Later, the widespread conversion of Negroes to Christianity was largely the effect of a wave of active Methodist and Baptist missionary endeavor that swept the slave states shortly before the American Revolution. Since that time the majority of Negro Christians have belonged to churches affiliated with one or the other of these two major evangelical sects.

Strongly fundamentalist Protestantism with its emphasis on the utter vanity of all things worldly and the glowing hope of glory beyond the grave provided a never ceasing source of consolation for a people who were utterly powerless to do anything to improve their own human condition.

Once they found that the Negroes could be kept quiet and contented by concentrating their religious worship on the life to come, white masters looked with favor upon the Negro ministers' vivid pictures of the rewards and punishments of the future life. The same white masters likewise were not unfriendly to the noisy, shouting, highly emotional type of worship and religious assent which the revivalist missionaries brought to the Negro from the countrysides and the Protestant churches and chapels of England and Wales.

As for immediate release, the liberation that the slave could not obtain here and now from outward bonds he could derive to a certain extent in psychological fashion through a highly emotionalized type of worship. All humbled and oppressed peoples can enjoy a certain degree of inner escape through exuberant, demonstrative action, especially when it is done in common as an expression of a common hope and belief. Out of this tumultuous worship came the precious cultural gift of the Negro Spirituals — about which James Weldon Johnson, who did so much to interpret Negro folk-made music to the American people, remarks:

> The thought that the Negro might have refused or failed to adopt Christianity — and there were several good reasons for such an outcome, one being the vast gulf between the Christianity that was preached to him and the Christianity practised by those who preached it — leads to some curious speculation. One thing is certain, there would have been no Negro Spirituals. His musical instinct would doubtless have manifested itself; but is it conceivable that he could have created a body of songs in any other form so unique in the musical literature of the world and with such a powerful and universal appeal as the Spirituals? Indeed, the question arises, would he have been able to survive slavery in the way in which he did? It is not possible to estimate the sustaining influence that the story of the trials and tribulations of the

Jews as related in the Old Testament exerted upon the Negro bards, and they sang, sang their hungry listeners into a firm faith that as God saved Daniel in the lion's den, so would He save them; as God preserved the Hebrew children in the fiery furnace, so would He preserve them; as God delivered Israel out of bondage in Egypt, so would He deliver them.

When a Negro sang: "Joshua was de son of Nun. He never stopped till his work was done," he referred of course to the sinner who was beginning his conversion and should keep up the job of self-reformation until he was in the ranks of the elect. But behind the biblical allusion was the thought that another work was to be done for the whole race and people, the work of freedom, and they should never stop till they should enter the Promised Land. It is sheer legend that the Spirituals represented simply and solely a naïve, childlike faith. On the contrary, they were sophisticated in the best sense of the word, conveying an underlying meaning, a symbolism, far beyond that of the rather grotesque images in which some of them were clothed.

Suffering is easier when endured in common, and Negro Protestantism helped to make things easier by its emphasis on community worship. In later years this led to the development of a great variety of social activities in the Negro Protestant church. These activities followed the curve of Protestant religious trends in the country generally, for religion here has always been shaped, to a certain extent, by the varying patterns of American culture. As a primitive appeal, shouting and singing lost their attraction. But the churches kept their hold upon the new generations by programs of all kinds of activities for young and old. As Deacon or Lady Chairman of a committee, an individual member, snubbed and a nobody in ordinary public life, became a person of no slight importance and was able to wield a little authority within a narrow but important sphere.

In this way the Protestant churches helped to form real leaders in the struggle for liberation and self-advancement. From being a local religious leader, the Protestant Negro minister in many instances developed into a leader on a regional or a national scale in his people's struggle for freedom. Many great leaders of the race found their start in church activities.

This became particularly evident in the field of education, the churches taking a prominent part in founding and conducting Negro colleges and universities and various institutions of secondary education. Many of these schools featured theological faculties. Lincoln University in southeastern Pennsylvania, the first Negro university in the United States and the only one established north of the Mason-Dixon line, is still the training ground for Presbyterian clergy through its Department of Theology.

With all their imperfections and compromises in handling the racial problem, the major Protestant denominations in the United States deserve a lasting credit for instructing vast numbers of the American Negro people in certain basic doctrines of Christianity. They gave them the hope of the Scriptures and the knowledge of the Saviour as well as the sacrament of baptism; they sustained their spirits in times of dire affliction and trained them in educational and in some cases social and political leadership. Finally, especially in later years, the various Protestant national religious organizations, including the Quakers, developed a galaxy of men and women from among their white membership dedicated to the work of promoting better race relations.

Protestantism's weakness as a social force lay in its lack of any central spiritual authority. This laid it open to numberless divisions and schisms as well as to passivity in the face of lay church leaders whenever they were determined to maintain a rigid pattern of white supremacy. Negro

Protestanism would naturally reflect the atmosphere of the epoch for better or worse. Present-day stress on social benefits and social activities is paralleled by a corresponding increase of such activities in the more "progressive" Negro denominations. The prevailing atmosphere of secularism and of contempt for higher supernatural motives is paralleled, according to reports of various Protestant church bodies, by a corresponding impatience of Negro youth with the otherworldly philosophy that so moved the older generation.

For the Negro who has been more or less actively affiliated with Protestant denominations, conversion to the Catholic Church means in many instances a break with certain greatly cherished values, certain precious associations. Unless his vision is wide enough to rise to a plane where his new ideals and their ideals are fused, the convert feels no longer as close as he did to the generations of brave men and women who by their lives and sacrifices wove the great fabric of Negro liberation in the United States. He misses a multitude of intimate features of today's close knit Protestant religious community, those which appeal particularly to simpler people. If the convert is of the more educated group it is not always easy for him to take up life anew, among his Protestant neighbors who know little or nothing about the saints and martyrs.

What, then, does attract the Negro to Catholicism? The only satisfactory answer to that question is: the grace of God. Certainly nothing would be more mistaken than to believe that any one formula has been, or could be devised, that would serve as *the* prevailing approach of the American Negro to Catholicism. Zealous missionaries have tried to devise such formulae, basing their speculations on Negro psychology, on the attraction of the Protestant worship, and so on. But the individual Negro is led to the Church in his own way, and generalizations are always misleading.

A zealous Negro convert friend of mine could not rest content until he should bring his old friend to the nearby rectory to talk to a Catholic priest and learn something of the Catholic faith firsthand. The idea was a good one, but unfortunately both pastor and assistants were away at the moment. Their place was taken by a somewhat crusty visiting clergyman, a total stranger to the place and surroundings. Uncomfortable and alarmed at this unexpected inquiry, he invited the inquirer and his anxious sponsor to leave the premises as soon as possible, which they promptly did. In utter dejection, my convert friend walked with his rebuffed companion in total silence. "You know what I think?" asked the companion after a few blocks had been passed. "Oh, I know what you think," grumbled my friend. "Let's not talk about it." "Here's what I think," repeated the companion. "That there man, he spoke with *conviction*. That's what I want in religion: I want conviction. He's convinced of the true church and I'll look into it."

Not only conviction but the sense of identification also plays its part, as was indicated in the experience of a young man, now in business in the North, with whom I talked recently. To my query as to what led to his conversion, he replied as follows:

> I can't say any one thing, Father. It just seemed to shape up that way. I grew up with all kinds of religious practice around me. But at college we all thought the only thing to do was to talk atheism. We did plenty of that, but it didn't make me feel any happier. Then I joined the Marine Corps, just to escape from myself. I ran into everything, good and bad, you can think of there. But I did notice one thing about those Catholic fellows. Whatever their behavior was, they did seem to have a sense of Deity — they could always come back to it, after things went wrong. God was there, waiting for them. I couldn't put my finger on any single item. But I felt

something drawing me and I picked up first one idea, then another. Finally I had to decide. Usually when you make an important decision, you put it off for some months. But all the parts fell right together; I was as completely sure as anyone could be.

It was strange when I first went to Mass. Nobody in the church seemed to be paying any attention to what was going on at the altar. Everyone was busy with his own thought and his books. Each one just talked to God, and went his own way. This seems so different from what we had in the Protestant service, where we all worshiped in common. But one thing has made a tremendous impression on me. You are at home everywhere in the Catholic Church. You have *identification,* and every fellow wants to be identified with something. When I was at Oak Bluffs the other day, that suddenly struck me. Here I am, I said to myself, in a completely strange town. Yet I could slip into confession in that local Catholic church; hear Mass and receive Holy Communion the next morning; and that would be the same anywhere in the whole wide world. I was identified not with this preacher or that parish, but with the whole world of God's Church.

The Negro brings to the Church something that is in danger of disappearing from its life in this country, and thereby putting American Catholicism out of touch with the rest of the great universal suffering world — a keen sense of social justice. In the past, the American Catholic Church built up its strength in great measure from multitudes of immigrant people, carrying in their veins a deep sense of social justice. They sought America to escape from cruel oppression, to worship God and raise their children in freedom. That belief in social justice nerved them to immense tasks, including the creation of parishes, dioceses, schools, colleges and universities, institutions and organizations of every description. It imparted a tremendous dynamism to the growing American Catholic Church. Today, we still need men and women in whom this spirit of social justice is alive.

The unfortunate element in the American situation is that so much of the Negro's spiritual courage, resourcefulness and energy has had to be employed in simply combating various inequities — qualities which could have been used, and should still be used, for the building up of Church and country. "One's heart is sickened," says the forthright American Negro author J. Saunders Redding, "at the realization of the primal energy that goes undeflected and unrefined into the sheer business of living as a Negro in the United States — in any one of the United States. Negro-ness is a kind of superconsciousness that directs thinking, that dictates action, and that perverts the expression of instinctual drives which are salutary and humanitarian — the civic drive, for instance, so that in general Negroes are cynically indifferent to politics; the societal drive, so that ordinarily the Negro's concern is only for himself as an individual; and even the sex and love drive, so that many Negroes suffer sexual maladjustments and many a Negro couple refuse to bear children who will inevitably grow up under a burden of obloquy and shame that would daunt and degrade a race of angels!"

It is difficult to convey a sense of this waste to those who have not themselves experienced it. It may and frequently does mean tangible loss, such as exclusion from paying jobs for parents of families, from decent housing where it is available for others than those of the minority group; and so on. Even more consuming of human patience, initiative, and self-respect are the innumerable intangibles, those that confront a mother who must explain to her children why they cannot buy an ice cream cone or a bottle of pop in a drugstore, why they cannot play or swim in a public park on a hot day, why they must be careful not to crowd up to the communion rail in church until the whites are duly retired from it. In numberless other places they will not meet all or any of these things, but any of them *may* be met, and most unexpectedly. Meanwhile, such an experience is wasteful of human life, and is a standing encouragement to seek compensation in literal waste and irresponsibility.

The Negro therefore is faced with a spiritual problem: whether to resign himself to this situation or to fight against it. Holy men and women have become saints by putting up with humiliations in heroic fashion. Pierre Toussaint did this for a lifetime. Countless humble souls lay these spiritual offerings upon the altar of sacrifice. Sometimes this is ignored, sometimes they are eloquently praised for their wonderful humility. A veteran French missionary from Africa said of his flock to me, "Ah, those are the *real* Catholic Negroes. They have no foolish American idea of trying to better their condition. They are dear to Our Lord's Heart."

Yes, they are dear to our Lord's heart; but are they dear for the precise reason that Père X assumed? Such saintly Negroes as I have personally encountered — and there are many of them — accepted their troubles for the simple reason there was no other clear course open to them. Inwardly they were acutely grieved by the conflict between the Church's clear doctrine and the un-Christian actions of some of her members. The thoughtful and pious Negro finds it, as a rule, difficult to understand how it is that in the question of discrimination Catholics are supposed to conform with rigid exactitude to the prevailing social pattern, while in other instances they are enjoined to follow a bold nonconformity to current usage — in economic or family morals, in the field of education, in the observance of Friday abstinence, and so on. Holy and humble souls can absorb, as it were, this contradiction and offer it up as a holocaust to the Creator, but when viewed from the outside, this same ambiguity has long been a solid roadblock to a generalized embracing by the American Negro of the Catholic Faith.

Hence the perplexity, where the Negro, who would like to identify himself first and foremost with the Universal Church, finds not the Church, not her Supreme Pontiff nor her hierarchy, but so many of her members continuing to identify him first and above all with an accident of racial origin: not through ill will, it is true, but through a widespread and not inculpable ignorance. This, as I said, gives rise to a basic spiritual problem, the problem of a man who finds evasiveness where he is entitled to love, who finds that while the one Church of Christ claims his soul with absolute authority, at the same time so many of its members warn him not to take her teachings too universally, too seriously.

The way out of this dilemma is through a great spiritual ideal, the ideal of interracial justice, in the full moral and theological sense of the words: the way of a total and adequately motivated, adequately implemented love. But neither the white man nor the Negro can set this ideal in motion alone. It is a joint effort in which each must do his laborious part. Here the two apparent contraries, humility and militance, fuse into one harmonious whole, which is the integral following of our Lord Jesus Christ, in the fellowship of His Mystical Body and in the role that Mystical Body is called to play in fighting injustice and bringing peace to the modern world. It will mean struggle, and it will mean humiliations, for nothing worthwhile is accomplished without pain: certainly nothing within the master plan of Christ's Redemption; and by both races a general examination of conscience must be made. The fact that the Negro is not to blame for his present situation does not excuse him from the arduous task of trying to better his condition both with and without the help of the more fortunate majority.

Resentment can turn the wrong way. Like the scarring radiations of Hiroshima, it can burn deep into a closed soul and leave wounds that take generations to heal. But the transcending of resentment can be the portal through which the soul of a liberated people can pass into the sanctuary of a higher fraternity. Experience has led the Negro people to a concrete understanding of certain fundamental teachings of the Christian faith, teachings supremely necessary for our time. These are the great *ethical* truths of social justice and the Natural Law with its corollary of universal human rights and duties, and the great *religious* truths: the unity of all men in the Kingdom of Christ and the corollary of universal charity toward all men in the house of the Father, the Church of the Redeemer.

Christians and Catholics, it is true, accept these doctrines without question. But acceptance is one thing; inward realization is another. The white Catholic is likely to consider them more as speculative opinions, often quite remote from daily life. Misuse of natural-rights teachings by some of the nineteenth-century Liberals created a rather lasting suspicion of these teachings among Catholics, even when they were proclaimed under authoritative auspices. But the Negro Catholic who has grasped these truths finds in them an immediate application to his own concrete situation.

It is not enough to protest rhetorically against the absorption of the individual by a this-worldly technological mass culture. If we wish to counteract its subtle influence we need a stronger weapon. This is the unadulterated natural-rights teaching of Christianity applied to all, to men of all classes and condition without fear or favor.

The most important field for realizing this idea is the interracial parish, where different races worship and pray and work, as part of one religious community. In more and more localities of the United States it has become apparent that the once so honored separate racial parish is not and cannot be a solution. No matter how devotedly, how yearn-

ingly the pastor shepherds his monoracial flock, the deadly
ambiguity still remains. It is exposed at every step, every
time a parishioner makes a move in the larger community.
The ambiguity can be removed only when all members
of the parish, *in all that pertains to the parish,* unite in
wholehearted co-operation and equality — whether this be at
worship, in the school, at recreation, or in parish organizations. It is only an evasion when a "mixed" parish is still
administered on a separatist plan.

In some instances, the interracial parish has originated by
deliberately abandoning the old separatist parish scheme.
In other instances, it is the natural result of population shifts
when the once "blessedly" homogeneous neighborhood is
invaded by "outside" groups. The pastor in such a case
can tolerate this change as a calamity, patiently doing the
best he can under the circumstances. Or he can regard it as a
God-given opportunity to prove right the Church's mission
program to the world. Thank God that so many Catholic
pastors in this country today are of this latter category.

Paradoxically enough, identification with his racial group
is in some respects an asset rather than a liability to the
Negro in his dealings with the white man. Were all
prejudice and discrimination suddenly to disappear, thinks
Professor Arnold Rose of the University of Minnesota, "it
is doubtful whether this group identification would last
long." But as long as this decrease is gradual, the trend
toward group identification at least for a time persists. In
Dr. Rose's opinion it has given the Negroes great self-as-
surance and helped them to build effective protest organizations and political power. It has also made them aware of
events throughout the country and throughout the world
which affect them. The positive and helpful, therefore, as
well as the purely negative and depressing aspects of group
identification make it all the more necessary for the Negro

not merely to be *accepted by,* but positively to *identify himself with* the higher unity both of Church and country.

From the preceding follows a deeply practical consideration that points to a special mission of the Negro people in our country and in our time. No pious exhortations to patience or humility can conjure away the Negro's deeprooted instinct to press for equal status. This urge is all the more significant since it is part of a world trend. As the Negro people of America advance in education, they are increasingly conscious of similar aspirations among other nonwhite peoples of the globe. The question in this instance is not how to change this sentiment, but rather to consider what direction it is going to take, and on this answer depends in great measure the spiritual future of our Negro fellow citizens.

The universality of the Church — the all-embracing nature of the supernatural Kingdom of Christ — is for the Negro a very real guarantee of his own place in the Kingdom.

The spirituality of the American Negro is in a very special sense the spirituality of the Church militant and the Church universal: a spirit which he has acquired not by any inherited tribal magic, but through the long, hard school of experience. Those who have come to the Church from without have brought to it certain deep spiritual insights which their ancestors acquired even under the meager spiritual fare with which they were nourished. It took, and it still takes, a virile act of faith to identify oneself with a Church which does not in every instance seem particularly friendly.

Here in the United States, the Catholic Negro is a minority (some 500,000) within the total (some 15,000,000) of his own racial group, as the entire group is a "minority," though the largest "minority," among the ethnic bodies of the nation. But as a member of the Universal Church, he is spiritual kin to millions of non-white Catholics around the globe:

their affairs, their advances, their hierarchy, priests and religious and outstanding lay men and women, are for him
a subject of legitimate pride. He is a citizen of an immense
and noble city. The respect that his person and his voice
enjoy abroad, especially among the vast and diverse non-
white peoples, is in inverse proportion to the indifference
which he has only recently been starting to overcome at
home. The voice of the American Catholic Negro has an
honored place today among the councils of his own race
and is becoming increasingly heard abroad. It is particularly
effective when heard in conjunction with voices of other
races, speaking not in isolation but in true fellowship, on
whatever level and for whatever high and holy cause men
choose to associate.

Our Christian spirituality reflects a purely individual
phase, concerning the private relations of each individual
with his Creator. But there is also a communal and an out-
giving phase. In the complete Christian picture the two
blend into one, not confusing those things which are distinct but co-ordinating them in one whole as the different
aspects of the human personality are co-ordinated into the
entire man in Christ. The long background of the Negro's
past offers to him today a ready entrance into this communal
and outgoing phase of the spiritual life. Its expression is
not a matter for facile rhetoric but for patient study and
for fervent, humble prayer and meditation.

LITERATURE AND CENSORSHIP

BY JOHN COURTNEY MURRAY, S.J.

IN THIS difficult matter of censorship the casuistry is endless. Therefore, since this talk is supposed to have an end, it will be better to omit discussion of cases. Instead, I shall attempt to define certain central issues and to state some of the principles that bear upon their solution. We shall not be concerned with the problem of censorship in the areas of news or opinion, or of public morality in general, but only as it arises in the fields of literature and the arts. Here the perennial issue of obscenity has recently come to the fore.

The discipline of the Catholic Church in this matter is stated in canon 1399 of the Code of Canon Law. Among the eleven categories of books whose reading is *ipso iure* prohibited to Catholics the ninth is this: "Books which have for their principal purpose the description, narration, or teaching of matter lascivious or obscene." However, this canonical discipline is outside our present subject, which deals with the issue of censorship as it arises in the civil order.

An argument is sometimes set afoot about whether "the state," abstractly conceived, has or has not some right of censorship over the media of communications. And there is the complementary argument whether the individual writer or artist has or has not a right to absolute freedom of expression. These arguments I leave aside. We can start from a fact of political history, that every government has always claimed what is called police power, as an attribute of government.

This power in itself is simply the principle of self-preservation and self-protection transferred to the body politic. It extends to the requirements of public morals, public health, public safety, public order, and the general comfort of society. The only question is, how far and in what circumstances does it extend to all these social values?

In virtue of the police power, society, acting through the agency of government, is entitled to impose restraints on property rights and on personal freedoms. The question is, what manner of restraints, under what conditions, is government thus empowered to impose, in restriction of rights and in restraint of freedom? These are the concrete questions that are relevant to censorship, which is, I take it, an exercise of the police power. It might, if you wish, be an exercise of what is called *patria potestas,* the emergency power which government is entitled to use, on occasion, to protect children and those who are *ad instar puerorum,* legally to be reckoned as children by reason by their helplessness. But the same concrete questions return: when and for what reasons and under what limitations is government empowered thus to act *in loco parentis?*

In addition to the problem of governmental or legal censorship there is the problem of censorship (at least in some wide sense of the word) as exercised by nongovernmental bodies — by civic committees or voluntary associations of one sort or another. We shall also have to consider this aspect of the problem.

The issue that is central in the whole problem is the issue of social freedom. More exactly, it is the issue of striking a right balance between freedom and restraint in society. This is the most difficult problem of social science, to such an extent that all other difficulties are reducible to this one. No complete discussion is possible here; I shall simply make certain assertions, general in themselves, but relevant to our special problem.

First, in society constraint must be for the sake of freedom. It seems a paradox to assert that the imposition of a constraint must be justified by an increase in freedom, since every constraint is a decrease of freedom. What I mean, however, is that the constraint must create a freedom in another respect. Traffic regulations, for instance, are a constraint on freedom of movement on the streets; but they are justified because they create a freedom to move — at least, nowadays, in some minimal sense! Tax laws are a constraint on your freedom to do what you want with your money; but they create other freedoms — to live in security behind a national defense establishment, for instance. The whole texture of civilization is a web of restraints, which deliver man from a host of slaveries — to darkness, cold, and hunger; to ignorance and illness and wearisome labors. Delivered from these base slaveries man is free to be a man, to live the inner life of reason and love, the classic life of wisdom, the Christian life of faith.

The problem of constraint for the sake of freedom is difficult enough when it is only a question of organizing the material conditions of life. But it becomes even more inextricable when it is a question of organizing communications within society; for in this field religious and moral, intellectual and emotional values come into play. It is easy enough to see that the "press" (understood to mean all the media of communication) can be the vehicle both of corruptive and of beneficial influences. It is easy enough to say that corruptive influences ought to be put under reasonable restraints. And it is easy enough to define what you mean by corruptive influence; it is one which destroys or diminishes the rational freedom of man, either by damaging his power of personal reflection or by exciting his passions to the point where they interfere with his rational control of his thoughts and action. On these grounds you can certainly make a case against sexual propaganda of certain kinds as corruptive of human freedom. The influence of inordinate and unregulated sexual passion on the life of reason in man is a commonplace of human and historical experience. The susceptibility of youth to dominance by carnal desires, to the detriment of rational freedom, is particularly well documented — and hardly in need of documentation.

However, when you have made your case against these influences as socially corruptive, you have only reached the threshold of the problem of social freedom. Many questions remain. For instance, when and under what circumstances do these influences become so corruptive that they require animadvertence by organized society itself? (It is presumed that the first solicitations of corruptive influences are resisted by the special resources of the family and the Church.) Again, what agencies are to be enlisted against these influences — the public agencies of government and law, or the private agencies known as voluntary associations? Either or both? And to what extent each? Above all, what is the norm whose requirements are to be enforced, in one way or another, against influences that are corruptive? It is, of course, the norm of public order. But what requirements of public order can be made valid against the claims of freedom?

Even supposing these questions to have been satisfactorily answered, a further complicating consideration remains. The fact is that the imposition of constraints, the limitation of freedom, has consequences. They are numerous; but two require special notice.

First, if you impose a constraint on freedom in one domain, in order to increase freedom in another, you may take the risk of damaging freedom in a third domain, with consequences more dangerous to the community. Social freedom is a complex, whose constituent elements are closely interlocked. You may, for instance, wish to "clean up" political campaigns by limiting the freedom of the contestants to attack each other's personal integrity; but the means you take to this end may damage the freedom of the electoral process itself. Every constraint has multiple effects; it may impose restraints on a freedom which you would wish to see untouched.

There is, second, a consequent consideration. Because social freedoms interlock so tightly, it is not possible to know antecedently what the multiple effects of a regulation will be. At best, the effect you want can only be foreseen with probability, not certainty. And unforeseen effects may follow, with the result that a regulation, in itself sensible, may in the end do more harm than good.

For this reason, the social reformer whose only strength is a sense of logic may well be a menace. For instance, if drunkenness and alcoholism are social vices whose effect is to diminish and impair the free will of men (as indeed they are), the logical thing is to ban alcohol. Here in America we learned by experience the disastrous effects of that type of mad logic. In contrast, the illogicality of the liquor law in Belgium commends itself. The retail sale of liquor in public bars is forbidden, but you can get liquor if you go to a store and buy two quarts at once! When you unravel its seeming lack of logic, you find that the Belgian liquor law protects the citizen against his own reckless impulses, but permits him the freedom to act deliberately. This, of course, is his essential human freedom.

I should call attention here to the somewhat unique difficulties presented by the problem of the public enforcement of standards of sexual morality. Jacques Leclercq, of the Catholic University of Louvain, who is no slight authority, concludes a brief advertence to this subject with this remark: "In short, it may be said that no government has ever succeeded in finding a balanced policy of combating unhealthy sexual propaganda without injuring legitimate freedom or provoking other equally grave or worse disorders."

Everybody agrees that debauchery of the sexual faculty is morally wrong, and that incitement to such debauchery should be legally forbidden. On the other hand, in the case of incitement as open as houses of debauchery, a view that goes back to St. Augustine's treatise, *De ordine,* warns against the dangers of attempting a total coercive repression of this particular incitement.

The strictness of traditional Catholic doctrine in regard to sexual lust appalls the libertarian; the laxness of the many Catholic governments in the same regard equally appalls the Puritan.

In 1517 the number of prostitutes in the city of Rome considerably surpassed the number of married women. And in 1592, under a Pope of formidable strictness, Sixtus V, there were more than 9000 prostitutes amid a population of 70,000. This was in the capital of the papal states. The figures are not indeed edifying; but perhaps they are interesting, not least when one considers that during the same era the newly constituted Index of Forbidden Books was being used with extreme severity by successive Pontiffs (Paul IV, Pius IV, Pius V) against heretical propaganda. To this day the Italian who is merely amused by the obscene *pasquinade* is deeply offended by the earnest inanities of a Baptist minister from Texas.

To the proper Bostonian all this is profoundly shocking. Just as to the Continental European, especially if he is a Latin, the spectacle of the U. S. A. is infinitely puzzling. A man is free to call error truth, and truth error, if he likes; but he is not free to use the notorious four-letter word which, in direct French monosyllabic translation, is celebrated as *le mot de Cambronne* (even though the General denied having used it on the famous occasion). Again the Supreme Court declares that the category of the sacrilegious is altogether indefinable, while the Post Office rules that Aristophane's *Lysistrata* is an obscene book. This is indeed puzzling.

Considerations such as these would seem to indicate that the problem of social freedom is insoluble, if by solution is meant a simple formula that is applicable to all cases and similar for all countries. However, a community can do one important thing: it can decide on the general orientation it wishes to give to its particular solution. We have done this in the United States. We have constitutionally decided that the presumption is in favor of freedom, and that the advocate of legal constraint must make a convincing argument for its necessity or utility in the particular case.

I would only add that the presumption in favor of freedom does not rest on doctrinaire grounds. Its basis was not the philosophic rationalism that called itself Enlightenment, but only a political pragmatism more enlightened than the Enlightenment ever was, because it looked to the light of experience to illuminate the prudential norms necessary to guide it in handling a concrete social reality that is vastly complicated. In this light the option was made for the civil freedom of the citizen under a government whose powers are limited, and under a rule of the law whose reach is likewise limited, chiefly by the axiom that the constraints of law must serve the cause of essential human freedom.

In our case, the consequence of this fundamental option which gives a basic orientation to our constitutional law is that freedom of expression is the rule, and censorship the exception. A more particular further consequence is the ban laid by the First Amendment (exceptional cases apart) on all prior restraint of communications, at the same time that the government reserves the right to punish, subsequently, communications that offend against law. The freedom toward which the American people are fundamentally orientated is a freedom under God, a freedom that knows itself to be bound by the imperatives of the moral law. Antecedently it is presumed that a man will make morally and socially responsible use of his freedom of expression; hence there is to be no prior restraint on it. However, if his use of freedom is irresponsible, he is summoned after the fact to responsibility before the judgment of the law. There are indeed other reasons why prior restraint on communications is outlawed; but none are more fundamental than this.

After this brief discussion of the central issue involved in censorship I come to my proposition. It may be briefly stated thus: censorship in the civil order must be a juridical process. In using the word "juridical" I mean that the premises and objectives of the program should be defined in accord with the norms of good jurisprudence; that the forms of procedure should be properly judicial; and that the structure and workings of the process should be sustained by the consent of the community. I should maintain that this concept of a juridical process should be verified, *mutatis mutandis,* in every form of censorship, whether governmental or nongovernmental.

Censorship exercised by public authority is obliged to be literally juridical, in the sense described. As a legal process this censorship is controlled by the canons of necessity or utility for the common good. That some degree of punitive censorship is necessary is sufficiently evident. Pornography, for instance, the kind of obscenity that is a perverse and vicious profanation of the sacredness of sex, seems to hold a permanent attraction for a portion of humanity. That it is a corruptive social influence is not to be denied; consequently, few would deny that its repression is necessary. Beyond this, how much more censorship is useful, and how useful is it? That seems to be the central question.

A preliminary answer is furnished by the principle, basic to jurisprudence, that morals and law are differentiated in character, and not coextensive in their functions. It is not the function of the legislator to forbid everything that the moral law forbids, or to enjoin everything that the moral law enjoins. The moral law governs the entire order of human conduct, personal and social; it extends even to motivations and interior acts. Law, on the other hand, looks only to the public order of human society; it touches only external acts, and regards only values that are formally social. For this reason the scope of law is limited. Moreover, though law is indeed a moral force, directive of human society to the common good, it relies ultimately for its observance on coercion. And men can be coerced only into a minimal amount of moral action. Again from this point of view the scope of law is limited.

Therefore the moral aspirations of law are minimal. Law seeks to establish and maintain only that minimum of actualized morality that is necessary for the healthy functioning of the social order. It does not look to what is morally desirable, or attempt to remove every moral taint from the atmosphere of society. It enforces only what is minimally acceptable, and in this sense socially necessary. Beyond this, society must look to other institutions for the elevation and maintenance of its moral standards — that is, to the Church, the home, the school, and the whole network of voluntary associations that concern themselves with public morality in one or other aspect.

Law and morality are indeed related, even though differentiated. That is, the premises of law are ultimately found in the moral law. And human legislation does look to the moralization of society. But, mindful of its own nature and mode of action, it must not moralize excessively; otherwise it tends to defeat even its own more modest aims, by bringing itself into contempt.

Therefore the law, mindful of its nature, is required to be tolerant of many evils that morality condemns. A moral condemnation regards only the evil itself, in itself. A legal ban on an evil must consider what St. Thomas calls its own "possibility." That is, will the ban be obeyed, at least by the generality? Is it enforceable against the disobedient? Is it prudent to undertake the enforcement of this or that ban, in view of the possibility of harmful effects in other areas of social life? Is the instrumentality of coercive law a good means for the eradication of this or that social vice? And, since a means is not a good means if it fails to work in most cases, what are the lessons of experience in the matter? What is the prudent view of results — the long view or the short view? These are the questions that jurisprudence must answer, in order that legislation may be drawn with requisite craftsmanship.

It is, in fact, the differentiated character of law and morals that justifies the lawyer or judge when he insists that punitive censorship statutes should be clearly drawn, with the margin of uncertainty as narrow as possible.

The net of all this is that no society should expect very much in the way of moral uplift from its censorship statutes. Indeed the whole criminal code is only a minimal moral force. Particularly in the field of sexual morality the expectations are small; as I have suggested, they are smaller here than anywhere else. It is a sort of paradox, though an understandable one, that the greater the social evil, the less effective against it is the instrument of coercive law. Philip Wylie may have been right in saying that American society "is technically insane in the matter of sex." If so, it cannot be coerced into sanity by the force of law. In proportion as literary obscenity is a major social evil, the power of the police against it is severely limited.

This brings up the matter of consent. Law is indeed a coercive force; it compels obedience by the fear of penalty. However, a human society is inhumanly ruled when it is ruled only, or mostly, by fear. Good laws are obeyed by the generality because they are good laws; they merit and receive the consent of the community, as valid legal expressions of the community's own convictions as to what is just or unjust, good or evil. In the absence of this consent law either withers away or becomes tyrannical.

The problem of popular consent to the order of law and to its manifold coercions becomes critical in a pluralist society, such as ours. Basic religious divisions lead to conflict of moral views, certain asserted "rights" clash with other "rights" no less strongly asserted. And the divergences are often irreducible. Nevertheless, despite all the pluralism, some manner of consensus must support the order of law to which the whole community and all its groups are commonly subject. This consensus must include, in addition to other agreements, an agreement on certain rules which regulate the relations of the divergent groups among one another, and their common relation to the order of law. In what concerns our present subject of censorship, I suggest that there are four such rules.

(For the suggestion of these rules I am indebted to Prof. Vernon J. Bourke, of St. Louis University: cf. "Moral Problems Related to Censoring the Media of Mass Communication," in Problems of Communication in a pluralistic Society *(Milwaukee: The Marquette University Press, 1956), pp. 130–131.*

Before stating them I would note that in the United

States at present all the religious groups are — from the sociological, even if not from the statistical, point of view — minority groups.

First, within the larger pluralist society each minority group has the right to censor for its own members, if it so chooses, the content of the various media of communication, and to protect them, by means of its own choosing, from materials considered harmful according to its own standards.

Second, in a pluralist society no minority group has the right to demand that government should impose a general censorship, affecting all the citizenry, upon any medium of communication, with a view to punishing the communication of materials that are judged to be harmful according to the special standards held within one group.

Third, any minority group has the right to work toward the elevation of standards of public morality in the pluralist society, through the use of the methods of persuasion and pacific argument.

Fourth, in a pluralist society no minority group has the right to impose its own religious or moral views on other groups, through the use of the methods of force, coercion, or violence.

I cannot pause here to demonstrate the reasonableness and justice of these four rules. I would only note that they are not put forth as rules that were made in heaven, necessarily inherent in the constitution of an "ideal" society. On the contrary, they are to be considered as rules made on earth, by the practical reason of man, for application in the conditions — by no means "ideal" — of a religiously and morally divided society. Agreement on them would seem to be necessary in the common interests of social peace. Their supposition is the jurisprudential proposition that what is commonly imposed by law on all our citizens must be supported by general public opinion, by a reasonable consensus of the whole community. At the same time they suppose that within a pluralist society the minority groups have certain definite, if limited, rights to influence the standards and content of public morality. The statement of these rules leads to the next subject.

In the United States there are a multitude of voluntary agencies which exercise some measure of surveillance, judgment, and even control of various media of communication. For the most part they shy away from the idea of being called "censoring" agencies. We need not quibble over the word; the frequent fact is that many of them achieve the results of censorship, even when they refuse the name. With regard to these agencies I should maintain the general proposition stated above — that their censoring should also be a juridical process, if not literally, certainly in spirit.

The juridical premise of their action is not in doubt. In the United States it is generally acknowledged that the voluntary association is entitled to concern itself actively with matters that relate to the public welfare. It is invidious to stigmatize all such associations as "pressure-groups," pursuing "private interests." The fact is that, in their own way, they can perform a public function.

The more difficult question concerns the methods used by these associations or committees. There can be no slightest quarrel when they use simply the methods of persuasion; that is, when they appeal for voluntary co-operation on the grounds of a common moral and social responsibility. Thus, for instance, many associations interested in decent literature and movies (surely a public interest) seek the responsible co-operation of producers and theater owners, of publishers and distributors, with a view at least to diminishing the volume of obscenity, or other objectionable features, in these media. Surely here all is entirely rightful and prudent.

Other methods — at the other end of the spectrum, so

to speak — seem to have at least the appearance of coercion. As an example one might take the organized boycott, against a merchant, a theater, etc. It is a sort of "consumers' strike"; it is sometimes accompanied by picketing; it normally involves some form of economic sanctions invoked against the offending party. What is to be thought of such methods?

It will be agreed that the use of formal coercion in society is reserved to public authority and its agencies of law. Coercion of a more informal kind — through economic pressures, etc. — is also employed by various associations that do not hesitate to identify themselves as "power groups." Such for instance, is a trade union. It does indeed seem a bit incongruous that other types of voluntary association, concerned with values that are spiritual and moral, aesthetic and cultural, should pursue their ends by what appear to be the methods of power rather than of persuasion. On the other hand, it is not possible to prove the position, taken by some, that an action like the boycott of a moving picture is somehow "unrightful," or "unconstitutional," or "undemocratic." No one can show that such an action lies beyond the limits of a primeval American right to protest and object. The action may indeed be strenuous; but the American right to protest and object is permitted to run to some pretty strenuous extremes.

This said, against the doctrinaire, it remains true that methods of action which verge upon the coercive exhibit some incongruity when used by citizen groups in the interests of morality in literature or on the screen. Even if they raise no issue of abstract right, they do raise the concrete issue of prudence, which, equally with justice, is one of the cardinal virtues. The issue rises most sharply in the case of Catholic associations. The chief danger is lest the Church itself be identified in the public mind as a power association. The identification is injurious; it turns unto a hatred of the faith. And it has the disastrous effect of obscuring from the public view the true visage of the Church as God's kingdom of truth and freedom, justice and love. Our purpose is to stand before the world as men and women of faith, and therefore of reason too, whose reliance is on the methods of reason and not of force. We would wish always to be men and women of courage, ready to face any issue; but also men and women of prudence, who understand the art of procedure, and understand too that we are morally bound, by the virtue of prudence, to a concrete rightness of method in the pursuit of moral aims.

It should be noted too that prudence is an intellectual virtue, a refinement of intelligence. It may therefore properly be asked, how intelligent is it to have recourse to methods that approach coercion in this delicate field of censorship? Few things are worse than to make oneself ridiculous. And when an effort to coerce is made at the dictates of stupidity, the result arouses ridicule as well as resentment.

This brings up the question, who is competent to censor, even in some extra-legal fashion? To say that all censorship should be a juridical process is to say by implication that it ought to be intelligently done. This means close attention to the qualifications of the censor. Here the example of the Church is instructive. In his reform of the discipline of censorship Benedict XIV laid great stress on the rule that the censor is to possess professional competence in the particular field in which he is called upon to pass judgment. Censorship is no job for the amateur. Like stress is placed on the censor's obligation to perform his task impartially, in the fullness of the judicial spirit that forbids the intrusion of any private likes or dislikes. In the process of censorship there is no room for the personal, the arbitrary, the passionate. The censor is not called upon for a display of moral indignation; he is asked only for a judgment, calm and cool, objective and unemotional. So too in the civil sphere, the less we have of moral indignation, and the more we have of professional competence and an unclouded faculty of judgment, the better it will be for the juridical nature of the censorship process.

In what concerns the problem of obscenity I would not discount the value of what is called the "common estimation" of men. People in general have a fairly clear notion of what obscenity is. And people in general can make, for themselves, a pretty good judgment on whether a particular work is obscene. Certainly the Code of Canon Law seems to suppose that the ordinary Catholic can make this concrete judgment for himself. I repeat, for himself. The question is, who can make it for others, i.e., as a censor.

Here a distinction is in order. Certainly the ordinary father and mother ought to be qualified to act as censors within the family. And to decide what their children may or may not be prudently exposed to, in the way of reading, movies, etc. But I should not think that the ordinary father or mother, *qua* such, is qualified to act as censor within society at large, or to decide what literature and movies may be displayed before the general public. Society has an interest in the artist's freedom of expression which is not necessarily shared by the family. If adult standards of literature would be dangerous for children, a child's standard of literature is rather appalling to an adult. If therefore any censorship is to be administered in the interest of society, the professional competence of the literary critic must play a role in the process.

Here perhaps the characteristic Catholic care for the welfare of children (often coupled with the typically American cult of the child-centered home) ought to be aware of a danger. The contemporary argument about censorship is sometimes described as a "battle between the literati and

the philistines." The description is snobbish, if you will.
But it would be lamentable if Catholics were to go over to
the camp of the philistines. After all, we do stand, not only
within the oldest religious tradition of the Western world,
but also within its most venerable tradition of intellect,
literature, and art. The tradition has produced great achievements in writing, painting, and the plastic arts. Not all of
them are fit for children indeed — not even the Bible in
all its parts. But that is no justification for any form of
philistinism.

In one further and final respect the process of extralegal
censorship ought to be juridical, pursued in the spirit of
law — that is, in its adoption of minimal aims. Fussiness is
out of order. There ought to be a few, only a few, areas of
concentration, in which a little bit (if not much) can be
done. I suggest that the chief area is the "pornography of
violence," as it has been called.

Mischief enough is done by the obscenities that occur in
the portrayal of illicit love (by literary hacks who never
learned what the genuine artist knows instinctively — that,
though art may "say all," there are certain things it is never
allowed to say explicitly). But here sex is at least rescued
from full profanation by its tenuous connection with love,
as love is still resident in lust. However, when sex is associated with, and becomes symbolic of, the hatreds and hostili-
ties, the angers and cruelties, that lie deep in men and
women, the profanation of the most sacred thing in sex —
its relation to love and to the hope of human life — is almost
complete. It could move perhaps only one step deeper into
the diabolical — in that association of sex and blasphemy
that pervades the Black Mass.

The image of the truly evil thing in the obscenities of
our day is seen on the typical cover of the "tough" kind of
pocketbook — the seminude woman, with a smoking gun in

her hand. The scene is one of impurity, but that is its lesser evil. The real evil is the violence in the impure scene. There is the perversion. If some restraint could be imposed upon this pornography of violence — so damning in its revelation of a vice in our culture — it would indeed be a moral achievement.

It is a good thing to keep our problems in perspective. Our chief problem, of course, is not literary censorship, but literary creation. This is true in the Church. She has no trouble in finding censors; but she prays continually that God may give her men of learning who can write the works that need to be written. The American Catholic community particularly needs to attend seriously to this problem of literary creation. Leo XIII is indeed remembered for his revision of the Index of Forbidden Books. But he was not the first Pope to point to the dangers of reading bad books. It is his great glory that he was the first Pope to say, in substance and effect, in a multitude of discourses, that today there is great danger in not reading good books. This is why I think it is a fine thing for the Thomas More Association to sponsor a lecture on censorship — once every seventeen years! Now it may resume the high apostolic function which it has been splendidly performing.

THE AUTHORS

THE MOST REV. KARL J. ALTER

The Most Rev. Karl J. Alter, archbishop of Cincinnati, is author of "Industry Councils." Archbishop Alter was born in Toledo in 1885 and ordained a priest in 1910. From 1914 to 1929 he served as director of Catholic Charities of the Toledo diocese. For the next two years he was director of the National Catholic School of Social Service at Catholic University.

In 1931 he was consecrated bishop of Toledo, a post he held until 1950 when he was named archbishop of Cincinnati.

Archbishop Alter has served as episcopal chairman of the social action department of the National Catholic Welfare Conference; chairman of the administrative board of the Catholic Hospital Association; treasurer of NCWC and for three years as chairman of the board of NCWC.

He is now vice-chairman of its administrative board and episcopal chairman of the lay organizations department.

REV. FRANCIS P. CANAVAN, S.J.

The Rev. Francis P. Canavan, S.J., who teaches political science at St. Peter's college, Jersey City, is author of "The Finality of Sex."

"I am not a professional moral theologian and have not dealt with the subject of sex and marriage in any other writing that I have done," says Father Canavan.

"But the subject of contraception is so much discussed today that I was concerned to work out an argument on it. Since so many people today are prevented by relativism and skepticism from accepting an argument based on rational principles, it seemed to me that the only way to meet them was negatively, that is, by taking the proposition that contraception is permissible and showing the conclusions that are implicit in the proposition. The assumption, of course, was that people would be unwilling to accept the conclusions and might at least get some doubts about the initial premise."

Father Canavan was born in New York City in 1917. His early training was in Long Island public schools. He was graduated from Fordham in 1939 and shortly after entered the Society of Jesus. In addition to seminary degrees in philosophy and theology, he has a master's degree from Fordham and a doctorate from Duke university, both in political science.

While working for his doctorate he spent a year at Oxford on a Rockefeller Foundation grant, doing research for his thesis. He is revising the thesis for a book on the political philosophy of Edmund Burke.

He has written for national Catholic magazines.

REV. E. M. CATICH

The Rev. E. M. Catich, head of the art department of St. Ambrose College, Davenport, Iowa, is author of "The Image of Christ in Art."

"I was a commercial sign writer and professional musician in and around Chicago before entering college," says Father Catich.

He studied at the Art Institute of Chicago and did graduate work at the University of Iowa and at the Gregorian university in Rome. He was ordained there in December, 1938.

Since 1939 Father Catich has been teaching art, music, and engineering at St. Ambrose College. He is a former president of the Catholic Art Association.

"He has produced distinguished work in the fields of sculpture, stained glass, calligraphy, oil and water painting and chalice design," say the editors of the *Catholic Messenger,* Davenport, in which his "Realities" article first appeared.

WILLIAM CLANCY

William Clancy, a consultant to the Fund for the Republic on Religion and the Democratic Society, is the author of "The Area of Catholic Freedom."

Mr. Clancy is a native of Detroit. He was educated at the universities of Detroit and Michigan and subsequently was a member of the faculties of Detroit and the University of Notre Dame.

He was associate editor of *The Commonweal* from 1952–55 and religion editor of *Newsweek,* 1955–56. Since October, 1956 he has been education director of The Church Peace Union as well as filling his Fund for the Republic post.

Mr. Clancy has contributed to many magazines, Catholic and secular.

JOHN COGLEY

John Cogley, journalist, is author of "Some Things Are Caesar's."

Mr. Cogley was born in Chicago and received his Ph.B. from Loyola university there. He subsequently made some special studies in philosophy and theology at the University of Fribourg in 1948–49.

He began his journalistic career as editor of *The Catholic Worker* in Chicago. He served, meanwhile, as director of St. Joseph's House of Hospitality. In World War II he was in the Air Force.

With the Rev. Martin I. Carrabine, S.J., he founded in 1946 the Catholic student magazine, *Today.* Two years later, he became associated with *The Commoweal* and in 1949 was named its executive editor.

He left *The Commonweal* in 1955 to do a survey and write a book on blacklisting in the motion picture industry for *The Fund for the Republic.* He was then asked to join the executive staff of the *Fund.* Currently he is working with Father John Courtney Murray, S.J., and Dr. Reinhold Niebuhr as the *Fund's* staff director on the project called "Religion in a Democratic Society."

Mr. Cogley's current connection with *The Commonweal* is as a weekly columnist. He also writes for *Look* and other national magazines.

MARTIN GLEASON

Martin Gleason, youngest of our contributors, is the author of "To All Its People." He is a senior in the college of arts and sciences of Loyola University, Chicago. His interests are in politics and public affairs.

Says Mr. Gleason of his article: "I believe the Japanese-American episode offers an excellent opportunity of how our free society can produce public policy compounded of ignorance and malice and destructive of the very freedom on which it rests. It is of particular significance for Catholics in that it points out the tremendous opportunity which exists for applying the principles of Christian humanism to the affairs of the community."

REV. RALPH GORMAN, C.P.

The Rev. Ralph Gorman, C.P., is editor of *The Sign*. The article "One View of Four Viewpoints" is actually a series of four vigorous editorials which Father Gorman wrote on varying viewpoints held by American Catholics.

Father Gorman was born at Binghamton, New York, in 1897, was educated in various schools of the Congregation of the Passion in which he was professed in the fall of 1917. He did graduate work at the Catholic University of America and at the Ecole Biblique et Archeologique, Jerusalem.

He was ordained in 1924. On completion of his studies, he taught Sacred Scripture at St. Michael's Monastery until 1935 when he became an editor of *The Sign*. He has been its chief editor since 1943.

Father Gorman recalls that the editorial on the ultraconservatives brought hundreds of letters, 90 per cent of them quarreling with his viewpoint.

"By the time the series of editorials was over, and we had received from 1500 to 2000 letters, I think the letters were probably evenly divided."

RT. REV. MSGR. REYNOLD HILLENBRAND

Rt. Rev. Msgr. Reynold Hillenbrand (S.T.D., Cavadre College, Rome), is the author of "Five Point Social Program." Msgr. Hillenbrand is former rector of St. Mary of the Lake Seminary, the Chicago archdiocesan seminary. He is pastor of Sacred Heart Church, Winnetka, Ill. He has spearheaded Catholic Action in the Chicago archdiocese. Msgr. Hillenbrand is general chaplain of the Christian Family Movement, the Young Christian Workers (college), and the Young Christian Workers. He is one of the founders of the Catholic Conference of Working Life of Chicago, formerly the Catholic Labor Alliance.

ERIK VON KUEHNELT-LEDDIN

Erik von Kuehnelt-Leddin, author of "Pollyanna Catholicism," is a scholar in the best European tradition, with a doctorate from the University of Budapest in 1937 and with further graduate work at the University of Vienna.

He was born in Austria in 1909, son of a scientist. His first language was French. Subsequently he learned German, English, Hungarian, Russian, and Japanese.

He has written for many American and English Catholic magazines and newspapers. He has taught at Georgetown, St. Peter's College, Fordham, and Chestnut Hill College. He has taught, too, in England.

His first book, a novel, *Die Anderen,* was published at Vienna when he was 21. Novels, sociopolitical studies, even a detective mystery are among his other books that followed over the years. And in a variety of languages.

Kuehnelt-Leddin has lectured widely in the United States, has visited all our states and most Canadian provinces and nearly all countries of the world except the South American.

He is married to the former Countess Christiane Goess. They live with their three children in a Tyrolean mountain village.

REV. JOHN LaFARGE, S.J.

The Rev. John LaFarge, S.J., is the author of "Christianity and the Negro."

Father LaFarge is a son of John LaFarge, American muralist and author and a descendant, through his mother, of Commodore Perry and Benjamin Franklin. After earning his A.B. at Harvard in 1901, he went to Innsbruck to study for the priesthood. He was awarded a licentiate in theology and ordained in 1905. Several months later he entered the Society of Jesus. Through his long years in the Society, Father LaFarge has been active in educational and missionary work. He is an associate editor of *America,* a weekly he formerly served as editor in chief.

He has been a leader in the National Catholic Rural Life Conference, the Conference on Science, Philosophy and Religion, the American Catholic Historical Association, the Catholic Association for International Peace, and the Liturgical Arts Society. He is a fellow of the American Academy of Arts and Sciences. Father LaFarge is chaplain and one of the founders of the Catholic Interracial Council of New York City. He has written incisively and lectured widely in this field. He has written eight books and a ninth, *The Priesthood of the Intellect* is in preparation.

CHARLES T. LUCEY

Charles T. Lucey, newspaperman, writes of "Hope for Tomorrow." This was his weekly column, "The Backdrop," October 17, 1955, an NCWC feature which appears in many Catholic newspapers.

Mr. Lucey, one of the country's better known reporters, is a native of Pennsylvania. He entered the newspaper business with the Erie (Pennsylvania) *Dispatch Herald* in 1923. He has served on the staffs of the *Toledo News-Bee,* the *Cleveland News,* the *Irish Independent* (of Dublin, Eire, where he was also correspondent for the *Universal News Service*) and the Birmingham (Alabama) *Post.*

He became Washington correspondent of the *New York World Telegram* in 1938, remaining with that paper until 1944 when he assumed the same post for the *Scripps-Howard* papers.

Mr. Lucey received the Clapper award for distinguished political reporting in 1952. In addition to his NCWC column Mr. Lucey writes frequently for *America.* He is married and the father of nine children.

U. S. REP. EUGENE J. McCARTHY

Congressman Eugene J. McCarthy is author of "The Christian in Politics."

He received his B.A. degree from St. John's university in 1935 and his M.A. degree from the University of Minnesota three years later. Rep. McCarthy has been professor of economics and education at St. John's and acting chairman of the department of sociology, College of St. Thomas. He is a resident of St. Paul, Minnesota, and a member of the Democratic-Farmer-Labor party. He was elected to the 81st Congress in 1948 and re-elected to the 82nd, 83rd, 84th, and 85th Congresses.

Rep. McCarthy has written for various national magazines on morality in government, the state and human freedom, the problems of censorship, and other subjects. He has lectured in various parts of the country and has appeared on numerous radio and TV programs.

REV. JOHN COURTNEY MURRAY, S.J.

Father John Courtney Murray, S.J., noted theologian, is the author of "Literature and Censorship." This was originally an address Father Murray delivered at the seventeenth anniversary celebration of the Thomas More Association May 4, 1956 in Chicago.

Father Murray, a native of New York, entered the Society of Jesus and subsequently received his bachelor's degree from Boston College in 1926 and his master's degree there in 1927.

In 1934 he received a degree in sacred theology from Woodstock College and a doctorate in the same field at Gregorian University, Rome, in 1937.

From 1927 to 1930 Father Murray was professor of Latin and English at Manila's Ateneo de Manila. He has been a professor of theology at Woodstock since 1937 and editor of *Theological Studies* since 1941.

Father Murray was visiting professor of philosophy at Yale in the academic year 1951–52.

He was given the Cardinal Spellman Award by the Catholic Theological Society in 1950 for his contributions to theological scholarship. He has received honorary degrees from Harvard, Notre Dame, St. Louis, and Georgetown universities.

Father Murray has contributed articles to *Encyclopedia Britannica,* the *Encyclopedia of Religion,* and has written extensively for periodicals of general circulation and journals of the learned societies.

THOMAS E. MURRAY

Thomas E. Murray, engineer and inventor, former member of the Atomic Energy Commission and one of the country's most distinguished Catholics, is author of "Though the Heavens Fall." This originally was an address by Mr. Murray at the Catholic University of America commencement in June, 1954.

Mr. Murray, a New Yorker, was graduated from Yale's Sheffield Scientific School in 1911 with a degree in mechanical engineering. Over the years he has been granted honorary degrees from sixteen universities and colleges. Among other honors he received Notre Dame's Laetare medal in 1952 and in the same year Yale's Engineer of the Year medal.

He began as an engineer with Metropolitan Engineering Co., and served as its president from 1912 to 1949 when it was merged with Murray Manufacturing Co. He was president of Murray Manufacturing from 1942 to 1949. He left these posts when he was named to the atomic energy commission.

Meanwhile from 1932 to 1940 he served as federal receiver for the $500,000,000 properties of the Interborough Rapid Transit. During his receivership there were no labor difficulties.

In 1943 Mr. Murray received a special award from the government for devising a method to manufacture shells which saved thousands of tons of strategic materials. About 25 per cent of World War II trench mortar shells were made by the Murray method.

About 200 patents in the electrical and welding field have been granted Mr. Murray.

When Mr. Murray's term as an atomic commission member expired in June, 1957, he was immediately asked to serve as a consultant to the congressional atomic energy committee.

Mr. Murray is married and the father of eleven children, two of them Jesuits. He and Mrs. Murray have 33 grandchildren.

MOST REV. JOHN KING MUSSIO

The Most Rev. John King Mussio is the first bishop of the Steubenville (Ohio) diocese. His contribution to this book is "Politics, Corruption and You," a subject on which he feels deeply.

Bishop Mussio was born in Cincinnati in 1902. He was educated at Xavier University, the University of Notre Dame, and at Mount St. Mary Seminary. He was awarded a doctorate in canon law after studies at Angelico University in Rome.

He was ordained at Cincinnati in 1935. He was chancellor of that archdiocese when named bishop of Steubenville. He was consecrated May 1, 1945.

"This article is the result of many talks I have given throughout the Diocese endeavoring to arouse our people to the necessity of ridding themselves of corrupt government," the bishop told the editors of *Realities*. And he added:

"It was to encourage our young people to enter politics and to have our people elect men who would serve the common good that this article was written."

WILLIS D. NUTTING

Willis D. Nutting is the author of "Order and Apathy." Mr. Nutting was graduated from the University of Iowa, his native state. He went to Oxford University for three years as a Rhodes scholar. In 1924 he became an Anglican clergyman. After six years in the Anglican ministry, serving in the British West Indies and in Colorado, he entered the Catholic Church. Mr. Nutting taught for three years at St. Teresa's College, Winona, Minnesota, and then went on to teach at the University of Notre Dame. He has been there since 1936 save for a one year's absence in Florida where he participated in an educational experiment. Mr. Nutting has written much for the magazine field. He has a particular interest in the adult Catholic layman, what he is and, says Mr. Nutting, what he should be.

FRANK O'MALLEY

Frank O'Malley, author of "The Culture of the Church," is a professor of English at the University of Notre Dame and a cofounder of the *Review of Politics* in which the article first appeared.

Mr. O'Malley was born in Clinton, Massachusetts, August 19, 1911. He received his bachelor's degree from Notre Dame, his master's degree a year later. He has been a member of the Notre Dame faculty since then,

In 1957 he was given the Annual Faculty Award for Distinguished Service to Notre Dame.

Excerpts from "The Culture of the Church" were printed in most Catholic newspapers and the article was commented on editorially by many of them.

HELEN CALDWELL RILEY

Helen Caldwell Riley, a native of Texas and a convert to Catholicism, is the author of "If Your Son Should Ask."

Most of Mrs. Riley's childhood was spent in Tennessee and Mississippi. In 1945 she went to Harlem Hospital School of Nursing. While in training there, Mrs. Riley became interested in the Catholic Church through, she says, "the warm friendliness and excellent example of the Catholic chaplains." She was received into the Church in 1947. One of these chaplains introduced her to the Catholic Worker and Friendship House movements and she served for a time as a Catholic Worker volunteer.

In 1948 before completing her nursing course she was stricken with tuberculosis and went to a sanatorium. While there she began to write — several articles for Catholic magazines and the beginnings of her first book, "Color Ebony."

Her disease arrested, she returned to Memphis and worked for a time as a practical nurse. Later the bishop gave her permission to open Blessed Martin House of Hospitality, following the Catholic Worker model.

Day care was provided for the children of working mothers and shelter extended to expectant mothers, many of them unmarried. She also sought to bring members of her race and white people together in a spirit of mutual charity.

Mrs. Riley was forced by a variety of circumstances to close Blessed Martin House in 1956.

She now lives with her husband and two sons in Southern California.

REV. JOHN B. SHEERIN, C.S.P.

The Rev. John B. Sheerin, C.S.P., author of "The Goal of Academic Freedom," is editor of the *Catholic World* which he says is the oldest Catholic magazine in the United States. For many years he contributed a monthly article to the *Homiletic and Pastoral Review*.

Father Sheerin is a native of Brooklyn. He received his B.A. degree at St. John's College and his law degree from Fordham Law School. He was admitted to the New York state bar in 1932 and was licensed to practice before the United States Supreme Court in 1938. In that same year he received his master's degree from Catholic University of America.

Father Sheerin was ordained to the priesthood in 1937 and taught English and oratory at the Paulist seminary in Washington from 1938 to 1944. For the next two years he was a member of the Paulist mission band.

The Paulist Information Center in Boston was founded by Father Sheerin in 1945 and he served as its first director. He has been an editor of the *Catholic World* since 1947, its editor in chief since October, 1948.

His articles have appeared in many Catholic magazines and newspapers.

GEORGE N. SHUSTER

George N. Shuster, president of Hunter College and author of nearly a score of books, contributes "The Poet as Witness" to this collection. This was originally given as an address in May, 1954, marking *Spirit's* twentieth anniversary.

Dr. Shuster, a native of Wisconsin, received his bachelor's and master's degrees from the University of Notre Dame. He studied, too, at the University of Poitiers. He was awarded a doctorate by Columbia University in 1940.

From 1920 to 1924, Dr. Shuster headed the department of English at Notre Dame. He went East and taught at Brooklyn Polytechnic Institute and St. Joseph's College for Women.

He became an associate editor of *Commonweal* in 1925 and managing editor in 1926, a post he held until 1938. He continues as a contributing editor.

Dr. Shuster joined the faculty of Hunter College in 1939 and was named its president in 1940.

He served as editor of the Century Catholic College Texts in English and has translated several works from the German. His own books show a wide range of interests and knowledge.

SISTER ANNETTE WALTERS, C.S.J.

Sister Annette Walters, C.S.J., is author of "Catholics and Mental Health." A psychologist, she is at present dean of studies at the College of St. Catherine, St. Paul, Minnesota.

Sister Annette is a native of Elmwood, Wisconsin, and a convert to Catholicism. She received her B.A. from St. Catherine in 1933 and her master's degree and her doctorate from the University of Minnesota. A member of Phi Beta Kappa, Sister Annette has done graduate work at the University of Chicago, the Catholic University of America, and Western Reserve University. She was a Fulbright research scholar at the University of Louvain 1952–53, investigating psychological services for exceptional children.

Sister Annette has lectured widely on various aspects of psychology to professional and lay groups, has been visiting professor at numerous colleges, has conducted seminars and teachers' institutes in nearly a dozen states.

She has written frequently for both professional and general magazines.

The article which appears in *Realities,* Sister Annette says, "grew out of a convocation I gave to the students and seminarians at St. John's University, Collegeville."

MOST REV. VINCENT S. WATERS

The Most Rev. Vincent S. Waters, bishop of North Carolina, is the author of "How I Lost My Prejudice."

Bishop Waters was born in Roanoke, Virginia, on the Feast of the Assumption in 1904. He was educated at Belmont Abbey, St. Charles College, and St. Mary's Seminary. He completed his studies at the North American College in Rome and was ordained there December 8, 1931.

He returned to his home diocese of Richmond and in 1936 was named its chancellor. He was appointed bishop of Raleigh March 10, 1945, and consecrated two months later.

His diocese is the tenth largest state in the Union. One familiar with the diocese who has characterized it as the country's "most missionary area," has added:

"Through Bishop Waters' efforts the Catholic Church is better known today through the cities, towns and countryside of North Carolina than ever before in her long history.

"A year before the Supreme Court ruled against segregation, Bishop Waters had declared that there was no segregation in the churches of the Diocese of Raleigh."

REV. ROBERT WELCH

Rev. Robert Welch, author of "The Catholic Church and American Democracy," is Catholic professor of religion in the University of Iowa School of Religion.

Father Welch, a native of Iowa, received his A.B. degree from St. Ambrose College, Davenport, in 1932. He studied for the priesthood at the Sulpician Seminary in Washington and was ordained for the Davenport diocese in 1936.

He was appointed to the faculty of St. Ambrose, where he taught history from 1940 to 1949. The last four years he served as chairman of the history department.

Meanwhile he received a master's degree in Latin American history in 1937 from Catholic University and did graduate work at the University of California 1937–40.

Father Welch was named to his present post in 1949.

He has written for the Catholic press, both in the newspaper and magazine fields.

MOST REV. JOHN J. WRIGHT

The Most Rev. John J. Wright, D.D., bishop of Worcester, is author of "The Mass and International Order." The basis of this article was a talk given by Bishop Wright when he was host to the 1955 Liturgical Week.

The bishop, a native of Boston, was educated in that city's public schools, at Boston College, St. John's Seminary, Brighton, and at the North American College in Rome. He was ordained in Rome. On his return he taught at St. John's Seminary and then became secretary to the archbishop of Boston. He was consecrated auxiliary bishop of Boston in 1949. On March 7, 1950, he was installed as the first bishop of the Diocese of Worcester. As bishop he has emphasized small parishes, programs of Catholic lay action, and the apostolates of the Catholic press and of radio and TV. He is episcopal adviser to the lay retreat movement in the United States and to the Mariological Society in America. Bishop Wright continues to preach retreats. He writes and lectures on spiritual subjects, particularly the Communion of Saints and the identity between Christ and the Church. He is the author of a book on papal social teaching and of many magazine articles. The bishop is a member of the American Academy of Arts and Sciences.

GORDAN C. ZAHN

Gordon C. Zahn, sociologist and magazine writer, is the author of "Catholic 'Separatism' and Anti-Catholic Tensions."

Dr. Zahn, a native of Milwaukee, spent eight years in the business world before returning to school after World War II. He is a graduate of the College of St. Thomas, St. Paul, Minnesota. He received his master's degree in 1950 and his doctorate in 1953 from the Catholic University of America. Since then he has been an associate professor of sociology at Loyola University, Chicago. Dr. Zahn spent the 1952–53 year at Harvard under a Social Science Research Council fellowship. With the help of Professor Gordon W. Allport of Harvard he obtained access to the letters written to Beacon Press after publication of the Paul Blanshard books. This is the basis for his *Realities* article. Last year Dr. Zahn was a Fulbright fellow at the Julius Maximilian university at Würzburg.

He has written extensively in the magazine field, particularly for Catholic publications.

Date Due		
JUN 2 7 '58		
JUN 3 0 '58		
OCT 6 '58		
FEB 1 '60		
JY 18 '60		
MR 13'62		
JUL 23 '63		
FE 14 '64		
JE 24 '65		
	PRINTED	IN U. S. A.